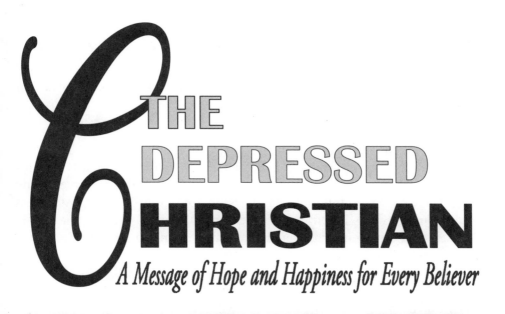

THE DEPRESSED CHRISTIAN

A Message of Hope and Happiness for Every Believer

C. Christopher Lindsay

Arrow Publications, Inc.
First Edition

CRl£O

Copyright ©2008
ISBN: 978-0-9798272-0-4
Printed in the United States of America
All Rights Reserved

Arrow Publications, Inc.

P. O. Box 10102
Cedar Rapids, IA 52410
Phone 1.319.395.7833
Toll free: 1.877.363.6889
Fax: 1.319.395.7353
Website: *www.arrowbookstore.com*

Cover Design: *A&D Productions by Debbie Christian* © 2008
Photograph by: *C. Christopher Lindsay* © 2008

Acknowledgements

My temptation is to disregard an acknowledgments section entirely—not because of a lack of sincere gratitude, but simply because the list is so long and the chance of forgetting a faithful friend, for me, too great. Nevertheless, I shall try my best. Pardon any inadequacies. My parents, Ed and Grace Lindsay, for <u>always</u> believing in me, how can I thank you enough? To Eddie, Teri, Jake and Jerrilyn, my family, my love. Thanks for the home-cooked meals @ 2538. To the editors who worked so diligently in making this book immensely better than when it arrived upon their desktop, Judy Morrow, Jerry Gramckow and Debbie Christian. Thanks so much, you're the best! To Ang, yes, I know, it's been a while. Just by being you, you helped me in Life. There's not many who can do that. Always grateful. To Theresa Martin, who was able to continue to re-read, again and again, even when I was not able. Thanks Iret. To Lawanda for your contributions, Sock Man thanks you! To Pastor Carlos and Maxine, thanks for seeing that which was in me even before I did. To all the Pastors and Teachers who's anointed teachings over the years have encouraged and enlightened. To Francis Frangipane's Ministry of Arrow Publication, thank you for being a window of heaven to so many, even me. To my Friend, Father, Savior and Help in the time of trouble, Jesus Christ of Nazareth…this has always been Your project, start to finish, thanks for allowing me to be a part of it. You are Good.

"You have turned for me my mourning into dancing;
You have put off my sackcloth and clothed me
with gladness, to the end that my glory may
sing praise to You and not be silent. O Lord my God,
I will give thanks to You forever" (Psalms 30:11-12).

☙❧

Dedication

To my grandmothers, without whom, this would not be possible. To Grandma Mary, seems we love you now more than ever. Miss you. To Grandma Ellen, love ya! See Grams, I really did write a book! (When's our next trip to Whole Foods?) Finally, to the Believers everywhere, who actually believe...

Table of Contents

Introduction

"For the Word of the Lord is right;
and all His works are done in truth.
By the Word of the Lord were the heavens made;
and all the host of them by the breath of His mouth.
For He spake, and it was done;
He commanded, and it stood fast"
(Psalm 33: 4, 6 & 9).

New Beginnings

Fascinating, isn't it? A few choice words by the LORD in the beginning created an entire universe. Not only was a physical world breathed into existence, but also its endless accompanying functions: quantum physics, organic chemistry, quadratic equations, philosophy, art, psychology, music, and on and on and on. Order, wisdom, and beauty were framed from a formless, dark void by just a simple word. The same occurred throughout the Bible, Old and New Testaments alike. God spoke a word to His sons and daughters, and their obedience changed the course of their history and the history of the world.

The same principle applies to you and me today. One word from God spoken into your life can create an entirely new reality for you. In fact, today, in this season, there is a word to be spoken into your life containing a wealth of unlimited potential waiting to be unleashed.

"...For I know the plans I have for you," declares the LORD, *"plans to prosper you and not to harm you, plans to give you hope and a future..."* (Jeremiah 29:11, Today's New International Version).

Yes, my friend, God has ordained, declared and decreed that you, too, have a wonderful future of hope, peace and good things, and not of evil. That's the beauty and amazing privilege of knowing and serving the all powerful, *loving* God of creation. Now you must begin to believe it in order to live it.

If you will allow His words to speak into your heart, to every matter concerning you, those words have the power to unlock the chains of hopelessness and despair, confusion and darkness, bondage, and fears. His words truly have the power to heal all that causes you to remain fragmented—be it in your thoughts or feelings, or even your body. There is a specific answer awaiting you, regardless of where you are or what you're dealing with.

With one word of direction—of hope or creative inspiration—the dark pages of despair, sadness, and confusion can be altered in an instant. That word has the power to produce in you joy and rest. Where there was only sorrow the day before, a refreshing love of life can return. Beauty can be seen again; happiness restored. That is what happens when God speaks. Worlds are changed—even yours.

I am a living witness. God spoke a word into my own life when I was about to die emotionally, spiritually, and mentally, and it changed the course of my life forever. At the height of my frustration and despondency, a simple Word from God turned my life around resuscitating peace, life, and happiness to a degree I never before thought possible. How I continue to thank Him for that. As you read this book, I fully expect the same will be true for you.

Good News

Therein lies some of the good news. This book was not written by some happy-go-lucky Skip who one day lost his job, got down on his luck, hung his head, kicked a rock, then suddenly became inspired the next day while watching a matinee movie and wrote a book about it.

For most of us suffering from depression, it's just not that easy. There is no one silver bullet. Like its victims, depression has many layers. Its remedy, and I do believe there is one, is no different.

"Heaviness in the heart of man maketh it stoop: but a good word maketh it glad" (Proverbs 12:25). The really good news is that this book is a "good word" for you. It will, as the verse suggests, make you glad. How can I be so sure? Trust me, my presumptions are not due to my own arrogance, but because the good words of this book are based on the good Word of God, the Bible.

The fact that you picked up this book suggests that you or someone you know has a heavy ("stooped") heart. The Hebrew word for stoop in the above passage is "shachah," which means to "bow down," "fall," or, literally, "to depress."

Perhaps that describes you? Do you feel like your heart and mind, your very life, is being struck down, wounded, hurt, paralyzed, and depressed? Maybe you feel like you are in a fallen state, your spirit bowed down, broken, and weary. Do you feel alone in your depression, your despondency reaching the point of physical pain, the shedding of tears, and the loss of appetite? Perhaps you feel as if you are literally withering away?

To make matters worse, many of us are tempted to believe that depression is a recent phenomena, and somehow contrary to the Christian walk. We feel, because of the words of others, that a depressed Christian is a walking oxy*moron*. To under gird this belief, a great many preachers decry how disgusted and embarrassed they are with depressed Christians. "Christians should be the happiest people in the world," they rave.

Personally, I believe that most who view depression in this way are the naturally optimistic types anyway; the used-car salesmen of the world; the cup's "half-full" sort. If they were to admit it—absent life's depressing circumstances along the way—they were probably happy even before becoming a Christian. Yep, they were probably born happy.

No, just as being a non-Christian does not make you unhappy, being a Christian does not make you happy. But it can.

Doesn't the fact that friends and family have no clue as to what we're dealing with, make depression even more difficult? Sure, sometimes they have bad days, but they're never depressed. They want to know what's wrong; they don't realize we haven't a clue either. They want to know the *cause*. They don't get that if we knew *that*, we wouldn't still be struggling to get out of bed each day. We don't really know how we got here. We just know that we feel down, way down, and there seems to be no way to pull ourselves out.

You see, my friend, contrary to popular belief, the Bible has a lot to say about depression. In fact, many of the greatest characters mentioned in the Bible—Elijah, Job, Jeremiah, David, Paul—suffered tremendously from depression. They gave powerful explanations for the causes of depression—and they told of a means of escape. You see, you may be so depressed that you no longer feel the need to eat. You feel like your body is literally wasting away in affliction. Sorrow and solitude may be piercing you to the point of tears. Yet, that also describes the writer of Psalm 102. *"Hear my prayer, O Lord, and let my cry come unto thee. For my days are consumed like smoke, and my bones are burned as a hearth. My heart is smitten, and withered like grass; so that I forget to eat my bread. I watch, and am as a sparrow alone upon the house top. For I have eaten ashes like bread, and mingled my drink with weeping…. My days are like a shadow…"* (Psalm 102:1, 3, 4, 6, 9, 11).

Even the great Apostle Paul declared his suffering was well beyond his ability to endure, to the point of despairing even of life (see 2 Corinthians 1:8). The powerful prophet Elijah thought he would be better off dead. He despaired to the point of actually asking God to kill him.

Yet many preachers scold congregants: "What about joy, saints of God? Where is your joy?" Consequently, in addition to our feeling weighted down by depression itself, we remain condemned instead of uplifted; we feel guilt and shame instead of hope for a better future; we receive more and more questions instead of answers.

Suffice it to say, much of depression is compounded by confusion. Accordingly, as you read this book, remain prayerful. Ask God to expose in you what needs exposing, to uproot that which needs uprooting, to change what needs changing, and to add what needs adding. *"Being confident of this very thing, that He who has begun a good work in you will complete it until the day of Jesus Christ"* (Philippians 1:6).

Therefore, over the course of this book, let's try to unmask the mystery of depression and hold it in proper view. Let's see if we can understand the fuller dimensions of life and not be overtaken by an overly simplistic view of life and God. Let's not be ignorant of our enemy. Let us expose. Let us conquer. Let us rejoice once again.

Finally, this will not be a quick journey, for depression runs deep. Be patient; growth takes time. Do the work, even if it hurts. Be honest with yourself.

Remember, if nothing changes, nothing changes. Finally, prepare yourself to view the battle over depression in a surprisingly new way. If you are willing, you will have a newfound ability to be uplifted.

Chapter One

The Happy People

"Blessed (happy) is he who puts His trust in the Lord"
(Proverbs 16:20).

I never knew the "happy" people existed until I met Natalia. She was wonderfully talented, funny, beautiful—and, best of all, she was my girlfriend. As we grew closer and began to peel back the layers of friendship via late-night phone calls lasting well into the morning, she finally had the nerve to admit to me that she was—*can you believe it*—a genuinely happy person.

Assuming I knew a bill of goods when I'd seen or heard one, I questioned her further. "So, Natalia," I asked, doubtful indeed, "in the morning, right when you wake up, *before* a cup of coffee, are you generally in a good mood, bad mood, or somewhere in the middle, 'flat-lining'?"

Without hesitation she responded, "Good. Why?"

Why? Well, for one thing, I thought, because that's unbelievable. I'd never heard of such a thing—to wake up and just be happy for no particular reason. I could understand if it were the first day of an extended holiday, maybe a Saturday, or even your birthday—but just because? This was inconceivable!

Oh the naiveté. (She was four years older than I.) She was so innocent, so untainted by the cruel, cruel world called, "life." (She grew up in East Oakland—a drug-and-crime epicenter—I, in the sleepy suburbs of San Jose.) I was truly astounded that day.

The Happy People

Thus I began my quest to unearth the mystery of "the happy people." What hidden ingredient did they possess that I lacked? Though often in the same station in life, their smiles seemed to last longer. Why were their days more joyful? Exactly why were their spirits more uplifted?

Did they have more neurotransmitters firing properly than I had? Did they have more of Jesus, more money, more intelligence (less intelligence?), more personality, more fiber in their diet? What was it? I was determined to know.

Before we begin to explore that most pivotal question: What makes for *the happy people*? — I'd like to briefly share with you my story. It may be quite different from yours in that depression has many faces and shares many varied stories, but this will be a helpful starting point for our journey towards eradicating depression's grip.

My Nightmare Begins

Oddly enough, depression struck me when I was a Christian. In the fall of 1990, I worked as a bank teller for a major banking institution. It was the perfect college-entry, part-time job. At that time, my life still *looked* good on paper. I had graduated from high school with an academic top-rating, voted "Best All Around" by my peers. I'd even received a significant scholarship to a prestigious local university. On top of that, I was a successful athlete, with trophies in several sports. I was the varsity football quarterback, and I had been voted the homecoming prince as a freshmen as well as homecoming king as a senior. It seemed my life couldn't have been better. Yet, even then, depression—along with its agents, *doubt and fear*—had begun its pursuit.

Fast forward ten years: I had just graduated law school. I'd spent a summer at one of the most selective internships in the country, working for the F.B.I. in the Office of the General Counsel in downtown Washington D.C. I was among the world's movers and shakers. Yes, it was supposed to be my time to put my enduring footprint upon the globe.

As a child, I'd always felt I wanted to do "something big." Now it was time. There were no more excuses for me not to do it. Schooling was over; I had earned a law degree. Coupled with Christ at the helm, I was thoroughly equipped. After all my past "successes" everyone was waiting for me to "Just Do It"—to hit my professional home run. All eyes were on me, and it was time for me to shine.

Yet, I couldn't even get a base hit. Fear and Doubt had not only caught up with me, they had completely overshadowed me. Though not in a physical sense, I was nonetheless crippled in life; both paralyzed and immobilized. Despite my best efforts, I could not move forward.

So, ten years after graduating in the top third of my law school class, I began working not as a lawyer, but as a bank teller. That's right! I was working at exactly the same job I had as a college teenager. Yes, while my law-school study partner was making just shy of six figures, I was making just over six bucks an hour! Can you imagine that? Can you imagine the shame and humiliation I felt? Can you imagine how my thoughts tormented me? The votes were coming in, and I was failing—no, I had failed. I was going down, and it seemed more and more probable that my best days were behind me. It wouldn't have been a stretch for me to feel that I was not going to amount to much. I felt many saw me as a fool—and how could I argue against such an assessment?

I was approaching my thirtieth birthday doing the exact same job I'd done just out of high school. I told others it was just a temporary gig while I was studying to retake the Bar exam, but I knew better. I knew the real reason.

Fear gripped me. I never felt confident enough to venture out into the unknown and risk failure. As a consequence, I only stepped backward — into the known, the familiar, the comfortable.

Doubt confused me. I was never fixed in my decisions for long, nor was I ever sure of what I wanted to do. A grand idea on one day was in the garbage heap the next. I was now captive to that Fear and Doubt, and I knew it. The hurt of that fact drew me down all the more. I had tried to fight my way out, but I was losing—I couldn't even *see* a way out. I felt the world condemning me, judging me, criticizing me—even mocking me.

As a result, I didn't want to be around anyone—especially family and friends. I hated their attention, their probing queries. I certainly didn't want to be around any Bible-"toting-and-quoting" Christians. I had a hard enough time just reading the Bible. The most I could muster was a glimpse at the Psalms. I felt the psalmist's anguish of heart. What I didn't need was a "just-trust-God" pep talk from a jolly old parishioner who'd never known a day of depression in his life. Heck, I knew enough Bible verses. I'd gone to church since I was a toddler. I could confidently bet that I knew more verses from memory than most pastors; I needed help, and I just wasn't getting it—not even from the Man Upstairs (or so it seemed). Even as a Christian, the best I could do was fall to my knees at night and beg God for a little help while I shed a few more tears on my already tear stained comforter. Thus began my continued descent as a depressed Christian.

From King to Conductor

FEAR. True, it had made earlier appearances in my life, but as a young person, the consequences of bowing to its voice seemed less noticeable and less injurious. Actually, I'd grown so accustomed to swimming in those currents of fear, doubt, and worry that it's difficult to determine when I actually began to drown in them.

I remember turning down the track coach and opting not to try out for the track team for fear that I would, contrary to the stereotype, lose a race to a "slow, white guy." (Please forgive me, but my thinking at that time was rather shallow.) I remember dropping out of calculus the first week for fear of getting less than a good grade.

I remember when my friends and I decided to try out for the big school play, "The Music Man." We (arrogantly) thought we'd transform drama from a "geeky" thing to outright "cool." I remember singing a song for the drama teacher. Then, during a volleyball match, the results were posted. My friend exclaimed rather jubilantly that I'd won the lead role. My first thought: "No way, Jose!" The next day I remember telling the drama instructor I couldn't do it.

"Why," he asked, puzzled.

"Well, duh," I thought to myself, "because I had no training in drama; because I'd make an utter fool of myself on stage, in front of all those people; because I was downright afraid." He tried to convince me otherwise. I, of course, wouldn't have it.

Then I remember getting re-cast—as the conductor. My sole line in the entire play: "All abooooaarrrdddd!"

Such became the ever-increasing pattern in my life—only as time grew, so too did the stakes. I was so afraid of what others thought. I was terrified of failing in front of someone, anyone. So instead, I'd quit before that moment of failure could strike. Sort of like "quitting your girl-friend" (as my grandmother called it) because, and only because, you knew she was going to quit you. Instead of going further in life, I began to shrink back to do only those things I knew I could do well — easy things — things without risk or challenge — things where I remained safe.

Because of such fears, I began to quit, run, and hide—to lower and lower states of existing. As I became older, the consequences grew more grave—and I was falling deeper and deeper downward. After college, I found myself digging ditches for a living -- literally. After law school, I was a bank teller, again.

Don't get me wrong; there's nothing wrong with being a bank teller. There's also nothing wrong with being a conductor, or a "C" student, or gas station attendant for that matter—if that's your destiny that God put inside of you. However, if within your divine destiny there lies more — if you are unfulfilled and not satisfied — if, for example, your true dream or vision is to be the president of a major Fortune 500 company and, yet, you're still working at a gas station—well then, *we've got a problem.*

That problem was eating away at me daily. To make matters worse, that problem became entwined in the already existent layers of depression within me. Soon I was beginning to become convinced that the best of my life was behind me. What a scary thought for a guy in his late 20s.

Bad Part

Now let me tell you what the really bad part was: I was a Christian. Not a casual one either. It wasn't that being a Christian itself was bad, but being a Christian made me feel worse. Why? Because I knew too much. I knew God doesn't give us a spirit of fear, yet I continued to battle fear (and lose). I knew God promised to lead and guide, yet year after year I remained without direction. I knew that His sheep hear His voice, yet I was hearing nothing. How could I know that I had eternal life yet continue living in this spiral of death?

It would have been different if I had been an atheist, or if I'd been wrestling with the question of life's purpose, or if I was struggling with some dark, heinous sin—and then wondered why I wasn't hearing from God. On the contrary, I was pursuing God as diligently as I could. I had no skeletons in my closet. I spent time in the Word and in prayer. I even taught Sunday school. Still, I was coming up short, way short. In my heart of hearts, I loved God. Yet, there was something blocking me. I didn't have the joy the Bible promised. I didn't have much of anything that was promised to believers. I knew there had to be more in this life, and I knew that the answer was Christ. Yet, Christ I already knew.

Even after knowing Jesus Christ, after being baptized, saying the "sinner's prayer," singing in the choir, etc., etc., etc., I still felt something was missing. I never felt at peace in my relationship with God. Daily, I struggled at what I thought pleased God. Yet, my Christianity could be characterized only by endless cycles of victories chased down by immediate defeat. I'd spend good quiet time with God on one day, yet defeated by the enemy in guilt-ridden thought patterns the next. This life of frustration was a roller coaster at best. Then, after all the dark years, after all the pain, fear, and shame, I began my journey out of the pit.

The Nightmare Ends

Just last night, while visiting with my dad over a late night waffle and orange juice, he congratulated me. He told me he was proud of me. He used to say that to me as a little boy. I hadn't heard it in a while, so I asked him why he said it.

"For sticking it out. For changing," he replied.

I could only laugh and shake my head. It was a no-brainer. If I was going to live at all, I *had* to change. To have continued down that course would have killed me. Maybe not physically, but to be living a life with only a fraction of joy, with only a fraction of my potential and purpose, was in fact killing me. To awaken daily to a life never fulfilled, always frustrated, only settling on a life far from my goals, ambitions, and dreams is *death*. Isn't it? I was living a life of "less than." What I wanted, what I yearned for, was a life of "more than enough."

My dad congratulated me because I was finally beginning to live in that life of more than enough. I'd switched tracks and found my path. No longer is my Christian life defined by guilt, despair, and frustration—with only a glimmer of hope of a bright future. Rather, I live each day with peace and joy. Imagine that. Though "saved" most of my entire life, only as of late have I felt like the new creation the Bible promises. I used to think that label was only relegated to those with a radically saved salvation experience, those who came to Christ after a lifestyle of sex, drugs, and rock and roll—not to those who were born in the pews. How wrong I was.

Listen. Maybe your "issues" have nothing to do with those I touched on. Maybe you have become hopeless, tired, and despairing for other reasons altogether. Maybe you have found yourself in a downward cycle of broken and betrayed relationships. Maybe you or a loved one has been afflicted by illness. Maybe you've been used and abused ever since your earliest memories. Maybe you're simply overwhelmed with life itself. Maybe you, too, are waking up to a life without purpose, without relationships, without peace. Maybe what is tormenting you is a life without passion. Maybe you're struggling with a seemingly unbreakable addiction, and it is becoming unbearable.

Though the causes may be diverse, the result is the same. We've found, to our horror, the pangs of depression. We've been living a life of less than—less than we desire, less than we're destined for, less than we dreamed of. So we have sadness, frustration, hopelessness, and sleepless nights to show for it. It is time to change.

"I waited patiently for the LORD; and He inclined to me, and heard my cry. He also brought me up out of a horrible pit, out of the miry clay, and set my feet upon a rock, and established my steps.

He has put a new song in my mouth – Praise to our God; many will see it and fear, and will trust in the LORD" (Psalm 40:1-3).

Say this prayer with me as we conclude this chapter: *"Father, I thank You that You have more in store for my life. I thank You that You have a better way. Lord, I thank You that Your Word is life. Father, I am in a horrible pit right now and I need You desperately. I am dying in so many ways, and I need You and Your life. Please, Father, You see my struggles. You see my pain, and You have seen my tears. I am crying out to You right now. I am calling upon Your Name for help. I look to You to bring me out, to rescue me, to save me and to heal me. I ask that You will teach me a new way as I continue to read this book and Your Word. I give You permission to have Your way with me. I surrender to You and am willing to change according to Your will. Turn my weeping to joy and my tears to gladness. I don't know how, but I know You can. Deliver me from depression forever, and into the abundant life that You have promised in Jesus. Help me, Lord. Save me. Rescue me. In Jesus' Name. Amen."*

CRID

Chapter Two
The Heart of the Matter

Beans and Rice

The height of my depression came when I was in Los Angeles, the "City of Angels." Then, I was convinced it referred to the fallen angels. Every day was a fight. I was constantly backed up against the ropes, being pulverized by life itself.

I knew God had called me there; I just didn't know why. I prayed continually, even over my bills. I tithed. I made it to church in time for praise and worship. In spite of it all, I could count the items in my refrigerator with my left hand, and the furnishings in my apartment with my right.

My dinners routinely consisted of legumes cooked with whole, brown rice and spinach (I was still a quasi health nut). Lunch was a standard peanut butter and jelly. Breakfast was a Krusteaz, "add water only" pancake with syrup, the imitation, two-gallon-jug-for-a-buck kind (thus, the quasi). I prided myself on my ability to eat for less than two dollars a day (those who saw my haggard appearance probably wondered why). My only comfort was the hope that the constant onslaught of police helicopters circling above my apartment complex would somehow keep the rent down.

I was a miserable wretch. I felt I was down for the count. Ever been to that place where you feel that your circumstances are completely hopeless? Ever felt there was no way out—only a continuous spiral downward? Ever felt like you were so overmatched that you never should have entered the fight? Ever wonder how you even got into the ring? Well, that was me.

Worse still, I felt no one was in my corner. I had no trainer, no cut man, and no cheering section this time around. I certainly didn't want to be around any and all of my, ever-so-sanguine, friends and family. No one understood what I was really going through in the still of the night. I had grown up a veritable, Saturday Night Live, "Superstar," having succeeded in most everything I put my hands to. Those were the good 'ole days. The nightmare — mine — had begun.

Remember now, I was still a Christian, and not a nominal one. I could quote scripture after scripture. I just couldn't lay hold of the promises of God—the promises of peace and joy and abundant life. I knew the words in the Word; they just didn't seem to be working.

For all my knowledge of the truth, I was still not free. Joy continued to escape my desperate grasp. Then, in the midst of my prayers and cries to God for help, an answer came.

Remember my quest to discover the secrets of "the happy people" from the previous chapter? Remember my desire to uncover what they knew that I didn't? Well, in this chapter, I would like to share with you their secret.

Yes, after extensive empirical research (I talked to a lot of people), my discovery came. Though I'm sure I have the right answer, I have a feeling you're not going to like it. That's why I remind you, I was a professional, too—at depression, that is. I was not a "happy person" who happened upon a bad day or two. I'm a veteran of this war, just as easily wired for depression as you. For you and me both, depression lasts longer and hits harder. So remember as you read on, we're on the same team.

So here's the difference that allows the happy people to remain consistently happier, and forces depressed people into reading books such as this: Happy people genuinely and consistently think positive about life and about themselves. They're natural-born optimists. Nine times out of ten, they are assured, confident, and hopeful. Let me put it another way: Happy people have happy thoughts. That's it! Period.

People who have gladness in their hearts have glad thoughts. Cheery people carry within themselves a constant hope. Granted, that hope may be totally unreasonable, without basis, and at times downright foolish, but the net result is the same: Happiness. Happy people wake up simply believing that this day will be their day. They believe life's twists will turn their way, and if, by chance, they don't, they still believe all will work out in the end. Those of us with a penchant for depression—well… don't. We are life's unsung pessimists.

I said you wouldn't like it, but it's true. I know we like to think it's deeper and much more profound because the problem seems to be so overpowering and overwhelming. Our pride persuades us that our opponent is much more formidable. To be sure, sometimes it is. For the most part, however, it isn't. Simply put, most of us who suffer the ever-present pangs of depression lack the positive-thinking patterns that energize the happy people. Take heart, however, for we are about to change that.

So, please, put away your stones and hear me out for when we really *get this,* life changes and joy awakens.

Prescriptions for Happiness by the Great Physician

Now before you start thinking this is my own Philosophy 101, let's ground this firmly in Scripture. Repeatedly, God's Word states, *"Blessed is he who puts his trust in the Lord."* In such passages the word blessed means "happy." The word *happy* means "exuberant joy." Practically speaking, exuberant joy means being in a good mood consistently, daily. It means getting out of bed in the morning, glad. It means being able to get up out of bed, period. It means a life free from depression's chokehold.

The word, "trust" in the above passages means a "refuge," a "hiding place." *Trust* is a place of safety, shelter and help. Consider also Psalms 43:5. *Why so downcast* [literally, "sunk" or "depressed"] *O my soul, put your hope* ["to patiently wait," "trust"] *in God.*

Over and over again, the Bible gives a brief, one sentence prescription for happiness: *"Put your trust in the Lord."* It's so simple it's almost insulting.

Here's how it works: When we give improper weight and validity to the wrong "thing," the forces of depression activate and advance. When we heed the overwhelming details of our day—the problems with our relationships, the crises at our jobs, the ailments in our bodies, the dimness of our future (when we give in to circumstances)—then peace and joy instantly dissipate.

As a result, we can't rest as well as we used to. We're more critical, cynical, and sensitive. We have anxiety attacks. Though our times spent with loved ones should be filled with gaiety, each visit is more like an internal gale storm. We're aloof to those around us. We have no spark; only sarcasm. Our countenance displays more zits than zeal. Our misguided focus paralyzes us and strips away life's pleasures. We can't work right, think right, or act right. Therefore, we can't engage life to the fullest. We've lost hope's light. The joy once springing up within has been quietly laid to rest.

We become impoverished, like a vagabond, pillaged of our heart's happiness. We have no refuge. Rather, our refuge is in the wrong place. Yes, we believe in God, but our mind's focus is on our circumstance and situation, not on our Loving and Sovereign Lord.

Yes, my friend, we do have a choice. That's why the Scriptures say to "put" your trust in God. These Spirit-filled authors knew that we all "put" our trust somewhere. The only question is "where" we will put it. We'll either put our trust in our own talents, intellect, friends, influence, money, and so on—or we'll put it in God.

This type of choice was mine during my season of unemployment. A man without work, without purpose, I felt the most miserable and despised of creatures on earth. The economy was in the throes of depression. I had a long list of reasons of why I had failed in life. The more I thought about that list, the longer it got, and the more deplorable I felt.

I shared these despairing thoughts with a friend who, in response, gave me this simple reminder: "Carmen, there are two sides to that story." She was right. The list of my successes was just as long. Better yet, God was on my side. What job couldn't I get? After all, is not the Lord my Shepherd, and shall I not want? Then and there, upon that hope, I began to fix my mind. Then, my spirit became uplifted.

Most assuredly, the more we put our trust in God, the happier we will become, and, dear reader, this is guaranteed! Remember that the *Bible says* putting one's "trust in God" is the ticket to happiness. Replete throughout Scripture, the prescription for an exuberant spirit is active trust. *If you trust in God, you will be happy.* Even Christ declared that the remedy for a troubled heart is belief in God (see John 14:1). It's a divine maxim. Trust is a principle for a happy, healthy, and secure life.

Why is this so? It's because a wholehearted trust that God will work out *every* situation in our life leaves no space in which depression can linger. Anxiety, fear, doubt, condemnation, and anger can find no room in a heart that trusts and is wholly convinced that God will come through. That person has hope. Where there is hope—real, expectant hope—depression can find no foothold. There remains nothing more to be depressed about. Everything is going to work out on our behalf—favorably. It's a vacation mentality. It is confidently believing that it's all going to turn out "peachy." Why? Because we trust.

This mentality has nothing to do with your current circumstances, so it's foolproof as well. It endures even when life is bigger than you are. It's not based on what others can do for you, so there's no need to be manipulated or swayed by others' opinions. It's not based on self-confidence, or self-reliance, so it rests not on your intellect or abilities or lack thereof.

Incidentally, I've found that folks with genuine, consistent happiness do this instinctively. Remember the *happy people*? They're already convinced that life is going to work out all right. It's the rest of us—the depressed—who must get this into our inner man—by any means necessary.

Vacation Blues?

Let's examine the evidence. To do so, think back to a time when you were glad. For those whose depression causes sleeplessness, recall a time when you slept soundly. For those who embody lethargy when depressed, resort to an event that popped you out of bed spry as a robin. Were you on vacation, about to go skiing, hopping on a plane to visit an old friend? Was it the first day of an extended vacation and there was nothing on your plate but a few irrelevant dishwasher spots?

When I face a full day of events that *I want to do*, chances are I'm going to wake up bright-eyed and bushy-tailed—regardless of the amount of sleep I've had the night before. I tend not to be depressed during vacations. During my month-long layover on the beaches of Mexico, I wasn't depressed once. While playing pick-up games of basketball at the park, I tend not to wallow in internal affliction.

However, the majority of my days are not spent in Mexico, on the basketball court, or on the ski slopes. Consequently, I did not always begin the majority of my days jumping out of bed ready to greet the world with a Coke and a smile. On the contrary, it would ordinarily take prescription-strength doses of coffee to pry my weary eyes apart.

Despite verses like Romans 8:28, I really didn't believe everything would work out for my good. My mind was never convinced of a hopeful expectation, but rather filled with pessimism and doubt. On any given day I never saw anything on the horizon to suggest mirth. My tendency toward over-analysis caused me to see too many possible obstacles and uncertainties along the way to ever allow my hopes to get too high.

I guess that's a nice way of saying I was negative, especially when it had to do with my own life estimations. I claimed to be a realist but let's face it, I was really a pessimist. Though I'd have never admitted it, I was one. Now, before you preclude yourself from the same category, hear me out. Are you free from worry?

Don't Believe Everything You Think

Happy people, consciously or not, constantly tell themselves they can. I'm willing to bet that most of us who consistently battle depression tell ourselves we can't. The happy people are convinced that happy days lie ahead, regardless of circumstances. The rest of us wait for proof beyond a reasonable doubt. This is depression's fodder.

Do you disagree? Just think about your depression. Trace its root. How much of it stems from unbelief or a lack of trust that all will work out positively? How much of your depression stems from your letting your circumstances overwhelm you? Do you doubt you'll make it, that you can do it, or that God will help you? How much of it is due to the fact that you don't believe a better day is in store? How much of it is a result of not having trusted in God enough to make Him your refuge, deliverer, and strength?

In our deepest despair, running rampant are these hidden thoughts: *I'll never have purpose. I'll never have a fulfilling relationship, or a fulfilling career. This project isn't going to work. This dream won't be fulfilled. This relationship is irreconcilable. I can't do it. I'll never lose this weight. It won't work; things won't get better. What's the use? Who am I? I can't. This is hopeless; my life is hopeless; I am hopeless.*

"For as he thinketh in his heart, so is he" (Proverbs 23:7).

Our thoughts will determine not only our judgment, but our journey as well. Remember, those with happy, positive thoughts are happy, positive people. Those with defeated, negative thoughts will feel—and live—defeated.

Another good friend who is a "happy person" stated that every day she simply looks forward to seeing what good things God's going to do. She expects it, regardless. So why don't we all do the same? Men and women of God, our thoughts will determine who we are. They can bring joy or depression. The choice remains ours.

Yesterday, seeds of doubt started to sprout in my mind and I began to "go down" like I used to in the old days. Though it didn't last long, I forced myself to trace back to the roots of this depression. It was a familiar pattern. I had questioned my abilities. Condemnation and confusion crept in. Fear, frustration, and despair followed. I doubted my capabilities, my opportunities, my dreams, the viability of my vision, its truth, and its coming reality. I had no hope or optimism of a happy future. I felt no guarantees of bright days ahead, and depression's waves began to pulverize me once again.

Not By Sight

Don't get me wrong, we have all the cogent arguments to support our doubts: *"I'm not qualified," "She's always like that," "It will never get any better," "I've never done that," "You don't know for sure," "They'll think I'm...."* Our concerns may even be valid. We disregard the fact that they bring us sadness. Instead, we put a premium on subjective probability. We project in our minds the obstacles, and our emotional health and well-being pay the price.

We, the depressed, care too much about having our thoughts line up with perceived realities. As a result, we wind up with hearts beleaguered. We sacrifice our happiness for logical outcomes. We become defeated before we even try. A hurdle arises, and we begin to doubt and hesitate. When we finally do try, the possibility of striking out at our first time at bat leaves us to give up altogether. We are so easily discouraged, so easily distracted. Yet God says, take courage, do not be dismayed, finish the course.

Meanwhile, the happy people couldn't care less about these "realities" and obstacles. They don't do the same math we do. It may well be blind faith, but at least their ignorance gives them bliss. Though their positive, grinning confidence flies in the face of reason, guess what? Their happiness remains.

The happy people's mental default is set to optimism. Those of us on the verge of a mental meltdown have our thoughts set for doubt. The consequences of doubt are confusion, fear, defeat, hopelessness, and depression. Ultimately, doubt leads to death.

Consider the ultimate path of depression: Suicide. It is hopelessness empowered. It's the belief that the chances of a happy future materializing are too difficult, impossible, impractical, or improbable.

What of laughter and mirth? They're based on the belief that a beautiful future awaits; it's resounding and defiant hope. What lies in the middle is the object of our considerations... our circumstances. For the despairing soul, circumstances are overwhelming. To the optimist, nothing is overwhelming. As believers, our outlook should be no different, for, with a loving, altruistic God dwelling on the inside, all things are possible and nothing is too difficult. Therefore, if God is for us, we should always believe that everything will eventually work out wonderfully, beyond our wildest dreams, as we are read in Ephesians 3:20. To the intellectual, the pessimist, and the atheist, that is a ridiculous presumption. They are right, naturally speaking. For without faith (seeing beyond the natural), it is impossible to please God (see Hebrews 11:6).

Opportunity Knocks

I bet I can hear what you're saying: "That's great for the happy people, but what about the rest of us?" Well, my friend, the great news is that we can become the happy people. We can cross over. You see, the good news is that we can reprogram these negative settings in our minds. Scripture tells us to do this. We are to transform our minds to the way the mind was originally programmed. What's great is that since we're setting our brain's defaults, we have the opportunity to set them all correctly.

You see, though the happy people have their thoughts programmed to optimism, in fact their optimism may be placed on the wrong thing. They may simply have a lot of *self-confidence* and believe they can overcome anything. Indeed, that will help them overcome *most* of what they encounter. However, eventually, life will become bigger than their self-confidence and this weak foundation will crumble. It may be a result of a failed relationship, business venture, or dream. It may not arise until they're lying on their deathbed but, sooner or later, life becomes bigger than we are.

However, if we have our optimism set according to truth, based on something bigger than life, even bigger than death, we can always rejoice. Always. Our foundation is set on things above and will remain solid beneath us as we endure life's realities.

Joy's Source

In the parable of the "talents," we learn that the faithful stewards are allowed into "the joy of the Lord." Interesting isn't it? God is joyful. In spite of all the death, violence, hate, division, and darkness that goes on in the world, God has joy. I find this striking. The Guy who knows everything is not down in the dumps but, quite the contrary, up in the clouds—happy. It's not because we serve a twisted and morbid God, but because He just happens to know that all will work out for the good — that ultimately everything turns out to be beautiful, righteous, and proper. This is about having a mindset elevated to God's truths. God's in control. Our trust brings us closer to God, knowing He's in control.

As I said earlier, I used to be the master of doubt and fear. Then, I began to change my mind. I began to gain unwavering trust that our God would take care of "it." ("It" meaning everything. "Everything" meaning **every** thing.)

This trust came by forcing myself, daily, for hours, to get into the God's Word. *"Faith [trust] cometh by hearing the word of God"* (Romans 10:17). Happy people may not need to spend hours in

God's Word to be mastered by positive, true thoughts. I did. As I began to read each day how God works—how God loves (how God *is love*); how God comes through (every time); of God's faithfulness, compassion, and benevolent intervention on behalf of His children—I began to trust. I began to realize the significance of God's name: *"The LORD, the LORD, Abounding in love, quick to forgive, slow to anger..."* (Exodus 34:6), and I began to trust Him more and more. As I adopted these truths, I consequently began to get rid of the lies: that God was angry with me, always out to punish me, always looking at my faults, failings, and frailties. I began to trust even more.

That trust gained momentum; it began to govern my thoughts in the morning, then in the evening. How, specifically, did I do it? In the morning, when my mind starts its natural course to become overwhelmed by the day's tasks or the ill state of some of my personal affairs, instead of letting them cast me down, I give them all to God. I trust and pray until that trust begins to grow and take root, until I'm actually confident that the Lord is going to handle it. I find my refuge in Him, and can walk away with joy because He has charge of those things now—and I don't. I pray until I have made Him my refuge regarding my career, relationships, family, personal "issues"—everything. I've found that when I do give Him everything, *completely*, He completely takes care of it all. I rejoice once again.

That trust allowed me to smile because I was trusting God for the first time in my life. Oh, yes, I'd been a Christian for years and years and years. I'd taught Sunday school, served as an usher, and sang in the choir, but depression still haunted me—until I started practicing that trust.

I put trust in motion before every visit to a neighbor, before picking up the phone, before a project—before my day. Then I just thanked Him for working it out, believing it would work out, even before it happened. I believed it until I could see it. Sure, it took a complete reprogramming of my mind. It's not blind faith, but faith mixed with truth. It's not easy, but it's worked every time. Why? Because it is written *"...whoever trusts in the LORD is kept safe"* (Proverbs 29:25b). Why? Because it is written *"...He is a shield to those who take refuge in Him"* (Proverbs 30:5b). Why? Because such verses are laced throughout the Good Book. It is a point of knowing that is intrinsically embedded in your brain. No surgeon or circumstance is able to remove this knowing.

Begin to see it yourself. Pinpoint those things in your life that cause you to feel hopeless, defeated, deflated, and depressed. Then believe that they can be overcome by God's grace and power working on your behalf. Believe it until you can see it. See yourself succeeding in relationships with God's help. See yourself losing weight with God's intervention. See yourself protected with God as your shield. See yourself freed from fear and anger, lust and lies, with God's hand upon you. See your future utterly and completely blessed. See yourself financially free. See your children freed from rebellion. Why? Because you've put your trust in nothing else but the loving hands of the LORD.

"My comfort in my suffering is this:
Your promise preserves my life" (Psalm 119:50).
"My soul faints with longing for your salvation,
but I have put my hope in your word" (Psalm 119:81).
"Some trust in chariots and some in horses, but we trust in the name
of the LORD our God. They are brought to their knees and fall,
but we rise up and stand firm" (Psalm 20:7-8).

Today, I have a solid defense against depression's attacks. Sure, it still tries every once in a while. Now I know where to go. More accurately, I know where to put my thoughts and trust. I put them in God. I put them on the truth that nothing is too difficult for me because I can do all things through Him. I give no room to lies that may try to invade my mind. I give no credence to thoughts that say I can't, or it won't happen. I've found that nothing is stronger. What can arise that's bigger than God? What's stronger than His love? This trust is based on God's Word. Nothing is more sound. My heart is lifted. Because I trust, I am happy. It is a reality that I can actually feel it for the first time. My friend, that same trust is available to you as well right now. God is yearning for you to actively put your trust in Him, today and for the rest of your days. That trust is within your reach this very hour. He is a very good and present Help in time of trouble. Allow Him to be yours.

As we end this chapter, say this prayer with me: *"Father, I come to You now in the Name of Your Son, Jesus Christ. Lord, I admit that I have allowed fear and doubt to rule, control and overshadow me. Father, forgive me for not trusting in You for every detail of my life. Forgive me for leaning on my own understanding and for walking by sight, and not by faith. I choose now, this day, and for the rest of my days to walk by faith, trusting in Your loving Name. Father, I put my trust in You for every issue in my life. I trust that You will be my shield and my strength. Loving Father, I trust that You will help me. I don't know how and I can't see a way out, but I still trust in You right now. I trust that You will make a way for me; that You will show me which way to go; You will rescue me from that which would try to harm me. Yes, LORD, for every thing concerning me, I place my trust in You and You alone. Thank You Lord for hearing me and answering me. Thank You for making a way. Remind me by Your Holy Spirit when I slip back to my former ways of doubt and fear, anxiety and anger. Help me by Your Spirit to change the way I think forever, that my mind would be renewed, that I would be transformed. Thank You Lord. I receive Your help right now. I receive Your peace. Thank You Lord. Thank You for Your love. I receive it now. Thank You Lord Jesus. I trust in You in O God. I put my trust in You! In Jesus' name, Amen!"*

Chapter Three

The Heart of the Matter Continued:

Practical "How to's" of Happiness

"Sacrifice thank offerings to God, fulfill your vows to the Most High, and call upon me in the day of trouble; I will deliver you, and you will honor me. He who sacrifices thank offerings honors me, and He prepares the way so that I may show him the salvation of God" (Psalm 50:15:23).

Shadows

Ever been overtaken by a shadow? Remember basking in the warmth of a sunny day when suddenly the air becomes colder, and the sky darker. You look up to discover the presence of clouds interrupting the sun's glory.

My life was somewhat like that. I had a great childhood: I played outside all day on Saturdays, and went to a great school with great friends. My parents were (and still are) all that good parents should be, I had no bed-wetting issues...but then, somehow, from somewhere, the clouds came. Shadows had overtaken me. I just can't remember the day.

It's difficult to trace back depression's first strike. Was it during high school, when I would bury myself in my room, endlessly listening to music, closing the door to family and the world around me? Was it the time I—though a stand-out athlete and academic—broke down crying uncontrollably in front of a complete stranger? Was it when I lay in bed, night after night, literally crying out to God, or was it the time I had to receive stitches to close up the large slit I had incised on my wrist?

Yes, it's difficult to pinpoint exactly the day I first understood that the beast I was battling was called, "depression." If I had to choose, I suppose it was when I began to turn off my home telephone ringer, then the answering machine as well. Eventually, I was unplugging the phone altogether for days on end. I told my closest friends, simply, "I'm going down," and I'd go down. There was nothing more to be said. There was nothing to be done. Depression struck hard and fast.

I realized then that this probably wasn't normal. You see, it wasn't that creditors were calling; it wasn't that I was trying to save on my phone bill. I just couldn't deal with life anymore, nor did I want to. I just didn't want to talk to or see family or friends—people I actually liked and loved—anymore. I just didn't want to be around them—or anyone for that matter. Somewhere along the way, hope had died.

How did I ever get into such a deep, dark pit? More so, how could I ever get out? If you've ever asked yourself these same questions, please continue on the journey with me.

Deadly Doldrums

The funny thing about a shadow is that it must take the shape of the pattern it reflects, yet without its substance or color; it's cold and lifeless. Isn't that exactly how we feel under the shadows? Our substance, our potential, our desires, even our ability to express life—happiness, joy, love, sorrow, anger, passion—all feel squelched somehow. Life loses its luster, the apple its sweetness. For most of us with depression, even the will to get out of bed, to be with others and, yes, even the will to live—are gone.

I felt the weight of darkness pressing its thumb harshly upon me, crushing me. I was suffocating from life itself, and I knew it.

"I'm dying here, Lord," became my familiar cry. "You're killing me." I'd been told that life was hard, but I was certain it wasn't supposed to turn out like this. Over time, however, I wasn't so sure. Are we to simply live in despair with no hope? Is hope for the "more" immature, naïve or selfish? Is the game of life to merely live, breathe, eat, sleep, exist and die, and the wisest of us would just get on with it?

Going Down

Indeed, during those times of "going down," I hated to come across Scripture passages concerning the pleasant promises of God. Those times, however, were fast and frequent, for the Bible is filled with such optimistic assurances. They frustrated me because I could find them on the page but no longer in my life. I read how I was blessed, but I felt cursed. God's Word said joy should define my life, but I lived in sorrow. God's promises of His presence, peace, and power seemed only an elusive, ethereal ideal on the cusp of evaporating altogether. Inevitably, I began to wonder what was wrong with me. I was convinced I had failed. Worse, I begin to wonder if I was a failure. Had I failed God so much that those promises were no longer available for me?

What changed all of that is what I began to share in the last chapter. I started practicing a simple, yet profound truth: I began to trust God. In this chapter I would like to continue by breaking this radical recipe down into daily, practical ways so that you can practice it too…and feel the joy of the Lord restored, for *happy is he who puts his trust in the Lord* (Psalm 40:4, 84:12).

Assume the Risk

I have found that just about every day brings unwanted and unforeseen events. I've also found that those events can cause needless worry, anxiety, fretting, and emotional energy. I've found that those unwanted or unpredictable events can cause depression, anger, fear, confusion, and doubt. I rarely find myself there anymore, and if I do, it is not a long visit.

To overcome depression then, I've learned to make some assumptions. In short, I'm living more like a fool, and I'm a lot happier as a result. I now assume that instead of this unpleasant or unwanted or *unwhatever* situation turning out the way I think it will, I trust that God will cause all things to result in my being blessed. (Remember, God declares He will bless our going out and our coming in!) (See Deuteronomy 28:6 and Psalm 121:8).

I assume that when I have to visit a person who is grumpy, moody, angry, and just plain mean—ten out of ten times, God will turn it into a blessed time in which I can minister some love, peace, and kindness. I assume God will bless those events that I don't want to go to, and that He will use me to bless someone. I assume God will bless any situation that has gone from bad to worse.

Thanksgiving

Then, after all my assumptions, I begin to praise God. I thank Him for what He's about to do. I thank Him when I wake up for what He's going to do—especially when I can't even see it coming. I thank Him until that thankfulness gets into my spirit. I thank Him until I have enough faith to kindle some joy on the inside. I thank Him until I smile because I believe He will do something completely "ridiculous." I thank Him until I smile because I know I'm a total fool for believing He will do just as He says He will do. See Colossians 3:16.

The crazy thing is, every time I do it, He does bless it and causes the outcome to be completely unlike what I would have originally expected. He causes my mountains to be moved. God enjoys to put His hands to our situations and show His magnificence.

I know for all the happy people out there this may not sound like a big news flash. As for us depressed folks—those of us who barely wake up with a pulse, let alone a spring in our step—it will provide heightened optimism. Some call this joy.

Today it's not so difficult for me to believe the impossible because God is showing me again and again examples of impossibilities made possible. I'm walking more and more into my divinely appointed calling. With the impossible possible, I can walk in fulfillment.

I'm not just talking about life's big-ticket items. This is about everything; every detail of our lives—children, jobs, marriage, health, relationships, attitudes, education—everything. It happened again for me this morning. I visited a person who makes the Wicked Witch of the North look like one of Santa's helpers. I didn't want to, but I knew the call to love was greater. I just assumed God would bless it and make it a profitable time, a time for His glory.

I thanked Him for blessing this time. I was able to smile as I walked to the front door because I knew I was "crazy." I knew I was asking God to do something totally improbable. I was asking God to show up and do the stuff God does—supernatural stuff. He did it so easily too.

Once upon a time, that morning would have caused me unrest. It would have choked any joy I could have mustered for the day. Not this time. Not ever again. I've learned to trust God for the impossible.

Only Believe

I've learned that with God all things are possible. I simply believe Him for everything. Remember, as "believers" that is what we are called to do: Believe. I believe He will bless my path, and I thank Him when my path looks bleak. I thank Him until I firmly believe it. I thank Him until I'm assured that when He examines my heart, He will find an unblemished and uncompromising faith in His care. Then, without fail, in His time, He comes through. That's why this is so much more than just blind faith or the power of positive thinking. This is no less than unlocking God's power in our lives. That power brings hope. Incessant hope. That hope brings joy. And that joy vanquishes depression—every time.

The way this happens today is not so unlike the story found in 1 Chronicles 5:18-22. There, three tribes of Israel mustered their military men, men trained for battle; men who "...*could handle shield and sword,*" to wage war against four other nations. The Bible states these Israelites "...*were helped in fighting them, and God handed the Hagrites and all their allies over to them, because they cried out to Him during the battle. He* [God] *answered their prayers, because they trusted Him.*"

These soldiers, the Word explicitly states, were helped and delivered because they cried out to God and trusted Him. They did not depend on their skill or training. They did not feel inadequate or unworthy. They did not stop and offer sacrifices to God. They simply trusted and God answered.

Such verses also suggest that if they did not trust, God might very well not have intervened. They would have been left in the natural. They may have won, they may not have won, but their trust in God moved His heart. Their trust led to His intervention. Their faith caused action. That's why this is not blind faith. It's faith and hope in a God who cares and who can and will overcome.

That's why God is so into our thanksgiving. Thanksgiving is faith in the midst of buffeting winds. It's faith that's able to give thanks to God even before our deliverance. We believe in something we don't see, and He knows our hearts belong to Him. Thanksgiving causes our heart to rejoice. Moreso, that trust acknowledges our dependence on Him. It acknowledges the truth that He is God, and we are not. That's the right relationship that we're always to be in before a mighty God. God then sees us properly aligned, and He responds at the perfect time. If faith calls God to action, why then do we fail to believe that our lack of trust may lead to God's inaction? Do we think our fate so pre-programmed that our chosen response to a crisis makes no difference? If we think this way, we are sorely mistaken.

In our difficult situations, God is often testing us to see what's in us, and He's trying to get us to think differently. In our difficulty, in our depression, we keep asking God to get us out. We think our depressed mood is because of our circumstances. God is waiting for us to believe that He can and will be who He says He is. He's waiting for us to look to Him for who He is: Almighty and Compassionate. He's waiting for us to look upon Him as would a child his parent, knowing that the elder will take good care of his child. When we realize this, and walk in that trust, our spirits become uplifted. We have peace and joy. We're removed from depression as we trust through the tough circumstance. *Then* God moves. Until then, God waits.

We, on the other hand, tend to believe that our situation's turnaround has nothing to do with our thoughts, or our faith. We believe that since God is sovereign, He's pretty much going to do what He's going to do. I sure used to think so. How wrong I was. Will you take a moment to examine whether you believe the same? Do you think your level of trust in God can actually make a difference not only in your attitude, but also in the circumstance's outcome? My friend, trust matters—and it makes a difference. I entreat you with all my heart, to try Him for yourself, daily.

Happy and Strong

"Rescue me from my enemies, for I hide myself in you"
(Psalm 143:8-9).
"He who dwells in the shelter of the
Most High will rest in the shadow of the Almighty.
I will say of the Lord, 'He is my refuge and my fortress,
my God, in whom I trust'"(Psalm 91:1-2).

What helped me put things in perspective? What helped me get my joy? What helped me start living? I came to the understanding that the Bible teaches that we are as strong as whatever we put our trust in. This realization is a powerful spiritual principle that must not be ignored. We are as strong as whatever we put our trust in, partly because whatever we put our trust in becomes our refuge. This is what the psalmist refers to when he mentions dwelling in God, resting in God, hiding in God, etc. The psalmist has put his trust in God. This is opposed to the wicked, who put their trust in riches, and in anything besides God. (See Psalm 52:8-9).

Consider the following: *"The idols of the heathen are silver and gold, the work of men's hands. They have mouths, but they speak not; eyes have they, but they see not; they have ears, but they hear not; neither is there any breath in their mouths. They that make them are like unto them: so is every one that trusteth in them"* (Psalm 135:15-18).

The psalmist instructs us that the one who puts his hope in something with no power will himself be powerless. The converse is also true. The one who puts his trust in something or someone with power, will be powerful. Consider the story of David and Goliath. The Israelite army had put their trust in what they could see—a nine–foot-tall, six-toed, ugly, stinky giant with, I imagine, halitosis, versus their small, paltry frames and shaking limbs. They were afraid and powerless. They were stagnant, never achieving victories, never attaining higher levels. By trusting in what they could see in the natural, they were incapacitated and defeated by fear.

The Bible says, *"Cursed is he who puts his trust in man."* The Israelite army had put their trust in their own training, their own brawn, their own talent and skill, and then matched that up with this huge, ugly Philistine. Consequently, the Israelites thought they were powerless.

Contrast that with David's trust. David courageously ran to the Philistine, as opposed to shrinking back in fear. David declared, *"I come to thee in the name of the Lord of hosts...this day will the Lord deliver thee into mine hand; and I will smite thee, and take thine head from thee..."* (1 Samuel 17:45-46). Rather than trusting his own scrawny frame or lack of military skillfulness, David had put his trust in God to save him. The outcome? David cut off Goliath's head, just as he had predicted. David had put his trust in God and had a God-given result.

Jesus taught that those who put their trust where it belongs, in God, would be able to perform unparalleled feats. He said those who have faith in God would be able to move mountains.

Back to the twenty-first century — what do we do today, when we feel like we're in a dead-end job, have no job, or hate our job? Our inclination is to put our trust not in God but in our resume. We consider what we've done in the past to size up what we're capable of doing in the future.

We put our trust in what we feel is possible given our experience and our talents, or lack thereof. We consider the job market, the stock market, and the real estate market to surmise our prospects. What is the result? We fret, worry, and stress. We get depressed because we are "realists," which means we naturally take the cup-half-empty view. We become as strong as our most recent, updated resume or bank account. That's as far as our confidence runs. That's as powerful as we get.

As a result, we accomplish very little because our trust is in ourselves, our sight, and the way we have sized up life. Fear of man will prove to be a snare, but whoever trusts in the LORD is kept safe (Proverbs 28:25).

Super Heroes

In Psalm 18, David declares he could run through an entire army, leap over a wall, bend a bow of bronze, leap like a deer, and run faster than a speeding bullet. Okay, maybe not the bullet part, but David truly thought he was super human.

No, David didn't have an insane delusion. He simply refused to equate his own limited capabilities with what he could actually accomplish with God on his side. He had put his hope in a supernatural God. He therefore concluded that he could do supernatural things. He had things to do—God things.

Beloved, if your thoughts are based on what you see or feel, or what's likely, or what's within your control, then you're too weak to do what God has for you. If your trust is in another, or in yourself, that's as good as it gets for you. Worse, you're cursed. *"Cursed is he who puts his trust in man"* (see Jeremiah 17). You can't do the things of God because you're not strong enough. On the other hand, if your trust is in God, then you are as strong as God Himself because He is with you.

Is it any wonder then that when Christ gave His most in-depth lesson to those with minds full of care and doubt, and to those with racing thoughts, anxiety, and worry, He characterized them simply by saying, *"O ye of little faith?"* Christ knew that when one adopts a heart of faith and trust in God, then worry, fret, doubt, and depression must flee. Christ, too, prescribed a hearty dose of trust in God for an aching, troubled heart. Why do we try anything else? We'll explore this together a bit more later.

So, You're Not Buying This?

I know what you're thinking. You're thinking this is too easy to be true. You cannot believe that the simple act of putting our trust in God has the power to convert depression to elation. Do you really think it's easy? My friend, if it were easy, don't you think you'd have tried it already?

Look, if I swore to you that you could banish depression for the rest of your life by simply tossing a shiny 1992 penny across your right shoulder while facing a northerly direction (and if you were to believe me), don't you think you'd be digging into your pocket right now?

No, this is not easy. Faith in an unseen power to do the impossible is difficult. Faith that a holy God will work on behalf of an unholy person is even harder. Knowing that none of it is based on our own works but His alone makes it all the more suspect. It can make sense only when we realize what a truly amazing God we serve. It makes sense when we recognize that our God is a God of goodness, compassion, forgiveness, and love. He IS benevolence. He loves. He cares. He wants our peace, safety, shelter, and best welfare. Lest we forget, in Christ, our sins have been paid for. We are holy *in Christ*. We are blameless *in Christ*. God is not mad at us. His anger toward and punishment against our sin was totally poured out upon Christ on the cross. Christ took up our sins, and gave us His righteousness. Therefore, God has nothing but abounding love, grace and favor toward us! Hallelujah! Remind yourself of this fact throughout each day!

Our spirits are united in fellowship with Him. My friend, in Christ you have been given the ability to fully trust God for all things in your life.

"Blessed (happy) is the man whose strength is in thee... O Lord of hosts, blessed (happy) is the man that trusteth in thee" (Psalm 84:5,12).

Objection: Relevance

I can't emphasize enough that what keeps many of us in depression is a troubled heart. The remedy is trust. David knew it. Solomon spoke it. The Israelites showed us. Christ reiterated it.

Fear and doubt are the kingpins of depression, the death knell of faith. Faith is a matter of seeing the natural resolved unlikely by seeing our God correctly. Faith puts all in His hands—each and every facet of life.

David was physically weaker and less experienced than Goliath, but his God wasn't. Through his God, David whipped the giant. The Israelite army had the same knowledge about the God of Israel, but they lacked the same trust. The difference in faith yielded distinguishably different results: One was faith and victory, the other fear and defeat. David ran and advanced, while the army stayed back in fear. The Israelite army succumbed to what they perceived as *reality*; David changed reality.

The same occurred when Peter walked on the water; he didn't consider the water's properties (solids v. liquids), nor did he worry about the turbulence. Instead he focused on Christ. His trust overcame the *natural* outcome. Fear brought it back.

What about us? Do we stay focused on the natural? Are we overwhelmed by our child's malady, our family's dysfunction, our sin's stranglehold, or the bleak appearance of our future? Or have we made a decision to change the circumstances, beginning with a belief in a God who has declared that the boundary lines have fallen for us in pleasant places? See Psalms 16:6.

When Saul was trying to kill him, David praised God in the midst of despair. That's the ultimate act of faith. Such trust can always make our future brighter, even when the clouds come, because you know where to look. Let us resolve to make that our habit, putting our trust incessantly in Him. David believed with all his might that His God would make the difference. Do you share that mighty belief?

Today, I'm a traitor. I am an optimist. I've traded my natural propensities for doubt's depression, for the joys of living in full and confident trust in God. I wake up feeling good. My heart is no longer heavy. I have a daily hope for good, for *God things* to unfold in my life. Those who know me notice the difference. I've slipped into the ranks of the happy people. I was not born into their number, but now, finally, I'm one of them just the same. I feel re-born, again. Though my spirit was saved years ago, only of late did the mind of my soul catch up. Today, the same can be said of you. It begins with trust.

Today, declare unto yourself in confident faith:

I will not die in discouragement.
I will see the goodness of the Lord in the land of the living.
God is my light, my salvation, my fortress, and my strength.
He will deliver me.
Yet will I trust.

Let us pray this prayer together: "*Father, I thank You for teaching me how to trust in You. Lord, right now I cry out to You for these issues in my life that are plaguing and tormenting me. (List those areas in your life.) Lord, I admit that these areas are overwhelming for me. They are bigger than me and at times feel as if they are suffocating me and even killing me. But, Lord, I know that You are bigger than all of them. I now know that I cannot look to these things, but instead, to put my trust in You. With each of these issues, I give to you and will rest in the fact that You will make a way, will provide, and will show me in Your time and way, how to proceed. I will not worry, fret or stress over any of these issues in my life. I will go to sleep in peace, knowing that You are watching over me and caring for me. Lord, You said, Happy is the person that puts his trust in You, and so Lord, I will rejoice and be glad that I have put my trust in You in all things. I thank you that I am holy before You in Christ. Therefore, Your grace is always at work in me, available to me. I receive it right now.*

Thank You for restoring joy back into my life. Thank You for giving me hope for my future with You. Yes, I trust in You! Thank You, Lord. I praise You. You are worthy of Praise. Lord, I bow before You and I bless Your Name!"

❧

Chapter Four

You Call <u>This</u> The Promised Land?

"...Which are a shadow of things to come; but the body is of Christ"
(Colossians 2:16-17).
*"Who serve unto the example and shadow of heavenly things, as Moses
was admonished of God when he
was about to make the tabernacle..."*
(Hebrews 8:5; also see Hebrews 10:1).

The New Testament tells us that the Old Testament histories are shadows, reflections, or patterns for the New Covenant—where we are today.

What first struck me about the passages listed above from Hebrews and Colossians was that I'd never heard of the Old Testament spoken in those terms before. Like some of you, I grew up in church and became a Christian at a very young age. As a kid sitting in Sunday school week after week, it didn't take long to learn the ropes. (Yes, you had to learn the ropes to get those graham crackers at the end of the lesson.)

What really took the pressure off my six-year old mind was the eventual discovery that "Jesus" was the correct answer to well over fifty percent of all questions posed. Better yet, even if it wasn't the right answer, what Sunday school teacher is ever going to tell you that "Jesus" is the wrong answer? (Man I loved those Graham crackers.)

At home, however, Mom would never have it. We had our own Sunday school—Monday through Saturday. So, over the course of my childhood, I got to know the best of the Old Testament boys, and not just the usual characters: Abe, Isaac, Daniel, Moses, and Samson. No sir. My brother and I knew them all: Uriah, Boaz, Mephibosheth, Melchizedec, Mordechai, Jabez. (Okay, maybe not Jabez.) So back at Sunday school, I became the "go to" man for all Graham cracker distributions.

Our Destiny's Past

What's remarkable about this *shadow* is that it suggests an application of the Bible I'd never heard of before, not even from Mom. Yes, I'd always known that studying the lives and stories of these robed and bearded ones would serve as an example of how or how not to conduct myself. I'd heard that it was a necessary precursor to what God would do in the coming Messiah. In all my life, I never knew that the story of Israel and all of its colorful cast of characters and adventures, both sordid and inspiring, are more than just a vehicle for behavior modification. *(Don't take time off work, have an affair with your neighbor's wife, get her pregnant and discretely have the husband killed.)*

The applications go far beyond that. The Old Testament is God's way of clueing us into what we, the partakers of the New Covenant, are getting into. The Israelite adventure is a preview of what we, today, can expect in our personal adventure with God in Christ. Why? Because God doesn't change. His ways were perfect then, so they don't need changing now.

Therefore, what God did with His people, the Israelites, He will do with us, for we, too, are His "Chosen People." Where God took the Israelites, He will take us. The bondage, the deliverance, the battles, the wanderings; all are a shadow of things to come for us. Thus, the more I studied the Israel-God relationship, the more I understood the human-God relationship. The more I grasped the life and times of the Hebrew nation, the more I grasped my own life and times.

Putting in O.T.

What does this have to do with depression? Everything. Depression is no ordinary ailment. Depression is a season of colorless, borderless, dissonance. Its influence is neither haphazard nor one-dimensional.

It attacks every facet of human existence; spirit, soul, and body. It affects our relationship with others, with God and with our self. Since depression maligns all areas of our being, we must address it beyond simply remedying the foods we eat, the thoughts we think, and the prayers we pray. We must attack it in every way it attacks us. Since it affects our life, we must understand life to the fullest extent possible.

The fact is, many today are depressed because life is unraveling in a disheartening and disconcerting manner. Life is confusing, perhaps more so now than before you became a Christian. The good news is that once we have a fuller grasp of who God is and how He works, the difficult questions, concerns, and confusions of life become significantly answered, alleviated and allayed. Life itself does not get easier, but how we go through it does.

Contained in the Old Testament experience, we see the parallels between the sorrows of the Israelite people and our own sorrows. Their confusions, fears, obstacles, and giants are ours as well. The Israelite journey is a shadow of our journey, and just as we are partakers of their promises, we are likewise subject to their pitfalls.

We need to understand both the Old and New Testament to really understand life. Nothing less will successfully contend with depression's grip. Fortunately, this understanding can restore color and shape to our borders and also produce needed harmony in our lives. It can bring balance and stability to times and events that seem anything but stable. In His Word, God has given us more than just a road map, it's actually a treasure map—a map to unlock the wealth of life that God intends for everyone.

In addition, in the Old Testament God promised to bless the Israelites in every way—in their physical bodies, their families, their land, their occupation, their possessions, their mind—in every thing. Time and time again David heralded that the Lord would be his portion and inheritance, not later, but now, in the *land of the living*. *The boundary lines*, he declared, *have fallen for me in pleasant places*. They *have fallen*, he states, using the past tense, not future. His son Solomon declared, *"Behold, the righteous shall be recompensed in the earth."*

In the New Testament, Christ told us that the kingdom of heaven is at hand, even *within us*. Paul tells us that all the promises of God are, *"yes and amen."* Christ said, *"Ask, and it will be given to you,"* and that, *"Greater is He that is in us than he that is in the world*; that we are, upon following his pattern of life, *blessed*. We have been promised not only everlasting life, but also an *abundant* life on earth as well. Speaking of the manner of life ordained by Christians, Romans 14 declares, *"For the kingdom of God is not meat and drink; but righteousness, and peace, and joy in the Holy Ghost"* (Romans 14:17).

What does this mean for us? It means that we not only possess the promises of eternal life with God in eternity, but we also have at our disposal the promises of a full, abundant life while living on planet earth. We have been given promises of joy and peace that are to be exercised now, in our immediate present, not simply during our much-awaited future. This is just as much God's desire as His desire for us to spend eternity with Him.

Now that we know that where God took the Israelites He will also take us, consider the following:

Ladies and Gentlemen, Welcome to the Wilderness: It's Worth Two Points.

"The Lord said, 'I have indeed seen the misery (affliction) *of my people in Egypt. I have heard them crying out because of their slave drivers, and I am concerned about their sufferings'"* (Exodus 3:7).

Note: Here God tells Moses that He had indeed seen the depression of the Israelites and had heard their cries. More importantly, God said He was *concerned about their suffering* and was about to do something about it.

Think about this: the Israelites cried, God heard, *and was concerned.* This is a familiar refrain in the Bible. It remains a light of hope today. If God says He hears our cries and is concerned, take Him at His word. Call Him on it.

So what about you in your depression? What's your routine in the season of suffering? What's your method of operation? Do you cry out to God? Do you look up? Do you press in harder at the altar?

Or do you close up? Stop going to church? Stop praying? Start drinking? Start eating? Start seeking others to meet your needs? I'm convinced today that the Lord lifted me out of depression because of the simple fact that I relentlessly and incessantly cried out to Him.

So, first and foremost, let's make up our minds to begin crying out to God daily with fervor. See for yourself that He is concerned.

Caution: Do not feed honey to infants!

"So I have come down to rescue them from the hand of the Egyptians and to bring them up out of that land into a good and spacious land, a land flowing with milk and honey" (Exodus 3:8).

Events for the Israelite nation escalated when God told Moses He was going to come down to rescue them and bring them up out of that land into a good and spacious land, the Promised Land.

God had Moses reiterate those two things to Israel's elders: One: *Rescue out.* Two: *Bring them into.* Remember that, just two things.

Over the course of the next twelve chapters in Exodus, God makes good on point number one: The Israelites do indeed get out. They were rescued.

Then, instead of God getting on with point two, a strange twist occurs. After the dramatic liberation from Egypt; the ten plagues; the Egyptians being wiped out in the Red Sea; after Moses, Miriam, and all the Israelites sing and dance to the Lord; Exodus 15:22 says Moses led them not into the Promised Land but, interestingly enough, *into a desert.*

God had promised just two things: 1) to rescue them out of bondage and 2) to bring them into the Promised Land—*milk and honey land.* He'd mentioned no wilderness period in between.

Had God forgotten to mention this minor detail? Did Moses take a wrong turn? Had he misunderstood God? Had Israel, characteristically, sinned? (They were, as we know, pretty good at that.) The answers: No, no, no, and no.

On the contrary, God *led* them there. Purposefully and without provocation, God brought them into a dry, dusty desert. This was no Vegas style desert. No all-night buffets, no Seafood 'n Slot Specials, no Luxor, no Caesar's, no MGM. In this desert there was no food, no water, nada.

In stark contrast to the plentiful Promised Land, this place was barren, lacking entirely those things the body needs: nutrition, shelter, security, stability, purpose, direction, comfort, capital, control, and understanding. God's people were stripped of all the comforts man longs for. Man wants to live. In the desert, almost everything is dying.

Welcome to the Wilderness

Now the significance of shadows becomes clear. Now it becomes necessary to pull back away from Israel and into our own lives and our own wilderness—our own time of hunger and depression. We need to place our situation squarely in line with a clearer view of God, His ways, and His time, as evinced in days of old. Remember, where God took Israel, He will also take us.

From the start, God intended to take Israel out of bondage and into a wilderness period. He intends the same for us. We should expect nothing less.

Instead, most of us forget this point or, like me, have never heard of it. We hit the panic button when hard times come. When suffering and affliction enters our life we begin to wonder what went wrong. We ponder what we must have done to set things awry. We assume we must have sinned. We blame ourselves. We blame God.

"He must be punishing me," we think. "I must have screwed up somewhere along the way."

Maybe you just got radically saved and God had been doing some powerful things in your life. Maybe you were delivered from things that had you bound all your life. The words of your prayers were barely off your lips before God answered with a miracle. All your problems seemed to have vanished. Now, all of a sudden heartaches have returned. Big time.

Frustrated, we turn to the promises in Scripture and proclaim, "But God, you said, 'by your stripes I am healed,' so why do I hurt so? You said, 'peace is mine', why then do I feel such unrest? You said victory is ours, so why do I keep coming up short? Lord, you said..., you said..., you said...."

Unfortunately, many of us have been sold a bill of goods about life and Christianity. We've been led to believe that a relationship with Christ means salvation from the wilderness. When things feel like they're going wrong, we think we must have done wrong. This couldn't be further from the truth. Yes, our relationship with Christ Jesus of Nazareth saves us from our bondage to sin. His blood has liberated us from the captivity of death and deception. Let me tell you this, He has not saved us *from* the wilderness. He has saved us *to* the wilderness.

My friend, if we are His, we will have a wilderness season; it's part of His perfect will and plan. So relax a bit. Every man and woman of God must go through it. It's okay. Really. The wilderness must come. It's a difficult place, but it's also a necessary place. You will feel pressed in by life, no doubt. You may even feel depressed. Though you name it and claim it in faith, you may not see all of the bountiful promises of Scripture unfolding in your life. Yes, it's a hard place, but it's not impossible, and you may not have done anything wrong to find yourself there.

Remember, for a place surrounded only by tumbleweeds and thistles, the wilderness season in our life is no less valuable. In fact, God planned it so. Due to His infinite love, He has made it so. So don't be mad. In fact, you should be glad. It means God has more in store.

So now you're asking, "What exactly did I get myself into with this Christianity thing? What's the real deal with this supposed loving God? First this thing with blood, animal sacrifices and death, now misery, affliction and wilderness -- is this God psycho or what? Why does He apparently get such a kick out of his children getting beat up? What is so good for us in the wilderness that we cannot obtain in the land of milk and honey?"

Answer: Death.

Death: You Gotta Love It.

In speaking of his own death (and ours if we are willing), Christ said, *"Except a kernal of wheat fall into the ground and die, it abideth alone: but if it die, it bringeth forth much fruit"* (John 12:24). He later states, *"Apart from Me you can do nothing"* (John 15:5).

God made it clear that we can do nothing for Him—nothing that lasts—on our own (Psalm 127:1). Since God does want us to do something, since He has called us to great works, He must get rid of our *selves* (which is incapable of accomplishing anything) so we can be filled with Him (in order to accomplish something). (See Philippians 4:13). We all have within ourselves a desire to live with purpose, to accomplish life's call, to do the work. Because God loves us, He wants this desire fulfilled in us even more than we do. He also knows that to do it, we must empty ourselves of ourselves. Even Christ emptied Himself (Philippians 2:7-9), so that nothing He did was of his own volition, but the Father's will (John 5:19).

The place of one of Christ's greatest "emptying" was Gethsemane (which means olive press). From the pressing of the olive, we get the oil, the anointing. Similarly, it's in the pressing of our lives where God may get the glory.

Here's a good rule of thumb: God always has our best interest in mind. In everything He tells us to do, in every command, in every leading, prompting, or prodding, it's always in our best interest to obey. Always. Are there any exceptions to this rule? None. Why? Because He loves you the most. The more a person loves you, the more you can trust that person. So, too, the reverse is true. If a person does not love you, you would not logically put your trust there.

I've heard this matter of trust best illustrated this way: Though a person may be an excellent mechanic, if he has a vendetta against you and hates you immensely, you're probably not going to take your car into his shop for a brake job, regardless of his skill level.

Yet, we have an all powerful God who loves us even more than we love ourselves, and He happens to be the best mechanic in town. So then, we can trust and obey every word and every ordinance from our God. It will always be in our best interest, always.

Thus, the reason for our time in the wilderness becomes more clear. Even our death can be a bit more palpable. Therefore, Christ tells His disciples that although they will have a yoke to bear and a burden to lift, his burden is easy and his yoke is light. Therefore, we understand that although the righteous may fall seven times, he "rises again." Therefore, we understand that our service to God, in Christ, is not an easy path but, rather, a perfect path.

Christ Crucified...You Too!

"The heart is deceitful above all things and beyond cure. Who can understand it?" Jeremiah 17:9.

"All of us have become like one who is unclean, and all our righteous acts are like filthy rags; we all shrivel up like a leaf, and like the wind our sins sweep us away" Isaiah 64:6.

How wonderful it is for man to recognize his wretchedness! It is actually vital to our health for you and me to recognize our absolute sinfulness and utter moral depravity. Each of us is wrapped in a robe of flesh that is hell bent towards selfishness and self-centeredness. When we begin to fathom our flesh's daily insatiable desire for independence and rebellion against God, we then begin to comprehend the need for that old man to be crucified with Christ. It cannot be fixed up by any other self-help teachings under the sun. There is only one remedy. Death by crucifixion with Christ. Yet with the death of the old man comes the resurrection. Yes, we lean fully and totally on the life of Christ within us. By faith we reckon ourselves dead to sin, but alive to Christ. We understand then that we have been crucified with Christ and it is no longer I who live but Christ…

"I have been crucified with Christ and I no longer live, but Christ lives in me. The life I live in the body, I live by faith in the Son of God, who loved me and gave himself for me" Galatians 2:20.

Counting the Cost

Therefore, He *"…led them all the way in the desert…to humble them."*

You can imagine then my surprise when I looked up that word "humble" in the large Strong's concordance of the Bible and found the word, "to depress." Yes, the Lord knows that apart from humility, we shall not even see the Kingdom of God.

"And he said: "I tell you the truth, unless you change and become like little children, you will never enter the kingdom of heaven. Therefore, whoever humbles himself like this child is the greatest in the kingdom of heaven" Matthew 18:3-4.

He places us in a wilderness season often for this very reason, to humble us. So that we may live a full life in Him, He brings us to a place where we no longer lean on the arm of our flesh.

*"That no flesh should **glory** in his **presence**"* 1 Corinthians 1:29.

Accordingly, it is imperative that we die. We especially must learn to die towards all of our efforts to please God. All attempts to live a righteous life based on our morality, goodness, acts of service, etc., must die. Only Christ's righteousness imparted to us makes us righteous – and righteous we are by such abundant grace! Die to self, the old creation. Die to selfish ambition. Die to pride. Die to ego. Die to bitterness and resentment. Die to selfishness. Die to lust, arrogance, deceit, and greed. Die to everything we desire more than our desire for God.

Unfortunately, some of us don't understand the plan of death. We grow more and more frustrated along the way, repeating cycles of broken dreams and abandoned plans. We feel stuck. We become resentful, even angry with God, blaming Him for our woes. We have errantly reduced Christianity to a self-serving doctrine. We think that if we toe the line long enough in Christian "service," and follow God long enough, we can cash in and have God fill up our Christmas wish list.

The longer it takes, the more frustrated we become. We continually fight instead of dying to the misdeeds of our flesh. Saints, God tests and examines the hearts. Will we follow Him, even if we know the gifts will never come? Yes, He is worthy of such devotion. Yes, it would still be in our best interest to do it, and I will show you why.

Only after we have reckoned ourselves as dead to our carnal man which rages against our spirit man can He truly bless us (Galatians 2:20). He can now trust us to obey Him, even in our time of bounty, because we've succumbed to the pinnacle test of our obedience: Learning death to self.

At this point, we no longer care what people say about us—we will obey. We do not care about what others think of us—we'll obey. We don't care about how we may look to others, the risks involved in obedience, and the threats to all of our accumulated security interests. We have died in the wilderness. We have submitted and committed ourselves to God. Therefore, we can obey and accomplish God's purposes for us in this life. We can be a vessel, a bond-servant, doing the Master's work. Jesus was continually dying to self, all the way up to Calvary. Listen to what the religious leaders proclaimed in that day, *"Teacher, we know you are a man of integrity. You aren't swayed by men, because you pay no attention to who they are; but you teach the way of God in accordance with the truth"* (Mark 12:14).

God brings us to hard, breaking times in our life, times of death, so that we might cry out to Him, humble ourselves before Him, seek Him and commit to Him and His ways. He brings us to the wilderness so that our trust will be in Him and Him only – for our righteousness, for our provision, for our peace, and for our prosperity.

Then, God will have our unconditional devotion. Then, we are able to give to God instead of continually wanting. Then, we can give to others. Then, we will seek every opportunity to be a blessing rather than receive a blessing. Then, our heart's desire is obedience. Then, we will be a force to be reckoned with as a Kingdom. Then, we begin to take on the character of Jesus Christ, Himself.

"...he forgetteth not the cry of the humble" (Psalm 9:12).

Die today, that you may live.

Dying Declarations

Wilderness times must come because God is perfecting us. Others may have obtained their promises in life without having to die, but He wants more from you. He wants more growth from you, so He prunes more. He wants you to inherit more, so you must sacrifice more. Therefore, He has perfectly and lovingly interrupted your life and caused you to detour into the wilderness. True, you may have done this to yourself, but God is big enough to use our mistakes for His good—if we let Him. Only make sure you also die to that which put you in error.

Certainly, hard times will come. We will be taken to the wilderness. However, we must always keep in mind the wilderness is only meant to be temporary. This is not our permanent lot.

"Though He slay me, yet will I trust Him" (Job 13:15).

Character in the Casket?

Let's talk about some things that will help us right now as many of us are struggling with depression in these very moments. God said He will take His children to the wilderness to test them and humble them. The word humble means—you guessed it—"to depress, to afflict, to deal hardly with...." Consider also that the ultimate level of humility is death. Paul implores us to *"Do nothing out of selfish ambition or vain conceit, but in humility consider others better than yourselves. Each of you should look not only to your own interest, but also to the interests of others. Your attitude should be the same as that of Christ Jesus...(who) humbled Himself and became obedient to death—even death on a cross"* (Philippians 2:3-5, 8).

God desires that we have the character of Christ. That character comes with a foundation of humility. That character comes when we no longer make our own wants and needs priority number one. We gain that character when we consider others more important than ourselves. We gain that character when we make obedience to God our priority over our own desires and pleasures. That character attribute will begin to alleviate many of our bouts with depression.

Many of you are troubled, despondent, anxious, fearful, and sad because things are not turning out the way you wanted. Loved ones are no longer in your life—and that wasn't in *your* plan. Your career isn't taking shape in *your* timeline—and that wasn't according to *your* plan. You had hopes and dreams, and they seem to be dashed against the rocks. You wanted to be happily married, and you're not. You wanted to be wealthy, and you're not. You wanted to be discovered, and you haven't been. You wanted to be famous, and you're not. You wanted him, and he didn't even notice you. You carry all of these broken dreams, all of these dashed hopes, and they are hurting you and bringing you down. They are the causes of your sorrow.

I learned an important principle a long time ago that stayed with me: *For every dream, there is the death of the dream.*

It is the essence of Christ's words to the Father: "Not my will, but Thy will be done."

Let me preface this by saying that I'm not advocating "settling." We are not to aim low just so that we don't get let down. What I am saying is that often depression comes from these frustrations, from the delay or even death of a dream. A resting and a peace can come in the midst of these when we say to our Father, *"Not my will, but Thy will be done."* When we give up *our* timeline, and *our* wants and wishes and say, *"Not my will, but Thy will be done"*—a calmness overtakes us. When we place ourselves and our present reality into His able hands, rather than asking for His hand to simply take care of our present reality, we find a comfort that is found nowhere else. As we say, *"Not my will, but Thy will be done,"* to the daily problems and crises we face—as well as the long-term desires and ambitions we have—we begin to discover His peace, and we begin to grow in His character.

(Let me also add that I'm not talking about becoming a walking door-mat for others. No, I'm not talking about being a "yes" man, who does whatever anyone and everyone asks. What I'm talking about is saying "yes" to what God is asking you to do. I'm talking about making His demands your top priority.)

Compassion in the Cactus

In the wilderness, as we are learning humility through hard times, our character grows because our compassion grows. Before humility is learned, it's easy to believe that *we* have earned our success. With this attitude, we feel we have the right to be harsh and cold with others. *"Pull yourself up by your own boot straps. That's what I did. Nobody helped me. Help yourself, you lazy bum!"*

However, the Bible says, *"What do you have that you did not receive, and if you received it, why do you boast as if you did not?"* See I Corinthians 4:7.

When our life gets hard, we learn to have compassion for others—for we want that same compassion from God and others. We realize we need grace and mercy to get through it, so we're more inclined to give grace and mercy to others. Our compassion grows, so too our kindness, patience, and gentleness. That's our character, and more than our comfort, God is most concerned with our character.

Brighter Days!

The solace in the storm is that the wilderness is *supposed* to be temporary, a training grounds, if you will — a test. It is imperative then, that we pass the test. You see my friend, when depression hits, when life feels hopeless, when all that you feel around you is darkness and cold, when your heart is broken, when your financial debt has buried you, when addictions have swallowed you up and the only possible direction it seems you can go is down, remember this: God has just handed to you your test. He wants to see what is in your heart. You are in the wilderness.

"The Lord examines the righteous" (Psalms 11:5).

Please don't forget why you are in the wilderness either. It is because God loves you. Now for those of you who are wondering about getting out of the wilderness, for keeps, well, that is the subject of our next chapter.

The following is a prayer for us as we endure wilderness times: *"Father, I thank You that Your ways are higher and better than my ways. I thank You for loving me enough to chasten and discipline me. I thank You for caring enough about me to not allow me to continue on my past course. Father, thank You for your continual forgiveness for the pride and error of my ways, for my selfishness, self-centeredness, and self-seeking ways and for wanting my way over Your way. Father, by faith I thank You that I have been crucified with Christ, that my old man and all of my sinful ways and nature is dead. I thank you that I have been resurrected with Christ and that the life and strength that I need now for life and godliness is found in Christ. LORD God, I choose Your way for my life. I will to do Your will. Each day, I make Your priorities for my life my own priorities. Lord, I choose to walk in the fruits of the Spirit today. No matter how difficult or how much it hurts, I will obey You and do what I hear Your voice telling me to do—please give me Your strength to obey You quickly. I put on the garment of praise for the spirit of heaviness. I clothe myself with the righteousness of Jesus Christ. I humble myself be-*

fore You and to my fellow man. I choose to love You with all my heart, soul, mind and strength and I choose to love my neighbor as myself. Lord, I thank You for bringing me into this wilderness to teach me. By the power of Your Holy Spirit, help me to learn what You would have me to learn in this season. Cut out what needs to be cut out of me. Add to whatsoever thing is lacking in my life. May I decrease so that You may increase. May You be glorified on this earth. I worship You. Even in this difficult place, Lord, You are worthy of my praise, thanksgiving and adoration. I praise you. I worship You. I honor You. I lift up Your name and I give You all the glory for the name of the Lord is to be praised. Forever I will praise You. Thank You for my life. Thank You for making a way for me. My hope is in You."

Chapter Five
Out of the Rut, For Good!

In previous pages we have explored the means to passing the Lord's tests—and placing ourselves in a position of promotion. Yet, with any real test (and this is a *real* test), there is the possibility of failing. Here, we'll explore the *biggies* of why many fail the Lord's tests, and continue to wander in the wilderness, stuck in life, unnecessarily. We'll explore them so that we can defeat them. We'll explore them so that we may finally pass the test, and live!

Reason Number One: Roaming Charges

"They that know thy Name will put their trust in thee" (Psalm 9:10).

There was a time in my life when I thought I was really smart. During that foolish (albeit blissful) era, I recall hearing a song about Moses by the legendary gospel artist, Shirley Caesar.

As she began to sing and talk and talk and sing in the way only she can, she repeated, "Nothing is impossible for God. Sickness is nothing for God," she sang, "Cancer, AIDS —all God's got to do is just bat His eye."

"That's not the issue," I muttered proudly. It is not a matter of whether God *can* do it but, rather, *will* He do it? I already knew without a shadow of doubt that God *can* heal the sick, however, *whether* God *will*, would always remain the question. As I grew older and a bit wiser— finally realizing that I knew nothing at all—I discovered that my thinking was very akin to the obtuse thinking of the Israelites. Though they knew God *could* help them, they doubted that He *would*. Isn't that just how many of us think? We wonder *if* God will help us, even though we're quite sure that God *could* help us if He really wanted to.

One complaint God had with the Israelites was the fact that their hearts erred (literally, *roamed*) from the truth because, God adds, *"They have not known my ways."* Then it hit me like the proverbial ton of bricks. When you don't know a person's ways, you don't know if he will or will not do something, even though you may already know the person could do it.

For example, if I were in desperate need of twenty bucks, I know I could call my dad and he'd provide it. I know this for two reasons. One, I know that on any given day my dad *could* spare an Andrew Jackson. Second, I know my dad's heart, and that he *would*, without fail, bail his son out in a time of need. That's just him; he has a giving heart. He'd rather starve to death than see his wife or children go without. This generosity conforms to his character. That's just who he is. Because I know this about my dad, I know what I can come to him for. I know I'd get the twenty bucks.

On the other hand, when you don't know a person's ways, the outcome is entirely different. If my dad had a checkered financial history or a hit-and-miss pattern of benevolence, my certainty in approaching him would be shaken. Further, if I'd never spent much time with my dad, I'd have no idea about his character or propensities. That result inevitably produces doubt. If your situation is dire, that doubt is accompanied by fear.

Similarly, the Israelites didn't know God's ways, so they became afraid and hopeless in their time of dire need. When surrounded by a place with no food or water, or when encircled by an unknown large army, their hearts grew faint and tired. They had no certainty that God would come through. They were left feeling despair, and depression settled in.

Likewise, when I didn't *know* God's ways, I lived with the constant undercurrents of the fear and unrest that this ignorance produced in my life. When I found myself in difficult positions pertaining to my relationships, work, direction, or identity, I was restless. I knew God could help if He wanted. I just didn't know if He would. To sum it up, I did not know God's ways.

"Therefore, holy brothers, who share in the heavenly calling, fix your thoughts on Jesus, the apostle and high priest whom we confess. He was faithful to the One who appointed Him, just as Moses was faithful in all God's house" (Hebrews 3:1-2).

In contrast, Moses knew God's ways and was fully confident and hopeful God would come through in desperate times, every time. Wouldn't it be nice to have a steady, resting trust with God in every area of your life—with respect to spouse, singleness, support, and survival? Moses knew God's ways because he asked God to show them to him. Moses said, *"If you are pleased with me, teach me your ways so I may know you"* (Exodus 33:13). When God taught Moses His ways, Moses never forgot them.

Moses grew to know the God of all creation by learning God's name. That, too, is how we learn God's ways—by learning His name and fixing our thoughts on Jesus, who has made us worthy to receive God's favor and love continually . Back then, a name defined a person. It encompassed one's character. To know a person's name was to know the person's ways.

"And the Lord said, 'I will cause all my goodness to pass in front of you, and I will proclaim My Name, the Lord, in your presence'" (Exodus 33:19a).

"And He [God] passed in front of Moses, proclaiming, 'the Lord, the Lord, the compassionate and gracious God, slow to anger, abounding in love and faithfulness, maintaining love to thousands, and forgiving wickedness, rebellion and sin. Yet He does not leave the guilty unpunished;

He punishes the children and their children for the sin of the fathers to the third and fourth generation'" (Exodus 34:6-7).

That is who God is. He's compassionate, gracious, slow to anger, and abounding in love and faithfulness. Therefore, His ways are compassionate, gracious, slow to anger, and abounding in love.

As a result, those who know His ways not only know that He *can* deliver, but also that He *will* deliver. Now before all the pessimists in the group run to the last part of God's name and nature (*...he punishes...*), don't forget that as Christians He has forgiven us and cleansed us of all unrighteousness, once for all. Therefore, we are on the north side of the ledger. Christ's blood paid the price of *all* our sins, past, present and future. *All* of our wrong doing has been paid for *in full* by Christ. No more punishment for our sins remains, only God's love and grace. How amazing is our God. How wonderful is the love of Christ! Thank you Father for the sacrifice of Your Son for my sins! Thank You Jesus for laying down your life so that I could have life! Thank You Jesus for Your blood which washes me pure! My dear friend, can I tell you that in Christ you are now under the grace of God – always – even when you mess up, the blood doesn't stop working. Even when we fall short, the Father's covering of grace through the sacrifice of Jesus on the cross remains. Therefore, there is now *no* condemnation!

Look again at God's introduction to Himself: "Compassionate." This is how God describes Himself. This is His Name. Doesn't that sound like someone you know? When Christ walked the earth, He had compassion for people. When did He turn down anyone who cried out to Him? When did He refuse one who ran to Him? He was always willing to endure the ridicule of the religious in order to see His compassion through.

Christ had compassion on the people because His very Name and nature is compassionate. God abounds in love and forgiveness; His mercies are new every morning, because that's His Name. That's who He is. It's the essence of who He is. Moses knew this and therefore trusted God. Always. In every situation.

Yet, the Israelites constantly lived in great fear whenever circumstances grew dim because their hearts roamed from this truth. Therefore, they were always filled with uncertainty and doubt when a crisis came along. God faulted them for not knowing His ways, but their hearts still roamed from the truth.

We also roam because we also forget God's nature and Christ's full payment for our sins. We roam at night with our anxieties tossing and turning. We roam in the morning with our thoughts racing. We roam because we let our hearts be governed by who we have made God to be, and not by who God says He is and what He says He will do for us. We equate the character of our earthly father to that of our heavenly Father. If we have been fortunate enough to have a good, kind, loving father then we tend to see God the Father in a similar light. Many, unfortunately, have fathers who misrepresent our Heavenly Father.

Accordingly, we await reprimands, whippings, and scoldings, instead of finding a strong tower, and "a very present help in time of trouble" See Psalm 46:1). We don't believe God is our healer and comforter, so we choose to deal with our sorrow through our own devices. We forget He is our peace and so we take mini-vacations in our mini-vans for mini-rest instead of turning to the GOD OF REST. In essence, we *choose to* have no hope, and because we have no hope, happiness continues to elude us.

Believers, it's time we become intimately acquainted with God's character. It's high time we understand not just that He can, but that—because of His compassion, because He is abounding in love, because He has already forgiven completely our wickedness, rebellion, and sin through Christ's work on the cross—He is willing as well. Until we understand this, we will never have hope, even though our faith believes He can. Consequently, we will never live in the joy He has in store.

Tinker the Thinker

Typically, when we find ourselves in difficult places we resemble more the doubting, unbelieving Israelite camp than Moses. Our thoughts and resultant actions mimic those of the Israelite army, rather than God's faithful servant Moses. In our hearts, we utter the same question, *"Is the Lord among us or not?"* In doing so, we test and contend with God Almighty.

What made Moses so special? Did he have the gift of faith? Was he simply doused with an extra measure of faith when God called him and so had an unfair advantage over the rest of the Israelites and us? Not at all. The difference was that Moses had a good memory.

When God called Moses, he was just as weak-kneed and afraid as the rest of his brethren. He ran. He failed in his purpose as a ruler of peoples. He had the same propensities to doubt, fear and tremble, as the guy next door. When God called him at the burning bush, he was filled with the same type of trepidation that his fellow Israelites demonstrated: "Who am I?" he asks. "What shall I tell them? What if they don't believe me...?" That's what I like about Moses. He naturally went down the road of fear and doubt, too. But he didn't stay there.

After repeated resistance, Moses finally gave into God's call and accepted the challenge. *I will be with you*, God tells Moses. God then gives him a demonstration of His power: He miraculously turns Moses' staff into a snake and his hand leprous.

Then, another miracle happened. Though not recorded in Exodus, something happened to Moses that changed him forever. It was something that gave him unrivaled power. It was something most people never attain in their entire lifetime. The Israelites at the time didn't. Many of us haven't. What was it?

It was trust. It was the simple fact that Moses believed God (see Hebrews 11:23-27). Although Moses displayed an incredible amount of fear, doubt, and insecurity on that fateful day at the burning bush, he also changed. Moses didn't forget what God told him there. From then on, in the midst of literal high waters, armies, and insurrections, Moses calmly rested in quiet confidence in God alone. From then on, Moses never doubted the supernatural, benevolent intervention of God again. Never. He may have become excessively perturbed at the Israelites, even disobedient, but he never doubted.

Yes, Moses had a good memory. Moses had one word from God—"*I am with thee*"—and from then on he never again doubted God's presence. Moses didn't forget.

On the flip side, the Israelites had a bad memory. God was with them throughout all the plagues against Egypt so that not even the hairs of their livestock were singed. God was with them by a visible fire and cloud continually, day and night. God personally directed their paths to a desert. Yet, *"In spite of all this, they kept on sinning; in spite of his wonders, they did not believe"* (Psalm 78:32).

Dare We Believe?

Similarly, God is asking us to stop doubting. God is waiting for us to stop asking *"Is the Lord among us or not?"* It's time to rest in His promises, and not continue to question the application of those promises to your particular crisis. Yes, He is with you even if you make a mistake, God is still with you. Believe that for your problem today, and "move," just as He told Moses and the Israelites. "What are you doing standing around and crying," God told them: "Go."

That's the mentality many of us need to adopt. Yes, we do need to check our motives and stay aligned with His Word. Many of us are in turmoil because we're afraid to move. We're immobilized by the magnitude of our circumstances. Many think there's no place to move. There may seem be no place to go. But there is—in God; in faith. No, He won't give us all the answers up front. You can be assured that God is with you, so start acting like you believe it.

Resolve in your heart that you'll never again question the nearness of God in your life and in your situation. Calmly trust in His presence. Know that He hears your cries. Learn to walk in that confidence. Rest in that confidence. Smile in that confidence. Find joy in it, and believe.

Reason Number Two: Does God know how to set the table?

We know God is compassionate and willing to help—and that He is near—but when faced with our problems, we can't seem to find a way out. We know of God's omnipotence, but we're in a fix. Your situation has gone from bad to worse, and your time is running out. Furthermore, in view of the horrid things hidden in your past, there is no reason to believe that anything new and positive will arise. You're experiencing lack in the vital signs of life: emotionally, spiritually, financially, socially, and physically. To put it bluntly, life seems utterly hopeless.

"Were there no graves in the land of Egypt that you have us die in this wilderness" (Exodus 14:11).

The Israelites were hungry in the wilderness. They had no food or water. Sure, they were now a free people, and the bad guys were behind them—dead—but at least back in Egypt they'd have eaten three squares a day. So they said, *"There we sat around pots of meat and ate all the food we wanted"* (Exodus 16:3).

Back home, in the slave quarters they'd still have been able to set their table every day with a fork, knife, napkin, and spoon. At least back there they'd have had a decent meal: *"We remember the fish we ate in Egypt at no cost—also the cucumbers, melons, leeks, onions and garlic"* (Numbers 11:5).

The Israelites were smart: They knew their math, sociology, language arts, and sciences. They understood the physical world, the laws of nature, production, and energy. They also knew that if they didn't eat soon they'd die.

They knew there was nothing in this desert to live on. They knew that if there was nothing living in the wilderness, there was nothing to eat. Life needs life to survive. The food chain is a living cycle. The only thing they were circling around was death. The Israelites put two and two together. Death plus circles equals death—imminent death.

So again, they began asking more questions. Again, they began testing God.

"They spoke against God, saying, 'Can God spread a table in the desert?'" (Psalm 78:19).

They were right. Logically, physically, and naturally, they'd made a valid point; they were being realistic. The Israelites did the math and knew they were coming up short. There really was no way they'd be eating any time soon, but they'd eclipsed God out of the equation. They left no room for the impossible. They left no room for the work of God.

What made matters worse for the poor children of God was that when the Lord did break through the natural and provided water from a rock, their inquiring minds wanted to know more.

Yeah, they said, *"But can he also give us food? Can he supply meat for his people?"* (Psalm 78:20).

Can you blame them for asking?

"When the Lord heard them, he was angry; his fire broke out against Jacob, and his wrath rose against Israel, for they did not believe in God or trust in his deliverance" (Psalm 78:21-22).

Of course we blame them.

We'd never tick God off like that. We've heard the Bible stories. We understand the "life application." God is omnipotent. Of course God can send manna from the sky.

In reality, the Israelites were afraid for the very same reasons we're so often afraid. They had no joy for the same reasons we have no joy. People, we are depressed for the same reasons they were depressed.

The Israelites trembled because they were faced with an impossible, fatal crisis and saw no relief in sight. Their hearts were in despair. Their minds raced with anxiety. The Israelites wouldn't believe what they couldn't see. They couldn't understand what didn't make sense. They couldn't hope in that which didn't conform to physical laws, or visible proofs. They only expected those things that take place every day. They expected that what happened yesterday would happen tomorrow. And they became depressed.

"Why so downcast o my soul, put your hope in God." The Israelites failed to put their trust in God for their impossible situation, and their souls were downcast. In the same way, we fail to put our trust in God for our impossible situations, and our souls, too, have become downcast.

We deny it. We think we trust God. We shake our heads: "Poor Israelites. Didn't they get it?" Didn't they know that God had water in that rock over there, and He would send down food from heaven in just a few hours? We knew that by the time we were knee-high in Sunday school. After all, we know God can do anything. The song "Nothing is too Difficult for Thee" is in our Top 40.

If the truth is to be told, we, like the Israelites, have trouble believing God will take care of the smallest details in our lives. So we, too, become worried; we fret. We suppress our fears, and that suppression subsides into deep-seated depression.

We don't really believe God for those things that keeps us awake at night, nor for the conflict with our boss, our spouse, or our siblings. We don't believe Him for our children or our in-laws. We just plain -- don't believe.

Again, I think many of us—especially those suffering from depression, in whatever form or degree—fall into the company of the disbelieving Israelites rather than Moses. I'm not saying we don't believe God to be our Savior. We do. We just don't believe Him to be our savior. Here's the meaning of my intentional redundancy.

Reason Number Three: Is Fear and Doubt Sin?

Yea, they spake against God, they said,
"Can God furnish a table in the wilderness?"
Behold, he smote the rock, that the waters gushed out,
and the streams overflowed;
But can he give bread also? Can he provide flesh for his people?
Therefore the Lord heard this, and was wroth: so a fire was
kindled against Jacob, and anger also came up against Israel;
Because they believed not in God, and trusted not in His salvation
(Psalm 78:20-22).
"For all this they sinned still, and believed not
for His wondrous works" (Psalm 78:32).

One reason we don't take all that has been said above seriously enough (and thereby stay in doubt, unbelief, fear, anxiety and depression), is that we fail to recognize the gravity of fear. We don't comprehend that the Israelites' unbelief in a supernatural intervention by God not only severely displeased God, but was considered by God to be an egregious act of sin (see Psalm 78).

Despite that truth, we would hardly consider our disbelief and doubt for the miraculous in our present situation to be sin as well. We tend to think of it as yet another harmless emotion. To test such theory, I asked a Bible college graduate which one she thought was worse: living in doubt and fear or an act of fornication. She considered the question a no-brainer. "An act of fornication, of course!" she retorted.

Nevertheless, the Israelite's unbelief, doubt, and fear about God's supernatural intervention not only was sin that severely displeased God, it was also the sin that kept them out of the Promised Land (see Psalm 78).

Yet most of us see our fear and worry as petty considerations regarding our relationship with God. We'd hardly consider our doubts and fears and unbelief to be sin or the very thing that keeps us from experiencing the promises of God in our lives. Instead, we like to consider only the "big vices" in determining whether we are living a life pleasing to God. We feel good because we haven't smoked a cigarette, didn't cuss on the freeway, and haven't had a Dos Equis in dos dias. Don't get me wrong, we shouldn't wink at issues of immorality, but we should look more intently at God's view of our unbelief. Whether we have a believing or disbelieving heart with respect to the difficult circumstances in our life, is of major consequence. And as we can see, He does look to see whether we believe: *"Therefore, since the promise of entering His rest still stands, let us be careful that none of you be found to have fallen short of it. For we also have had the gospel preached to us, just as they did; but the message they heard was of no value to them, because those who heard did not combine it with faith"* (Exodus 4:1-2).

Would you consider the following, although sobering (and a bit lengthy), illuminating Scripture?

The Lord said to Moses and Aaron: "How long will this wicked community grumble against me? I have heard the complaints of these grumbling Israelites. So tell them: As surely as I live, declares the Lord, I will do to you the very things I heard you say: In this desert your bodies will fall - every one of you twenty years old or more who was counted in the census and who has grumbled against me. Not one of you will enter the land I swore with uplifted hand to make your home, except Caleb son of Jephunneh and Joshua son of Nun. As for your children that you said would be taken as plunder, I will bring them in to enjoy the land you have rejected. But you- your bodies will fall in this desert. Your children will be shepherds here for forty years, suffering for your unfaithfulness, until the last of your bodies lies in the desert. For forty years - one year for each of the forty days you explored the land - you will suffer for your sins and know what it is like to have me against you. I, the Lord, have spoken, and I will surely do these things to this whole wicked community, which has banded together against me. They will meet their end in this desert; here they will die" (Numbers 14:26-35).

Imagine that, because of fear an entire generation of Israelites was unable to obtain God's promises. They were too scared to confront a people bigger, stronger, and faster. It's not so difficult to believe their unbelief. It happens all the time—even to us.

The Israelites didn't believe they could do what God had called them to do—so they didn't. They thought they'd die—so they did. Sobering? The Israelite's hopes for the Promised Land were not dashed away because of any dark, wicked, or twisted act. It wasn't because of their idol worship. It wasn't because someone was caught lying, cheating, stealing, or fornicating. They were simply afraid. Because of their lack of trust, they lost God's promise, and this time, there were no second chances.

Does it seem that God was being a bit unfair? Does His punishment seem disproportionate? Surely, there are enough sins to worry about without having to add to the list fear, worry, and a tinge of unbelief. What's the big deal?

Here's the big deal: God said the Israelites' fear-induced failure to go up and fight the Canaanites was an act of "provocation" (see Numbers 14:11). What's mind jarring is provocation literally means, "to scorn," "despise" or "contempt." Their unbelief was actually a pronouncement against God that He was small and insignificant, worthless and impotent. That's how God sees our fears when we respond contrary to His Word. We consider Him worthless.

In the same vein, the Psalmist declares that the Israelites "limited" the Holy One of Israel by turning back (see Psalm 78:41). Similarly, the Bible says that because of their unbelief, or lack of faith, Jesus was not able to do in His hometown the same miracles He had performed in so many other places.

God told the Israelites to go up and fight. He said go "up." Instead, they shrank "back." God said take it, but instead, they left it.

Our lives aren't much different. We, too, want deliverance from depression. We want to enter the land of promise and obtain the joy and peace that is given to us by His Word. We want to go up. , but to go "up" we must face some insurmountable odds. We can either believe His Word that we can do all things, or we can treat Him and His Word as small and insignificant and shrink back, remaining incapable of progressing and prospering in our lives.

Can I tell you that when I began to trust God to take care of me and my life, when I began to verbally repeat, over and over, "Thank you, Lord," "Thank you, Lord," regardless of the situations in life I found myself in because of that trust taking hold of me, my life began to change. Direction, purpose, peace, inner-healing, all began to come into my life, but first *I* had to change. First, I had to **trust**.

Reason Number Four: When we forget about Forgiveness

Some of you still feel you can't trust God because of your sinfulness. I know, because I felt the same. If so, you're underestimating the power of the blood. I know, because I did, too.

This is how we errantly think: We *feel* we really can't trust God to be our constant help and hope because we believe He will always have a valid reason for not helping. We feel that our constant sin and disobedience keeps us from any hope of being helped by God. "Why would He help me," you think. We assume God reasons as we do, so we *errantly* believe He says, "Well, I would help her in this situation, but she hasn't read the Word or really prayed in over a week." Or, "He yelled at his son last week, and lied the week before, so he's going to have to work this little problem out on his own."

We feel condemned by our sin and that it has jeopardized our ability to rely on God, so we rely on our self—and sink deeper still yet into our depression.

But, that all changed for me when I began to understand the power of the cross and the blood of Jesus Christ. Then, I began to realize that

Christ paid for *all* of my sins, and that my spirit-man was *totally* purified. I began to realize that God sees me in the clothing of Jesus' righteousness. This is the place where you need to remember the cleansing value of blood of Jesus over your life. Remember our study before about what God calls Himself in the Word. His name is, *"Forgiveness of wickedness, rebellion and sin."*(See Exodus 34).

I am cloaked in this robe when I enter the Presence of God. I can enter the Throne of the Holy of Holies with confidence that my petitions will be heard. I am a child of the King and welcome into the Presence of God. Not only that, but He is "Abba" my Father, my Daddy! I'm not only Holy because of Jesus' blood, I'm an adopted child of God, just as much invited into the realm of God as Jesus Christ, Himself. That means I am purely Holy.

I am purely righteous, and I am purely beloved. You see, many of us have become stuck in life because of condemnation. We, consciously or not, condemn ourselves for not living "good enough" — and that condemnation crushes our ability to rise in life. Condemnation comes when our eyes are fixed on our self — and our sin and mistakes, rather than having our eyes fixed on Christ and His forgiveness, and our good standing before the Father as a result. Sadly, many of our finances, relationships and lifestyles remain in shambles because of this shame. My friend, take your eyes off of yourself. Stop *trying* and *rest* in the finished work of Christ as your righteousness. Dwell in the full acceptance of God concerning you because of Christ's gift to you on the cross. As you immerse yourself in this truth, in the truth, then right living will come. Then, the riches of God's favor can run through your life like a flooding river, press you past the areas that you have become stuck and stagnant! Rejoice in the Lord all ye people!

That's when I began to realize that I didn't receive God's goodness and favor because of *my* works — not because of anything that I did, but because of *God's* work, I have become His own. My sins — past, present, and future — are paid for, in full. I am in right standing with God, right now, even as I speak. I can run to Him as MY loving Father. Well, then, I started running, and as I ran, I began to ask Him for things a son needs. Remember that little verse that says *"You have not because you ask not...?"* (James 4:2) You, right now, you, can do the same—run to Him. Know who you are in Christ: You are His own, Holy and Beloved.

Start asking God for things you never thought you should ask for before. Ask Him for things like extreme joy, never-ending, peace, and ultra clear direction and power (See Colossians 1 and I Peter 1). Ask Him to help you with that thing that has been haunting you. Know His ways, and then get happy because you know a good God who not only can, but *will* come through. Then know that just as Christ resurrected from the dead, so He will resurrect us — and find hope resurrected within you. See Romans 8:11. In this knowledge, you will finally find rest and joy. Awaken your hope — joy awaits you.

You can grow while you are in a state of hope and faith. Worry, anxiety, and stress dissipate. You now enter God's promises of peace and joy. Entrance to this place begins with a believing heart. Though it is not *all* about faith, we must acknowledge and accept the fact that faith is monumental in finding rest for your soul and begin to activate that belief into our own, everyday lives. Pray for God to remove all doubt from your heart and mind. Begin to believe God for what seems impossible, like peace, joy, and a sound mind. Start thanking Him for it even now!

Act as if God is actually real. Even pretend, if you have to, that He really is concerned. Imagine that He is just waiting and hoping for you to step out and believe Him for every concern in your life. Then, go on and imagine that He is full of love for you. Continue to imagine that He looks on you with compassion. Finally, fill your imagination with thoughts of His total forgiveness toward you. If you would live like that for just one day; you will see Him work. Then you'll experience His amazing glory.

Because of His character and His ways, you can believe and trust God in *your* crisis, today. Rest there, and stay there.

"And they that know thy Name will put their trust in thee..." (Psalm 9:10).

Conclusion: What's To Do In The Wilderness

Remember, the best thing you can do when you're in the wilderness is to realize that you are in the wilderness. So, relax a bit. Don't trip out, freak out, or skip out. Our provisions may be scant—daily manna, so to speak—so break out the Top Ramen and Cup O' Noodles and enjoy. Never forget that He's with us continually, just as He was with the Israelites, so He *will* supply your daily needs. He sees and is concerned. Know that—and hold onto it—even if you don't see His hand in the particular predicament.

Learn to walk by faith. Listen to the Word, not your circumstances, because what you see in the desert is nothing. Get to know God, trust Him through your lack. God may be silent at times, but He's not deaf.

What is there to do in the wilderness? *"The Lord, the God of the Hebrews, has sent me to say to you: Let my people go, so that they may worship me in the wilderness"* (Exodus 7:16).

We are to worship God in the wilderness of our lives. Worship in the wilderness is the ultimate act of trust, of faith. To praise God, the Jehovah Jireh, the Lord our Provider, in the midst of a barren place is a powerful demonstration of faith. *"And without faith, it is impossible to please God"* (Hebrews 11:6).

"...feeding them with manna, which neither they nor their fathers had known, to teach them that man does not live on bread alone but on every word that comes from the mouth of the LORD." See Deuteronomy 8:3.

God wants to feed you and nourish you with something you've never known, and which your parents hadn't known. He wants to feed you from His presence, not from your own plotting, planning, and plowing. He wants to speak to you in an intimate way, words of life and sustenance. His presence, His words, can satisfy your soul like no person nor job can, like no amount of money or recreation can. His satisfaction endures to the end. It comes as we humble ourselves before our Mighty, loving God, that He may exalt you in due time. What a privilege it is to be able to come before the Father of all each day, into His very presence, His throne. What an honor it is to do His bidding, to be His servant, His slave. There is no greater blessing or joy in all the earth.

"However, when the Son of Man comes, **will** he **find faith** on the **earth?**" See Luke 18:8.

Let us pray together: *"Father God, I come to you now in the name of Jesus Christ of Nazareth. Father, I confess that I have roamed from You for many days and for many reasons. Father, I have rebelled against You and have walked independent of You and Your ways. I did not know Your ways or Your Name, and so did not trust You in every area of my life. I did not fully receive Your grace in Christ but trusted in my self. I acknowledge to You my doubt and fear is sin and that I have prevented Your work in my life because of it. Father, thank You for Your forgiveness through Jesus Christ and His blood and death on the cross. I thank you that You said under the New Covenant in Christ's blood that You will remember my sins against me no more! Father, I know now that You are a God who is full of compassion and mercy, who is over-flowing with love for me and slow to anger. Lord, I know now that You reward those who diligently seek You. I choose now to seek You with my whole being. I will wholeheartedly trust in You alone for all because You alone are Good, all of Your ways are good and loving, and because You are the All-Powerful God. I will believe You for the impossible. I will have hope even when all seems hopeless— because You have called me to walk in great faith. So I call upon Your Name for peace in my life. Lord, I look to You to be my Healer. I look to You to be my Provider. I look to You for all things, for You are the great I AM. I thank You because You are with me and You are my God and strength. Thank You for your joy and Your blessing upon my life. In Jesus' Name."*

CR80

Chapter Six
Depression's Best Kept Secret
Part I

It was in high school that I first remember a friend suggesting I join the FBI. To be sure, it was because of my ultra-squeaky clean upbringing. That upbringing began in pre-school at a small, Baptist school near our house. It ended at graduation ceremonies from Valley Christian High School in San Jose, California. To the outsiders looking in, our school motto was "we don't cuss, drink, smoke, or chew, or go with girls that do." I scrupulously stuck to that motto—which is probably why I didn't have too much trouble getting into the FBI for a summer internship following my second year of law school. Not that the application/interview process was easy, in fact, it was downright intense—right down to the polygraph examination.

I Spy, the FBI

A polygraph exam is deceitfully difficult. It can play tricks on your mind as nothing else can. Not that I had anything to hide, but with all the wires and electronic gizmos hooked up to my arms, chest, and fingertips, it didn't take much for my thoughts to begin racing wildly. I tried to shut down the free-fall of ideas, but couldn't. I was in a quandary, and the exam was starting. I actually began to think this machine could literally read my mind. Let me tell you, that really sends your mind reeling! The polygraph examiner was ready to begin and I needed to be focused. The problem was that I was anything but!

Question: "Sir, Could you please state your full name?"

Each question, even the most simple, elicited a thousand thoughts, some relevant, some so far left I began questioning my own sanity, much less veracity. I tried to remain calm and composed.

Answer: "Ummm."

I couldn't focus. My thoughts were all over the map. I felt the early onset of a cold sweat. Suddenly, I knew that if I didn't snap out of this soon I would never make it into the program.

Question: "Are you or have you ever been in communication with a subversive government or had contact with any agent of such?"

How could they ask me such an outlandish question? Of course I hadn't; but when he mentioned words like "agent," "contact," and "subversive," my mind was off and running to the latest James Bond film.

That, of course, led to thoughts about the never-ending debate over who was the better Bond? Moore? Connery? Brosnan? True, Dalton never had a chance, but... *Stop it, Carmen*, I thought to myself. *You're going to betray yourself.*

But I couldn't stop it. I would never betray her majesty's secret service. I just hoped they wouldn't notice.

Answer: "Ummm."

Yes, my mind was fast afloat on the stream of consciousness, headed for disaster.

Sure there were some easy ones:

Question: "Have you ever taken drugs?"

Answer: "No."

Question: "How often do you drink alcohol?"

Answer: "Rarely."

Question: "Have you ever stolen?"

Answer: "No."

Then there were the ones that sounded easy but really weren't if given enough thought:

Question: "Did you ever cheat in school?"

How could he ask me that one? *Ever?* Who could remember such an academic nuance? I had never cheated in my life, but then again, hasn't every one cheated at least once?

So maybe he meant been *"caught"* cheating, and what did he mean by school? Is pre-school school? Do those mandatory, preschool nap times count? Sure, I peeked, my eyes opening surreptitiously now and again while lying on those colored cots. Who didn't? It was so enticing.

But is preschool-peeking cheating?

Yes, I was losing it, and fast. If I didn't stop this psychological train wreck, I'd certainly fail the polygraph and lose all hopes of winning this internship. I tried to stop thinking, but how do you do that? When do we ever stop thinking? Unless…that's it, Carmen! Start napping. Now.

But what if I peek?

"The Road to Enlightenment is long and difficult…
so bring some snacks and a magazine."

> —Anonymous quote written on the T-shirt
> of a guy I saw at the coffee shop.

Needless to say, I did get into the FBI's summer internship, had a great time, and made some great friends. Truly, I will never forget that polygraph experience. That whole experience, however, reminds me of how my "squeaky-clean background" helped. Yet, what happens when a squeaky-clean background hurts?

In this chapter and the next, we will explore that subtle killer of the Christian walk called, legalism. I know this subject well, and it is my hope to alleviate you from the pain and suffering always accompanied with it.

Too Good to be True

Growing up, by most Christian standards, I was doing a great job at this thing called, life. Sure, I wasn't happy. Maybe I was suffering a bit from depression, but since I wasn't doing *this*, had never done *that*, and was constantly doing the *other*, I was, necessarily, on the straight and narrow. Shouldn't I then be happy?

I was doing everything I knew to do right, yet felt like I was all wrong. I was always under the impression that if I did right, I'd be happy. As it turned out, I wasn't. That's what made it even more scary and confusing. Sure, if I knew I was being disobedient in some area then I could understand and explain my lack of joy, but, what about when your slate is clean?

I understood from my Sunday School days that once I reached the pearly gates I'd find happiness on the streets of gold; but I wanted to be happy in my life *now*. I even knew that being a member of the Kingdom of Heaven meant standing alone at times during difficult hours on earth. It does require sacrificing some earthly pleasures for the sake of the eternal. Yet, the King also says in His Word that the Kingdom of Heaven is a matter of righteousness, peace and joy in the Holy Ghost—and that the Kingdom of Heaven is at hand, even within us. My question was, "Where *is* this joy?"

Incidents in the Life of a Neighbor

"But when the commandment came, sin sprang to life and I died. I found that the very commandment that was intended to bring life actually brought death" (Romans 7:9-10).

This chapter covers one of the biggest pitfalls to depression, yet most of us never realize we have fallen here at all. For me, personally, it was one of the most liberating truths to ever reach my soul. To illustrate this truth, I'd like to introduce you to a recent acquaintance of mine, Marilyn.

Marilyn grew up overseas in a loving home with a loving father who loved God and loved his local church. This small, cozy, neighborhood assembly provided a warm welcome to all. It also happened to prescribe rules such as no make-up, no jewelry, no pants for women, no red clothes (red, of course, being the "color" of sin), no movies (to do so would be to "sit in the seat of mockers"), no dancing, and the list goes on and on. Basically, the church had rules that made you feel that if you were having fun, you were, necessarily, doing something wrong. Of course, these heavy-handed regulations were never discussed over the pulpit. Rather, they were neatly implemented in whispers in quiet corners of the sanctuary, off to the sides, in the aisles, in the parking lot after church.

Nevertheless, my friend Marilyn always loved the Lord. Even as an adult, she spent most of her waking hours in church, singing in the choir, serving in the various auxiliaries. Then, not really knowing when or why, her love went cold. She continued her church attendance but with reluctance. She battled unclean thoughts. Her adherence to the proper dress code began to wane during times alone. She'd slip in to the movies on an early Saturday afternoon, wear a toe ring the next, and maybe even buy a secular CD, all of which were considered deplorable by her church's rules.

"Incontrovertible sin," her conscious accused. But she couldn't help it—she *liked* it. So she hid it, and continued. She dabbled further and further into the "prohibited." Most of it was harmless, and some were quite deadly, but no one had taught her to wisely discern. She was made to believe that all things outside "the church" were bad, so she was naïve... a feast for the enemy and he knew it.

Since she could hide it, and since she could keep it mostly in her mind, she did. All she had to do was wear what was "right" and do what was "right" in front of the "right" people.

Eventually, a war erupted within her. Though her actions plagued her with guilt, they brought her pleasure as well. One day, she decided to try harder to cease and desist from all of her "wicked ways." She resolved to go to church more, pray more, and listen to more Christian music. Truly, she became sincere in her desire to please God. On other days, however, racy, lustful thoughts controlled her, compelling her anywhere and every-where but to God. She was ill-equipped to handle this war that was going on inside of her and felt as if she was on the road to implode. "I'm going crazy, Carmen," she confessed. "It's like I don't know who I am any-more."

Crowded Space

Consciously or not, those of us who have adopted religious or legalis-tic tendencies have erected tight and narrow fences that surround us on every side, constricting us. Though we cannot see them, those fences constrict our every movement. Eventually, the fence of legalism closes us in so that what was once supposed to be for our good now brings us into bondage.

Many Christians, including me at one time, live out their Christianity from within their soul, mind, will, and emotions. Instead, we're meant to live out our Christianity from our spirit-man. When our walk with God is limited to our soul, we create rules to measure our relationship: "Did I say a prayer today, listen to Christian music, call my grandma, shun swearing, elude lying, and avoid anger?" Soon, those rules can begin to predominate and expand. That fence gets so close we can barely take a step without tripping over it. We can't freely move our arms. We can't freely move at all. That's what began to happen to Marilyn. That fence of rules around her—against her day and night—was pushing right up to her very being. Eventually, she began to resent it. She needed some space.

Fascinating how the law kills (see 2 Corinthians 3:6). Trying to keep the law suffocates the life right out of a healthy, happy believer. Al-though she didn't realize it, my friend began to push back because her view of Christianity prohibited her from doing things entirely proper for a saint of the Most High God. The religious rules and regulations she'd assimilated began to encroach further and further into her "space," con-stricting proper expressions of her personality, tastes, interests, and crea-tivity. In effect, the rules, which she thought were the essence of Christianity, had figuratively hedged a tight, constricting fence all around her, confining her movement, and preventing her from becoming all that God had designed her to be. Her "religiosity" instead of true Christianity had her in shackles, bound hand, foot, and mind.

She liked classical guitar music, so she bought a "secular" CD with classical guitar music. She enjoyed fiction writing, so went to the movies to enhance her creativity in that area. The wonder of storytelling was an element of her creativity. Yet she knew that her fellow congregants would condemn her if they found out. She could not share her joy in her new found creative and God-given ability with the people who she considered an extension of her family.

Her "religion," which she falsely equated as her relationship with God, told her this was, "all wrong." Her religious rules were trespassing on her very being. That fence line of religious prohibitions was forcing her to abandon aspects of her God-given personality. Her reaction then was to push against that boundary.

She wanted nothing more than to burst out of those constraints. Yet, she believed that such a "break" was not a rebellion against godless rules, but against God Himself. She was left feeling tormented. Eventually, she did break out—in her mind, in her thoughts, in her soul. Religious legalism had closed her in. Now she was breaking out. She burst open that door with such force that all became welcome—the good, the bad, and the horribly bad. She wanted space from rules and threw the proverbial baby out with the bathwater.

She was now overreacting to the overreaching prescriptions of her church. She hated herself for feeling that she had betrayed God in her heart. Though, on the outside, no one even suspected it, she had indeed changed.

"Carmen," she expressed to me sadly, "I feel like I'm going insane." Unless she was able to rid herself of religion, of this legalism, she would soon begin to live like the Pharisees. On the outside picture perfect, but on the inside rebelling and rotting.

All Things in Moderation

Granted, many of us have not grown up with such far-reaching legalistic doctrines. I think that more of us have than we realize. Take a moment and answer the following questions. When the Bible states "*...those who are led by the Spirit of God are sons of God"* or, *"So I say, live by the Spirit..."* do you struggle to understand what that really means and how to apply it in your life? When you read *"walk by the Spirit"* does that seem a bit mystical, ethereal, and in the company of Obi-Wan exhorting the young Luke Skywalker to "use the force"? I know that for a time in my life, I struggled to understand these concepts. "Great," I'd say to myself, "you tell us to live by the Spirit, but could you please also tell me HOW?"

If you are that person, legalism may be a factor in your life, and that factor may be a huge contributor to your daily struggle against depression.

Speaking of struggle, here's another question I'd like for you to answer. Do you find yourself on a roller coaster of guilt over not spending enough time in prayer and reading Scriptures? Do you find yourself—if you're really honest with yourself—continually criticizing others and judging, based on their actions, whether they're living a "good" Christian life? What would happen if you saw your pastor walk out of a movie theater, drink a glass of wine, or drive an expensive car? Would critical thoughts come to mind? If so, then read on, this chapter may be just for you.

Finally, one last, simple question: Do you feel you are becoming more intimately acquainted with your Lord and Savior? Are you getting to know Him more and more each day?

It is imperative that we understand that a healthy life is not regulated by man's ordinance, but by God's Word and His Spirit. Unfortunately, it was not until much later in life that I realized that God is not a God of rules. In the perfect state of the world—in the garden—there was but one prohibition. There was only one rule. So, then, why do we put on others more than God puts on them? Why do we put upon ourselves more than God puts on us?

Imposed regulation from church doctrine suffocates our healthy likes, tastes, interests and freedom. It inhibits the unique life and creativity that we each have to offer the Kingdom – each other. It breeds unnecessary weariness, frustration, and rebellion. This is why those who are living a life entangled by legalism will never find happiness. Legalism suffocates. God's breath refreshes.

True, it may not be healthy for *me* to go to movies at this time, or to see certain movies. God may have even revealed to me that I shouldn't go to the movies at all, but that doesn't mean He's given a blanket prohibition on movie watching, and by no means is it a license for me to put that upon you or anyone else. Each one of us is to work out our own salvation with fear and trembling. That means I spend time with God. That has nothing to do with going to church, listening to Christian radio, wearing "Christian" t-shirts, or going to the movie house. On the contrary, our love for God, His Word, and His Spirit—not manmade rules—dictate which actions we are to curtail and when. Further, our walking with the Spirit should more than just guide us toward the things to avoid; the Spirit leads us to the places He would have us go, to the people with whom He would have us speak (as well as the words to speak), and even the business ventures we ought to begin.

The problem with rules is that they replace relationship. With religion, you never need to know God, you simply do the checklist. A Christian who lives simply by rules feels that, in order to be in good standing with God, all he has to do is carefully follow those rules. Since we will always fail the checklist, peace of mind will always elude us. This lifestyle wholly ignores the entire aim of Christianity, which is to know God more and more intimately (see John 17:3). That is why there was a time in my life when I was "doing" all the right "Christian" things, but still felt I wasn't drawing any closer to God. Concerning my friend, Marilyn, after all those years in church, she still felt she didn't even know God. There was no relationship with the loving Father – only rules.

Similarly, if we live under the law, in any way, we'll never feel worthy enough to continuously be able to trust God wholeheartedly for every detail in our life (and therefore find rest in our circumstance), or draw near to Him daily (and find rest in His presence).

Yes, brothers and sisters, legalism kills. We will delve more into this subject in the following chapter. For now, just recognize that legalism is a fatal barrier to experiencing a life of joy. Because legalism is a close cousin of depression, we must be willing to address it squarely. So as you read the next chapter, ask the Holy Spirit to prepare you to pull down every entanglement of legalism within you. As you do, you will discover grace anew, and the joy that follows.

Say this prayer with me: *"Father, I thank You for delivering me from the curse of the law and from living a legalistic lifestyle. I thank You for Your Spirit that lives inside of me and that You have called me to live by the Spirit. Thank You for teaching me how to walk in accordance to the Spirit. Thank You for teaching me the sound of Your voice from all others. Thank you for freeing me from being controlled by my emotions, or by my understanding. I choose Your Spirit to lead my spirit. I will follow Your voice. I will not allow man-made rules to replace my relationship with You. I declare that I am free from false guilt and condemnation. Thank You for allowing me to find my life in the Spirit. I thank You that the fruit of Your Spirit is joy. I thank You for allowing me to experience You and Your Spirit and Your love and joy more and more each day. I thank You that I have liberty in Christ. I thank You that I am no longer under the curse, but in Your blessing. I am free to live my life to the fullest, In Jesus name, Amen!"*

Chapter Seven
Depression's Best Kept Secret
Part II

When my mother "got saved," she got saved. Reared since infancy in a religion that riddled her with guilt, she no longer swam in the sludge of shame and failure. She was ablaze. She didn't "play" church. She didn't "act" Christian. She was. She spent hours at the park alone with God. From sun-up to sun-down, Sunday through Saturday we heard her singing praise hymns throughout the house.

Mom would blanket us in prayer every night, and not the "Now I Lay Me Down to Sleep" type either. Consequently, my brother and I went, not only to Sunday morning church, but Sunday evenings as well, and Sunday school, Vacation Bible School, camps, retreats....

As part of her genuine commitment to the things of God, if my mother came across a passage in the Scriptures imploring her to act, she acted; if to cease, she ceased. So when she came across the Proverb that said, *"He that spareth his rod hateth his son,"* she spared not. When she discovered the exhortation *"Do not withhold discipline from a child,"* she withheld not. When she learned that the Word said, *"Chasten thy son while there is hope, and let not thy soul spare for his crying,"* she chastened—and we cried. When she read, *"Foolishness is bound in the heart of a child; but the rod of correction shall drive it far from him,"* she began unbinding and driving.

Needless to say, spankings were no infrequent event in our household. It didn't stop there. Mom carried the rod of correction everywhere we went — tucked in her purse, under the seat, on top of the refrigerator, strapped to her waist; no place was too remote, no distance too far, no setting too obscure. She'd been known to pull over on the Interstate if we needed a good flogging. En route to school, on vacations, on the train, the plane, even the automobile—it was all fair game. All she had to do was look at us with that Clint Eastwood sort of squint and we boys fell in line faster than a private first class on the first day of boot camp.

She was never angry, upset, and she didn't even yell when she whipped out the rod of correction. When she pulled off the side of the road to commence the thrashing, it was never in a fit of rage, never a quick blip to the face. She was always calm, gentle, and loving. Mom always shared with us the ample justification for each occasion. Believe me, there was always, always, ample justification for the occasion. She was so sincere with the "This is going to hurt me more than it's going to hurt you," spiel that we were tempted to believe it.

Our spankings were always followed by an expression of unconditional, undying, tender love.

In retrospect, it's easy to understand my tendencies toward living under the law, believing Christianity is more about living by rules and regulations than out of a heart of gratitude. I completely understand how common it is to reduce our Christianity to rules rather than relationship.

Choose One and One Only

Regarding your standing and relationship with God versus religion, you either put your trust in your own works or Christ's work—there's no in-between. Paul declares in the third chapter of Philippians that he would rather be found in Christ—to "know Him"—rather than have his own righteousness. Instead of taking pride in his own "righteous" accomplishments, he considered them as "dung." (In today's vernacular, that

word would look something like @#$!. For now, we'll settle for "dung.")
To place our trust in our own righteousness is to be cursed, for *"...cursed is he that puts his trust in man..."* (see Jeremiah 17:5).

Can A Christian Be Cursed?

To put your trust in our own ability to measure up to God's standard is one of the most prideful positions man can take because it is a statement to God that we don't need Him, and His work or His cross. Pride separates us from God. Pride defeats us so that we cannot inherit God's promises, including His joy. Pride brings the curse, for God *opposes the proud.* Pride caused Lucifer to be banished from among God's own angels... from the position of Angel of Light. Lucifer fell from being the angel closest to God to being an angel in opposition to God's ways. It was all because of pride.

To be aligned with God means recognizing that we can do nothing to earn our way into His holiness. We draw nearer to God as we acknowledge that He alone has saved us from all of our sins through Christ's work on the cross, the shedding of his blood for you and I. That acknowledgement brings the blessing, for *God gives grace to the humble.* It's this blessing that brings us out of legalism's stronghold of depression. Those that are blessed by the hand of the Lord are lifted up. Those who are not are pressed down.

For years life was hard for me, and it showed. My friends had always known that I strived to please God. They respected that, but that was my problem. As a Christian, I was striving to please God instead of realizing that, merely by being in Christ, I pleased God. I didn't absorb into my heart which I knew in my mind already. God does not love us because of or in spite of. He simply loves us. That's what He does. That's who He is. It would be a long time before I assimilated this understanding.

Instead, I continued striving. I was striving to have longer and longer quiet times in prayer and the Word, feeling guilty on the days I skipped. I was constantly striving to witness more, serve more, and pray more. As a result, I could never really relax. I was constantly plagued with condemnation. I could never enjoy the beauty of life. I was never *in* peace.

Sure, I could laugh, at times, but a foundation of joy in my life escaped me. I was incapable of enjoying a sunset, a sunrise, or a Sunday. I was constantly aware that I was a spiritual being but never cognizant of the fact that I was also a human being, with all of the accompanying glorious shortcomings, frailties, and emotions. I was fighting a losing battle. Constantly striving, I was constantly failing. I was overwhelmingly hard on myself, beating myself up day after day.

I was depressed, sad, and weary. I could never find what it took to make happiness last for longer than a few fleeting moments in the day. Such frustration penetrated my heart deeply. Though I knew I was a Christian, I felt accursed.

Paul wrote, *"For as many as are of the works of the law are under the curse: for it is written, Cursed is every one that continueth not in all things which are written in the book of the law"* (Galatians 3:10).

Just as with most modern systems of jurisprudence, if you are guilty of breaking one law, you are a criminal and subject to lawful punishment. You don't have to break the entire penal code to be found guilty. This is also true with the Old Testament laws: If you broke one law, you were guilty. One lawless act brought the curse or worse, a stoning. It was all or nothing. As a result, the substitute animal punishments were an integral part of the religious and social order of God's people. Mercifully, God poured out His righteous punishment on a living animal instead of a living man.

In the New Testament, God's crowning act was revealed to us at Calvary, as He poured out His righteous punishment on His beloved Son Jesus, for you and me. He who knew no sin became sin – that we may be found righteous. God imputed to Jesus our sins and imparted to us His righteousness. How great is His love for us! Receive that love and grace today my friend! That is our path to victory!

Concerning the New Testament church of Galatia, Paul feared that they were about to fall back under that same curse, which meant alienation from God and a defeated life: *"Christ is become of no effect unto you, whosoever of you are justified by the law; ye are fallen from grace."* (Galatians 2:21; 5:4).

I finally gave up. I quit. I told God about it. I simply cried out for Him and for His grace—His favor and power given to me for my life, even though I didn't deserve it. Then something inside me took hold. It clicked. I began longing to spend time with God. My prayer life skyrocketed. His Word suddenly became alive. I began to find rest and peace. In short, I began to prosper.

Don't Worry, Be Happy.

"As we said before, so say I now again, If any man preach any other gospel unto you than that ye have received, let him be accursed" (Galatians 1:7).

Paul felt so strongly about the destructive power of legalism that he'd have a curse placed on the person who preached its message. In Philippians Paul calls "dogs" and "evil workers" those who espouse the profitability of works done in the flesh. The Galatians who had been taken prey to it, he called bewitched, fallen from grace, and in danger of bondage. More so, Paul states that the law brings condemnation and death. It is the law that actually empowers sin. The law makes us aware of sin – it is like an instructor or tutor that makes us recognize how sinful we are and how severely we need a Savior. The law is not the Savior. Living under rules can never clean us up, in fact, it only makes us see how dirty we are. No wonder we feel condemned — those of us who have lived under the law. Paul states, therefore, that once we come to the Savior, we no longer need the tutor. There is no more need to live under the law because we are now under grace. That grace propels us forward in Christ, not away from Him. That grace allows us to want to run to Him, not away from Him because of guilt and shame. Praise the Lord!

Paul considered his religious perfection as dung because he knew there is an inverse relationship between observing the law and knowing Christ. Paul knew that as legalism increases, our closeness with Christ—and our ability to walk in His power, His peace and His presence—decreases. Grace and legalism are at polar extremes. We will live our lives under one or the other. In one is life, the other is death. *"For if righteousness cometh by the law, then Christ is dead in vain"* (Galatians 2:21). With legalism, you are on your own. Even your righteousness is on your own terms. That is what humans like. Thus, the Scripture says *"...each of us has turned to his own way."*

It's easier to relegate your religion and your religious experience to rules and works because there is no accountability there. There's no need to come to God because you don't need God if you're going to abide by rules and rituals. There is no need to abide. There's no need to come clean. There's no need to draw into His presence. Therefore, our prideful ways go unchecked.

Under works, then, there is no need to submit. *Wrong, you say: You have to submit to the rules themselves.* I disagree. Under the law, you can always find loopholes. There's always an exception to the rule, especially for the one who is in charge of the accountability. That's why the Pharisees were guilty of not practicing the myriad of rules they espoused. We can always rationalize sin. That's what we do. We justify ourselves and judge others. Still, we remain un-reconciled to God. Deep down we know it. So we either run from what we know—to avoid the truth—or we deny the truth altogether. In either case, the fruit of joy in our life continues to rot because we remain unclean.

We feel we only deserve that with which we have worked, sweated, and toiled over. Besides, obtaining all of God's benefits and promises merely by faith in Christ seems entirely too easy and too cheap. We feel that if this thing called Christianity is as big as Christ says it is, then we've got to work for it.

In truth, the law of the Lord is so high, so pristine, it can never be achieved by man's effort. That's why Christ said even to be angry with a brother is as murder, and to lust is as adultery. He laid down the true law first so that we could see the need for Him, the Savior of the world.

What we fail to realize is that the call to faith, and having the fruit of the Spirit as a result of faith, requires daily abiding. Our life, then, is found in abiding with Christ, our Savior.

Headed for Self-Destruction

"For all the law is fulfilled in one word, even in this: Thou shalt love thy neighbour as thyself. But if ye bite and devour one another, take heed that ye be not consumed one of another" (Galatians 5:14-15).

The church in Galatia had also forgotten about that ever-continuous command called, LOVE. Instead, they were mired with in-fighting, back-biting, and "devouring" one another. Paul warns them to take heed of this, lest they even consume ("use up" or "destroy") themselves. As they veered toward a religion of flesh-based works, their spirit man was growing weak and tired. Their flesh was strong and robust, but their spirit became gaunt and faltering—they were headed for self-destruction.

Under legalism, there remains perpetual guilt and self-hatred. Thus, by stifling our ability to love our self, we become incapable of loving others, for it is written, *"Love your neighbor as yourself."* All we're left with is a critical attitude of our self and others. This attitude begins to kill not only our walk with God and our joy, but our friendships as well. We then begin to associate only with others who are just as critical, con-demning, and backbiting as we are, and we justify it by saying everyone else is "not living right." We think we're being persecuted for righteous-ness instead of realizing that we're relying on our own pride and faulty doctrine.

Unfortunately, that rings true of many of us Christians and churches today. How hypocritical we are when we "worship" God with our mouths during praise and worship and then whisper to our neighbor ill-spirited words against another brother or sister. God cannot be mocked.

We are not fooling God. We reap what we sow (see Galatians 6:7). Then we wonder why we have so many interpersonal relationship problems, and so many unhealthy relationships.

Unchecked, legalism depends on the flesh to see you through. The works of the flesh are outlined by Paul as follows:

"The acts of the sinful nature are obvious: sexual immorality, impurity and debauchery; idolatry and witchcraft; hatred, discord, jealousy, fits of rage, selfish ambition, dissensions, factions and envy; drunkenness, orgies, and the like. I warn you, as I did before, that those who live like this will not inherit the kingdom of God" (Galatians 5:19-21).

To the legalists of His day — to the Pharisee who we strive not to be, Jesus said the following:

"You are like whitewashed tombs, which look beautiful on the outside but on the inside are full of dead men's bones and everything unclean. In the same way, on the outside you appear to people as righteous but on the inside you are full of hypocrisy and wickedness" (Matthew 23:27-28).

Some name calling isn't it? Christ was not happy when confronted with the doctrine of works demanded by these Pharisees. Inside, they were full of wickedness. Unfortunately, many people we know today are in jeopardy of becoming the same.

It's time to replace duplicity with humility, cruel words with kind ones, slander, lies and gossip with psalms, hymns, and spiritual songs. Make up your mind to have a tongue that builds up and never tears down. God desires mercy not sacrifice. God desires hearts that speak words of life, encouragement, and compassion to each other more than He desires the "sacrifice" of praise songs. Better yet, as Christ would say to us, do the one without neglecting the other.

Christians Just Want To Have Fun

"What has happened to all of your joy?" (Galatians 4:15a, NIV).

Finally, Paul had heard that many in the Church were no longer having "fun." The Galatians had once been happy. At the time of Paul's epistle, they'd lost it. They'd replaced it with a confidence in their own efforts to pursue and please God. Although there is never any happiness in that pursuit, it remains the tendency of man to go there anyway. It makes us feel good.

It is imperative to our soul's happiness that we recognize that legalism kills. Most of us deny we're living under the law. We know we can't earn our salvation. We can even quote from memory the supporting Scriptures to back us. *"For by grace are ye saved through faith; and that not of yourselves: it is the gift of God; Not of works, lest any man should boast"* (Ephesians 2:8, 9).

In reality, however, we do continue to look to our works to see if we measure up to God. We look to our works (our most recent recollection of sin) to determine if we qualify for God's favor, His Spirit, and His blessings.

Yet, Paul asks the Galatians, *"Received ye the Spirit by the works of the law, or by the hearing of faith? Are ye so foolish? having, begun in the Spirit, are ye now made perfect by the flesh?...He that ministereth to you the Spirit, and worketh miracles among you, doeth he it by the works of the law, or by the hearing of faith?"* (Galatians 3: 2, 3, 5).

The concept is similar to that which we discussed in earlier chapters regarding salvation. We believe God will be our Savior from death and hell, but not that He will be our Savior during the difficult times on earth. So, too, we recognize that works and observing the law won't get us to heaven in the future, but we use those tactics as a spiritual barometer to determine whether and what we will receive from heaven today.

As a result, many of us begin our prayers with "cleansing"—pleading for God to forgive our sins. We somehow believe this is necessary to bring ourselves rightly before His throne of grace. We still believe that our cleanliness is up to "us." We believe the law, and, in turn, our lawlessness, affects our relationship. This has the guise of humility. In reality, it is pride. It indicates that we believe we can come to the Father only after we straighten up any sin issues committed since our last time of prayer. This is nothing other than basing our standing with God on works.

In contrast, God's example of prayer given to us by the Lord places "confession time" in the middle of the prayer outline. We are to come to Him—*"Our Father"*—and ask requests of Him—*"Give us this day, our daily bread"*—even *before* our time of repentance of sin, *"Forgive us our debts...."*

Just as Christ told His disciples that they were already clean—only their feet needed to be washed—we are already clean before God. That's why Christ said He must wash us, or we can have nothing to do with Him. He alone washes. We cannot.

In the same manner, in the Old Testament, the article used for ceremonial washing before entering the sanctuary of God was not a bathtub but a basin. The whole body did not need to be washed, just the dust of one's feet. Their bodies were already clean. In addition, the basin was not placed outside the tabernacle but inside, indicating that they were already able to enter the gates and the courts of God's throne.

We too must remember that the blood and the blood alone allows us access into the very throne of our loving God of all creation. If you think your sin keeps you out, then you must think you had something to do with your salvation in the first place. Our acceptance with God was never based on our lack of sin, nor will it ever be. Thank God for that.

We were forgiven, justified, and made right before God when Christ became our Savior, and we continue to stay forgiven, justified and made right before God because of the Savior – His loving grace poured out upon us with blood – the only thing that takes away sins. His blood has already washed us, once and for all (see Hebrews 10:10). Our salvation can rest in nothing else. We can rest in nothing else. Therefore, we can boldly enter His throne of grace.

If this were not so, if we could have done it on our own, there would have been no need for God to send His Son. If this were not so, Christ was lying or demented when He said, *"I am the way, the truth and the life, no man comes to the Father but by me."*

Please know that the enemy of your soul will use religion, tradition, man's ego, societal pressure, whatever it will take to keep you from fully appreciating the magnitude of God's forgiveness, the exchange that crucified Christ who became sin for us and gave us the very righteousness, love and favor of God instead of the penalty of our sin. Since we continue to believe a part of it is based on our self-effort, we remain less than grateful, and thankful and appreciative of the amazing, indescribable work that was accomplished on the cross. Therefore, we love less. However, Christ declared that He who is forgiven much, loves much. Indeed, we all have been forgiven much. Yet, many Christians do not recognize they have been forgiven of much because they think they have to earn a portion of it. If we would only see the righteousness purchased for us and receive it, knowing that it endures and remains even when we fail, how much greater would our love be for the Lord. Knowing the greatness of His forgiveness makes us love Him greatly. That love drives us to obedience, for Christ said that if we loved Him, we would keep His commandments. Do you see that our obedience is born out of love for Him? That is why the grace of God teaches us to live correctly, not the wrath of God (See Titus 2:10-15; 3:1-8).

Unfortunately, this is how our tainted minds due do legalism, think: Something seemingly unfortunate happens – we lose our job, are forced to find another place to live, become sick, receive an unforeseen bill in the mail, etc., and we immediately think God is punishing us or that we must have done wrong for this to happen. We feel condemned. We blame God. We blame something or someone. Believers, can I tell you again that God is not angry with you! He cannot be. He is holy and He has already poured out the fullness of His wrath upon Christ. Therefore, wrath no longer remains for those who are in Christ! There remains only grace – expressed in love – the favor of God to us even though we do not deserve it. Remember, His new covenant states that He will remember our sins against us no more (Hebrews 8:12; Colossians 2:13). Yes, God will lovingly discipline His children, but He will not punish. Think of how you discipline your children. If they did not feed the dog, would you discipline the child by shooting the dog in the head? Of course not! So if we, though evil, would not do such a thing, how much more would an infinitely loving God never discipline in such a severe manner. Folks, stop condemning yourself for being sick, for being overweight, for losing your temper. Stop condemning yourself as a husband, wife, employee or employer. Instead, start remembering that you are forgiven and made holy through Christ's death on the cross for you. That's grace – and that makes us live right – it is not condemnation!

Beloved of God, the Lord does not take such draconian measures to discipline us. You must realize, however, that the deceiver of our souls, would attempt for us to believe it. He is the accuser, so that's what he does. He accuses you of your sins. Unfortunately, many of us have believed his lies. We continue to think God is angry at us when we fail. How then can you expect anything good from an angry God? You cannot, and as a result, our ability to trust God in faith is squelched. No, Christ is our propitiation. He is our mercy seat. That means that Christ has taken our place of punishment. God's wrath toward the believer has been fully appeased. Yes, there remains a wrath reserved for those who continually reject Christ, and for Satan and his cohorts, but not for the believer.

Let me give you another real example: I have a friend who honestly believed that every time she sinned, that her fellowship with God was broken and that she would go to hell if she didn't confess that sin. So I asked her if she believed that exceeding the speed limit was breaking the law of the land. She said, "Yes." I then asked her if that was, therefore, a sin. Again, she answered in the affirmative. So I put forward to her this hypothetical: I asked her if she was driving down the freeway at 66 miles per hour (one mile per hour over the posted speed limit) and she then suddenly collided with another vehicle and immediately died, having had no time to ask for forgiveness (for the sin of breaking the speed limit law), would she go to hell. After thinking about it for a minute, she stated, somewhat sadly, "Well, yes, I guess I would."

Is it any wonder why such an individual would be tormented by depression and confusion? How can you trust God in the midst of such uncertainty and fear? You cannot! You can't have child like faith in God when you are confronted with (what you think is) an angry God.

Sadly, many of us have family members and friends with tempers, mood swings or stay angry with us for hours and days on end. We, then, as Christians, are susceptible to believe that our Father has these same traits as well. Alternatively, we beginning to read the Old Testament and believe we are still bound by the same "rules" and operating under the same terms and conditions.

Let's look at the thinking process of my friend who thought that she was separated from God because of breaking the speed limit. She had the erroneous belief that *only* her past sins were covered by the blood. For every sin committed, a new covering of blood needed to be applied. Yet, this was the process under the Old Covenant where the blood of mere animals was sufficient to cover a man's sins. That is why the process needed to be repeated time and time again for every new sin committed. Amazingly enough, this is exactly how some of us believe the sacrifice offering of Christ Himself works as well. My friend, don't you think that the blood of the Lamb of God, who takes away the sins of the world, offers a little more efficacy and power than the blood of a bull? Of course it does!

"Furthermore, every [human] priest stands [at his altar of service] ministering daily, offering the same sacrifices over and over again, which never are able to strip [from every side of us] the sins [that envelop us] and take them away--

Whereas this One [Christ], after He had offered a single sacrifice for our sins [that shall avail] for all time, sat down at the right hand of God, then to wait until His enemies should be made a stool beneath His feet.

For by a single offering He has forever completely cleansed and perfected those who are consecrated and made holy.

And also the Holy Spirit adds His testimony to us [in confirmation of this]. For having said,

This is the agreement (testament, covenant) that I will set up and conclude with them after those days, says the Lord: I will imprint My laws upon their hearts, and I will inscribe them on their minds (on their inmost thoughts and understanding)."

He then goes on to say, **"And their sins and their lawbreaking I will remember no more."**

Now where there is absolute remission (forgiveness and cancellation of the penalty) of these [sins and lawbreaking], there is no longer any offering made to atone for sin.

*Therefore, brethren, since we have full freedom and confidence to enter into the [Holy of] Holies [by the power and virtue] in the blood of Jesus, by this fresh (new) and living way which He initiated and dedicated and opened for us through the separating curtain (veil of the Holy of Holies), that is, through His flesh, since we have [such] a great and wonderful and noble Priest [Who rules] over the house of God, us all come forward and draw near with true (honest and sincere) hearts in unqualified assurance and absolute conviction engendered by faith (by that leaning of the entire human personality on God in absolute trust and confidence in His power, wisdom, and goodness), **having our hearts sprinkled and purified from a guilty (evil) conscience** and our bodies cleansed with pure water. So, let us seize and hold fast and retain without wavering the hope we cherish and confess and our acknowledgement of it, for He Who promised is reliable (sure) and faithful to His word"* (Hebrews 10:11-23, Amplified).

I know that's a lot of scripture, but did you catch verse fourteen? *"...by a single offering he has forever completely cleansed and perfected..."* Christ's death on the cross for you has forever and completely cleansed you and perfected you. That's grace! That's love! In addition, as verse twenty-two states, our hearts have been purified from a guilty conscience! Our iniquities have been/and are continually being washed and covered. We can have complete confidence in our standing before God – even if we blow it! There is no longer a need for more blood and begging for forgiveness – our forgiveness remains...and remains! Our sins – all of them – even the ones you will do tomorrow, have already been paid in full by Jesus. Folks, this is the good news! This is the gospel of Jesus Christ! Today, we don't have to spend our time and energy *trying* to become righteous or *trying* to please God (i.e., the world religions of our day). God loves us as He loves Christ because we said, "Yes," to Christ, putting our faith in Him. Now, we can spend our time loving and serving Him and others, not performing works to attain our salvation.

But now the righteousness of God has been revealed independently and altogether apart from the Law, although actually it is attested by the Law and the Prophets,

Namely, the righteousness of God which comes by believing with personal trust and confident reliance on Jesus Christ (the Messiah). [And it is meant] for all who believe. For there is no distinction, Since all have sinned and are falling short of the honor and glory which God bestows and receives.

[All] are justified and made upright and in right standing with God, freely and gratuitously by His grace (His unmerited favor and mercy), through the redemption which is [provided] in Christ Jesus,

Whom God put forward [before the eyes of all] as a mercy seat and propitiation by His blood [the cleansing and life-giving sacrifice of atonement and reconciliation, to be received] through faith. This was to show God's righteousness, because in His divine forbearance He had passed over and ignored former sins without punishment.

It was to demonstrate and prove at the present time (in the now season) that He Himself is righteous and that He justifies and accepts as righteous him who has [true] faith in Jesus (Romans 3:21-26, Amplified).

According to Romans 3:21-26, declare to yourself that you have been justified (declared righteous in God's sight) freely by God's grace through the redemption that is in Christ Jesus. That's right, this is the truth concerning you: "I have been declared righteous in God's sight through Christ." I would encourage you to make this, or something like it, your daily declaration of faith, and who you are in Christ Jesus. Yes, let the grace of God uplift you. This is the grace that propels us to live by the Spirit. This is the grace that propels us to right action. This is the grace that keeps us from sin! (See Romans 6:14). Our understanding of our righteousness will begin to manifest in our behavior. Negative thoughts (like guilt and condemnation), leads to negative behavior (like secret sins and addictions). No longer let the lie of condemnation depress you. You are hidden in Christ. God loves you as His own. Imagine loving someone enough that you would be willing to sacrifice your own child. My friend, that is the love of God for you. Receive the riches of His grace, His inheritance for you in Christ. If He spared not His Son for your eternal life, how much more will He take care of all your needs in this life!

Yes, begin to say these words aloud, daily: "I have been declared righteous in God's sight through Christ!"

A New Path Discovered

I've found that God brings us to difficult places so that we'll simply give up. That act—as we stop with our own efforts, and even die to ourselves—choosing to rely on Christ's power within us — allowing the Holy Spirit room to act, and move within us and for us. Then it's no longer I who live, but Christ who lives in me (see Galatians 2:20). In this place there is no more frustration, guilt, and struggling to try to please God. In this place we're no longer trying to figure out what Jesus would do and *trying* to do it. Here we simply *cease trying* and *let Him* do it through us.

Last night I spoke with an old college friend who was in crisis, and we discussed this very thing. "So how do you actually put this "giving up" into practice?" she asked. For me, it started with a simple prayer. It was my simply telling God that I was through. "Lord, I give up. I can't do it, and I need you to do it. I no longer place myself under the law of trying to please you. I receive your grace instead."

Then I began to tell Him my laundry list of things—everything I was giving up on. I just began believing He'd do it. Then, I began to apply that exercise, that prayer, to not just one moment in time, but to a continual prayer throughout the day. So even on my day off, even going to lunch with a friend, at work on a project, whatever it was, I told the Lord, "I can't do it. I don't want to do it. I don't want to be the one speaking or doing; let it be You. Help me Lord. Holy Spirit, help me."

That was when I began to see victory and rest. You will find rest and victory in the same.

*"[Be] confident of this, that He who **began** a **good work** in you will carry it on to completion until the day of Christ Jesus"* (Philippians 1:6, emphasis added).

Got Boredom?

Just as God's Spirit compels us to action, legalism compels one to boredom. Consequently, I truly believe that many today who feel the pangs of depression are actually suffering from boredom. Yes, I know that our schedules are full and the day-timer crammed. Yet, internally, we remain bored. We carry on the façade of contentment in our "busyness." That's not to say we're not challenged by life, and at times overwhelmed. I believe it is because of our need to seem busy. The more our cell phones rings and the fewer hours we have free on our daily calendar, the more popular we feel, as if popularity could fulfill our happiness. We soon find that those on our calendar want, want, want and we are usually left laying on our bed at night, staring at the ceiling unable to sleep for the 30 cups of strong coffee we drank that day just to stay up with all we thought we had to do. We lay there wondering where the day went and our hearts sink as we see our lives flash before our eyes since we never do accomplish the things that we have hidden down in our hearts – those dreams of destiny that God has called us to do. We have been caught up in the engine of present-day life. Though fully alive, we mostly feel dead. We smile, but are sincerely *unhappy*. We have become spectators, yet we've been created to be active participants. Deep down, we know it, and that's what hurts.

Unfortunately, I used to be a spectator of life as well. In my attempts to do everything right, I ended up doing nothing at all. I was too afraid I might mess up. I was too afraid I might step out improperly or in an untimely manner. I was waiting for life to come to me. I didn't take risks. I never ventured out of the box. I simply waited, and thus never obtained or produced fruit. Then, I waited some more. Mired in my own guilt, I continually robbed myself of the joy of my salvation—my complete and total forgiveness in Christ.

Sadly, I think many today are waiting for life to come to them instead of seizing it. In reading the Bible, you will quickly discover there's a lot of war and bloodshed going on. This is a fight. We are to fight, resist, stand firm, hold fast, and press on. Unfortunately, I couldn't; I was too afraid to do any of that. My own religion made me afraid. I felt like I was walking on a tightrope, a very tight rope, to please God. I was putting my trust in myself and my ability to live "perfectly," and that brought me constant failure and shame.

To help us understand, let's go back, again, a few pages in time. I realize the Pharisees get picked on a lot in Christian circles, but since Christ did it, why break tradition? Their religious order and those whom they represent continue to provide some provocative truths we should discuss.

We know that the Pharisees were as legalistic as they come. They had all the glitter of a life-giving faith, but most were completely dead on the inside. They followed the letter of the law and were, culturally and physically, God's very children. Their hearts, however, were far from God, to the point that Christ called them the, "sons of the devil."

This terribly religious class trusted in their own abilities, were smug in their own knowledge, and loved the esteem of others rather than the esteem of God. They sought only that which would draw the accolades of men. As a result, the Pharisees were mostly onlookers of life. Their life was consumed with observing, judging, and condemning. They were spectators.

They went out to "see" John the Baptist baptizing. They remained in the background, condemning, while *watching* a few men and women in faith bring their sick to Jesus. They *saw* "sinners" walk into the house to eat with Jesus.

The Pharisees weren't the most popular people in town. They were negative, judgmental, and condemning. They weren't welcome at many parties. Others didn't like to be around them. Who would? Who would want to live life under such restraints? They engaged in life to critique, not to partake.

They were boring because they had tied their own hands with do's and don'ts. They had to live perfectly, which, in life, means very little will be done. Life is rarely, if ever, perfect. Since they'd already judged others, they lived in fear that they too would be judged. Therefore, they could never take risks, they could never live passionately—they could never live. All they could do was the same-old, same-old, traditional church stuff.

There is no growth in legalism, either personally or corporately. You can't do much because rules dominate your life (and, naturally, the line to join their ranks is pretty short). Therefore you become stale, rigid, and dry. All that's left to make you feel better is the judgment you can lay on others. Really, these people can *seem* busy because they stay busy condemning others, and what is so dangerous about this behavior is that they truly think, like Saul – before he became Paul – that they are doing the work of the Lord. This is the deception of this mindset and how it draws more and more people into the same trap.

The Pharisees had to disassociate themselves from others. They had so many rules that they couldn't do much lest they stumble into their own legalistic pitfalls. Still, they continued to condemn. However, internally, they knew they remained empty and unfulfilled. They were unhappy people, so they took out their gloom on others, making them live up to a standard that was beyond their abilities.

On the contrary, we saw multitudes being drawn to John the Baptist, to Peter and Paul, and to Christ. Christ was a party favorite. They were the movers and shakers in life. They only condemned those who condemned others because they knew this was hindering the liberty that God intends for all. Further, these men and women attracted folks. The anointing of God draws men; legalism repels. When Jesus is lifted up, He promises to draw all men (1 John 12:32). We have tremendous freedom in God through Christ. It stems from a clear understanding of His love that He lavishes upon us daily. It's reinforced by our understanding of our adoption as Sons and Daughters of God in Christ. We are holy. God has paid for our sins. We are to praise Jesus for this and quit trying to work for it. Quit making others work for it, and quit allowing others to make you feel that you must work for it. Simply live in it.

My friend, daily appreciate the salvation God has given us. Be glad He has made you righteous. No longer live your life under the law. Rejoice in His grace given to you—then give that grace to all those around you.

*"And we have such trust through Christ toward God. Not that we are sufficient of ourselves to think of anything as being from ourselves, but our sufficiency is from God, who also made us sufficient as ministers of the new covenant, not of the letter but of the Spirit; **for the letter kills, but the Spirit gives life**"* (2 Corinthians 3:4-6, emphasis added).

Pray this prayer aloud, releasing control of your life to God: *"LORD God, I give up. I give up trying and striving in my own efforts to please you. I recognize that apart from You, I can truly do no thing. I will no longer trust in my own righteousness and my own good works to try to please You or obtain Your favor and help. I recognize and acknowledge that it is only by the finished work of Your Son Jesus Christ, His blood shed for me on the cross, that I can come to You. I thank You that Jesus' blood is totally sufficient for my complete righteousness and that I can come to You each day boldly and receive help, strength and favor in my life. Father, I look to Your grace to keep me from judging others; or being critical of those around me, my loved ones, even You--and also myself. I receive Your grace for my life. I receive Your acceptance of me. Guide me to the priorities in my life that keep me in accordance with Your will. I return to You right now, Loving Father of all creation. I return to You through Jesus Christ, not rules nor of obligation. I thank You that there is no condemnation for those that are in Christ Jesus. I thank You that I am in Christ Jesus by faith. Thank You for Your strength. I rely upon You for all aspects in my life. Thank You for the peace that You have given me. Thank You for the inheritance that is mine, In Jesus' name. Amen."*

Chapter Eight

Prevented by Our Past

Part I

"Sorrow is better than laughter,
because a sad face is good for the heart.
The heart of the wise is in the house of mourning,
but the heart of fools is in the house of pleasure"
(Ecclesiastes 7:3-4).

What Do You Expect

Due to particularly painful past events, I was incapable of watching sports on television. It's not that I didn't love sports. Quite the contrary, I lived for them and played them every chance I had. I just wasn't able to w*atch* them. Consequently, I didn't always fare well during "sports talk" with the fellas.

On a good day I'd have sneaked a peak at the sports page earlier, memorizing a few scores and a few key names to go with it. On a bad day I wasn't so much concerned about "which" game we were talking about—Falcons vs. Giants, Nets vs. Suns—but rather, "what" game we were talking about (football, basketball, baseball, or hockey). I was totally clueless.

Needless to say, it didn't take long before I took a little "heat" for my Susie Homemaker oblivion to the ever-so-wide world of sports. The guys assured me though that at the very least my wife, if I ever got one, would love me for it. There'd be nothing in the way of her having the full lot of me all day Saturday *and* Sunday to run man's most dreaded and disdained tasks: the legendary "Honey-Do-List."

I must admit, however, my reasons were not so altruistic. Actually, they were quite pathetic. The problem I had with watching sports was with my memory. Watching sports affected my ability to function properly. I couldn't go forward. I wanted to, desperately, but felt constantly constrained. I was stuck, emotionally and mentally. Granted, I'm not suffering from Alzheimer's, dementia or anything of that sort; but it was a debilitating disease nonetheless.

The problem I had with watching sports was not from a lack of knowledge or practice. As children growing up we played every sport in the book—except maybe cricket. Sports were so big on my block that we permanently spray-painted yard-lines, end zones, and field goals on the street's pavement. We played sunup to sundown.

Our parents had to force us to come in and eat, but who had time to eat? There was leather to catch, plays to plot, opponents to tackle, and cars to dodge. We even played neighboring blocks for regional championships. Come time for college, the head coach of the local university's football program paid a visit. Soon afterward, I found myself signing matriculation papers. I was, as planned since boyhood, well on my way to the pros. This had been a lifelong dream.

And that was that. The rest was history, and when I say history, I mean, *(his/tæ/ré) 1. the branch of knowledge dealing with past events. 2. a continuous, systematic narrative of past events as relating to a particular people or person. 3. the record of past events and times, esp. in connection with the human race.* -- Random House, *Webster's Unabridged Dictionary,* ©1998.

Indeed, something had happened. That something's name was, "Reality." A big fish had swiftly become a minnow—my pond was swallowed within the proverbial ocean. When I went to play football, I felt alone, out of place and overwhelmed. I shrank back and lost all confidence I had in my ability to be that football player I thought I was. I was thrown into the camp of the unknown, and as you also recall, I have never been very comfortable in the area of unknowns. I liked to be where I am sure of victory or I don't go there.

Well here I was, literally dropped off in a strange place where I knew no one and no one really knew me. Inevitably, the absence of confidence makes it impossible to be successful in the sports arena.

With each passing practice, my gridiron dreams faded. With each passing week, my heart sank another notch deeper into depression and despondency. This thing I thought I wanted to be my life, this thing I thought *was* my life was devastating me. I was horridly realizing the dream was not anything like my immature little brain had conjured up in my innocent little boy's head. The fame and fortune, I realized too late, came only after years of hard work, broken bones, sweat, being knocked around, being beat up, being the Rookie. Now, also remember, I had an incessant need to be successful at everything I did on the first try – the first time out – there was no room for failure and the learning curve was not for me. Watching something you had laid on your bed night after night, dreaming for as a child, materialize into your life's darkest nightmare was life's major disappointment – my major disappointment was in myself.

I buried this deep in the recesses of my psyche, not to be spoken about. Watching television sports only reminded me of this failure, and although I really did not equate my dislike with televised sports with this pitiful segment of my life, I would not allow myself to even broach the edge of the topic, even in light and friendly banter about present-day sporting events, with my friends. It was off limits, to them, and especially for myself.

Whereas I realize many other starry-eyed high school athletes have to deal with harsh reality as well, my problem, however, was that I didn't... deal with it, that is.

Sure, I moved on and found other pursuits, talked about other things, and stopped playing two-hand touch in front of my parents' house, but deep down, something had died. I simply opted to ignore it.

So I shrugged my shoulders and moved on, forgetting about this slice of history. My conscious memory wiped it out completely. It was as if there was never a dream in the first place.

Meanwhile, clandestinely, my depression deepened. Years had passed since those wispy dreams of younger days now old. Then, on a beautiful Southern California spring weekend, I found myself at a prayer retreat for a time of spiritual rejuvenation. I had no particular agenda and no particular "issues" to be resolved. I was simply seeking greater direction and growth in God.

As two older and wiser men of God who had no previous knowledge of me began to pray for me, I began to weep uncontrollably. I tend not to do that. Suddenly, thoughts of the *football nightmare* as well as a great many other failures and painful events rushed to mind like a flood. I was struck by a rush of spiritually induced recall. Instantly, I realized that shattered hopes, aspirations, and dreams had quietly and secretly shackled me.

They had racked my brain with blame, regret, and frustration. Deep down, I felt I'd failed. If only I had practiced more, been more disciplined, more aggressive, less fearful, older, younger, stronger.... Yes, even less naïve. These thoughts overwhelmed me.

For years, unable to swallow these humbling thoughts of my own failure, I'd blocked out the truth. I couldn't imagine how to discuss it, so I closed the door, never realizing that those memories and thoughts of failure kept me from moving forward. My desperate attempts to obliterate my past kept me there.

I couldn't step forward into my future because I was mired in the past. Then, without warning, after all this time, these thoughts rushed in, seemingly from nowhere. Prior to that point these broken dreams and their accompanying guilt were not even part of my conscious. They had been lying dormant. I did not go to them; they came to me. The Holy Spirit brought them. It was time to get healed.

How we Heal

"This one thing I do, forgetting those things which are behind, and reaching forth unto those things which are before, I press toward the

mark for the prize of the high calling of God in Christ Jesus" (Phillipians 3:13b-14).

I think one reason God gives us a season of wilderness is to give us the opportunity to get rid of the baggage from our past. Some of us cannot let go of a relationship well outside of God's will because we remember the many make up and make-out sessions and have forgotten the far more numerous painful break-up sessions. As a result, we have trouble moving on with the present. We think our best days are behind us, suffocating the hope of our future, and killing our joy. We are being lied to, and it's eating our lives away.

My inability to forgive myself for failures in the past kept me from enjoying the present. I simply carried on and never adequately dealt with the issues of the past. I did not feel the need. I had suppressed those memories. Only by the help of the Holy Spirit did I realize they still lingered and haunted. As a result, my road down the "should'a, would'a, could'a," was long, winding and, at times, devastating.

After all those years, I still felt the effects of deep-rooted frustrations of failure and guilt. Unfortunately, regret's resolve is relentless. It slowly creeps its way into our lives in the form of apathy, passivity, and sorrow. Though for many years it was a silent, subconscious force, it was a great force of my depression nonetheless. I was locked in the shadows of my past and did not even know it—imprisoned and unaware.

Many of us remain incapable of forgiving and forgetting—our self and others—because we, too, look back. Friend, looking back only leads to frustration. It causes regret, sorrow, anger, blame, and ultimately, bondage.

The One to Watch

"He regarded disgrace for the sake of Christ as of greater value than the treasures of Egypt, because he was looking ahead to his reward.... These were all commended for their faith.... God had planned something better...." (Hebrews 11:26, 39, 40).

Great women and men of God look ahead, not behind, and have learned the necessity of letting go of the past.

The one person who had every reason to live a backward-looking life but never did, was a guy named Moses. Moses never talked about his days in Egypt, even though he was "the man" back in "the day." He never spoke of his past power, position, or status. He never spoke of his extensive education and training. Though never a slave, he never hung that fact over his formerly enslaved brethren.

More so, only by a mistake made in a split-second decision did he miss out on being a major player in the greatest civilization known to man. Moses blew it and had every reason to blame himself. His life would never be the same. He went from being a man of nation-wide respect and notoriety to becoming an obscure sheepherder, all because of his temper.

In spite of all that, Moses never looked back. He didn't wallow in his own failure. He didn't lay stuck because of past screw-ups.

So was Moses in denial? Was he suppressing? No. He knew his life had purpose. Moses had to go through his own personal wilderness before he'd be ready for the big one with the Israelites. Moses had his own past to deal with. He had his own frustrations to resolve. Moses had to have his own understanding of his life—his plans and purposes—tweaked by the sovereign, loving God.

Moses had to forgive himself for his mistakes. Moses had to learn that God can work all things—even Moses' criminal record—for the good of His beloved. Moses had to die to self and adopt God's vision. Moses had to prepare for his true purpose. Therefore, Moses had to let go of the past and have the faith to smile at his future. Moses was able to do all this because he was on to *something better* (see Hebrews 11).

Consider those who chose to do the opposite: Just after being freed from slavery from the Egyptians—while they were in the wilderness—the Israelites said this to Moses: *"We remember the fish we ate in Egypt at no cost—also the cucumbers, melons, leeks, onions and garlic"* (Numbers 11:5).

Never mind that the Israelites lived and died their entire lives in service to the Egyptians. Never mind that the Egyptians despised them. Never mind that the Egyptians felt they were superior to them. No, Egypt was the happenin' place to be, and the Israelites were just happy to be at the party—albeit as caterers and cooks, not as invited guests.

Moses didn't need to look back because he was on to bigger and better things. He was convinced that his future was brighter than his past, and friends, Moses, if anyone, had a pretty bright past. If *God* wasn't trippin' over Moses' past blunders, why should Moses? If God had forgiven him, why shouldn't he forgive himself?

Moses was now doing a God thing. Moses knew that with God, the future only gets better. As a side note, take a peek at the end of Revelation. We have a bright future, too! Moses was forward looking because forward is always the better route for God's people. Always. Moses didn't need to talk about the days of driving his ornate, Egyptian chariot; he had a better — higher calling. Moses didn't allow his past to affect him because he knew more was in store.

The same is true for you and your future. God has more in store. To rid yourself of depression, you too must be convinced of this reality. God has a better place for you here and now, on earth, but you can't see it because you're dwelling in the past. Consequently, we resist His taking us there. We're ill-prepared for the God-task in front of us. We insist on living in boxes, going through storage, and strolling through memory lane. Even when we do finally put those memories to the side, we do it without adequately dealing with them. We opt instead to simply push them deeper and deeper within.

Yes, we blew it, but move on anyway. Moses blew it. He even killed a man, but Moses still had a bright and beautiful future. So do you. Yes, some of us have been abused, badly, but so were God's children under slavery. They were abused at all levels as well. God had a better plan, a brighter day ahead for them. Moses was wholeheartedly convinced of this. In order for you to move out of your depression, you'll have to believe the same. We will continue along this same course in the next chapter, but for now, ask the Lord to show you areas within your heart that are in need of His healing touch. Get healed now so that you can fully enjoy the future that awaits you.

"Sorrow is better than laughter, because a sad face is good for the heart. The heart of the wise is in the house of mourning, but the heart of fools is in the house of pleasure" (Ecclesiastes 7:3-4).

Say this prayer with me: *"Father, I thank You that You have good things in store for my life. Lord, forgive me for thinking that my life is best lived independently of You. I thank You that You have called me forward, to something better. Lord, in various areas, I have been stuck and mired in the past. I have let the past hold me captive from my best. I have not been able to give you my best because I have not let go of some things in my life that You are asking me to let go of. So Father, right now, I let go of living in the past. I let go of any attachments to things, peoples or habits that are not of You. I refuse to allow my past to keep me from looking forward--to my future, to my calling and to the wonderful plans that You have for me. Thank You for being the God of the living, and not of the dead. I let go of the dead places in my life and choose to move forward with You, wherever and however You may lead. Thank You for a bright future in You. I rejoice in my present and my future. I thank You that with You, all things are possible. I wait patiently upon You and the blessings in store for me as I walk in Your way. In Jesus name, amen!"*

Chapter Nine
Prevented by our Past
Part II

"Sorrow is better than laughter, because a sad face is good
for the heart. The heart of the wise
is in the house of mourning,
but the heart of fools is in the house of pleasure"
(Ecclesiastes 7:3-4).

Injured, Reserved

Some time ago I found myself at a Lake Tahoe ski resort first aid office. A few of us had made a one-day, banzai run to the slopes, and my friend got a bit too much air off a jump and blew out his knee. In addition to a few other overly-zealous, injured trailblazers, one unfortunate bloke was brought in who had just dislocated his shoulder. When the doctor removed his shirt, you could see that the top of his arm had been thrust back beyond the socket and into his back. As excruciating as it looked, the guy was not in pain—he simply couldn't use his arm. I was at the next table, and I overheard the doctor talking to him. The doc tells him it's going to hurt a bit, and then does something I never would have expected. The doc takes off his own shoe, lifts up his foot and places it firmly against this poor guy's shoulder and neck. Then he grabs the guy's arm—the one that's out of its socket—and begins to pull it forward, quite firmly, I might add, while at the same time using his foot to keep the lad from coming forward. All the while, the guy is screaming bloody murder. Full voice, at the top of his lungs, he's screaming in pain as the doctor vigorously pulls forward on his arm while at the same time firmly pushing back with his foot, trying to thrust the shoulder forward into place.

The next thing I remember, I'm inhaling smelling salts—the kind they use to wake up the knocked out loser in a boxing match. My brain is on fire; I look up, and the entire medical staff is surrounding me. That's right, the one person in the room who is actually injury-free, is the focus of the entire first aid team. I had fainted!

I was humiliated, to say the least, but the story makes a great point. You see, just like the dislocated shoulder, our heart and soul (emotions, will, mind) can be dislocated or broken. The Bible speaks of a heart that can be damaged in a variety of ways—bruised, crushed, shattered, and so on.

Since we can't see this heart, many don't realize it's injured. However, just like the skier in the story who would have had his arm, and ultimately his life, greatly impaired if not corrected, many of our hearts are greatly impaired because past damage done to them is not corrected. Sure, the injured skier could have chosen to not go through the pain of the doctor's realignment. Even without the full use of that one arm, he no doubt could have survived, worked, married, maybe played some other recreational sports. Nevertheless, he'd always be limited. Due to a desire to avoid pain, his life never would reach its full potential.

This is the way with the heart. Years may have passed since an event that caused us great sorrow or pain, and our heart was broken, but now all we see are the results. We just can't seem to enjoy life. We may have a great spouse, a great job, and great kids, yet something inside of us isn't as it should be. We're not happy, and we don't know why.

For some, a hurtful word was said to us and we are still holding on to it—still holding it against that one who spoke it. Truly, some are still stunted and stuck emotionally at that same moment in time those words were uttered no matter how many years ago it may have taken place. That's right, some of you are still stuck in 1988 because a person said a mean or cruel comment against you. Sadly, you still can't get past it and have lost a myriad of grand, life moments ever since. Though you think you are making the other person suffer, you are the one sick and withering away. You can't enjoy fully the good blessings in your life because you are still angry and bitter. My friend, give up your right to be angry! If you do not, you will never be able to enjoy the good that comes each passing day. Unless you surpass that cloud of critique and contempt hanging over you, you will never feel the warmth of brighter days.

There are some of us who carry along a constant sense of guilt and shame. We feel inferior to everyone else. We feel like everyone is talking about us, even laughing at us. We don't feel smart. We don't feel attractive. We don't feel loved. Some of us also have persecution issues, we are always the victim, constantly being hurt by others, or so they think.

Worse yet, we don't love ourselves. Actually, we don't even like ourselves. We feel condemned. We can't delight ourselves in God because we feel God is mad at us. We're no longer excited about life. We have no vitality, no desires, no dreams, and no vision. We have nothing in our life that excites or ignites our passion. We don't sleep well at night and live in a fog during the day. We feel life is hopeless. We're irritable with others. We may have Jesus, but we're still not happy. We may have God in us, yet we still feel empty. Deep inside, we know something's wrong, but we just don't know what.

If you are experiencing any of the above symptoms, you may be suffering from a wounded heart. Please don't reduce that to just a romantic love loss, although it may be that, but I'm talking about a past that caused a measure of sorrow. It may have been quite traumatic: a parent who left you; a relative who raped you; a friend who rejected you. You may have wounds from words or fists.

You may not have been wounded by something that happened to you. Wounds occur equally and painfully from the lack of an event. The Bible states that, *"Hope deferred makes the heart sick"* (see Proverbs 13:12a). For some, waiting and waiting for a desire or dream that never arrives, can break a heart and spirit: A relationship that never came to fruition;

the apology never offered; the job that never arrived; the love that failed; a wish that never landed. In time, the wait itself can wear us out. Over the course of years, that "hoped-for" event never occurred, and sorrow struck. Because these things happened long ago, we don't make the connection that our unhealed past hinders our present.

Many of you are thinking you've already dealt with your past by leaving it behind you, by moving forward, by not dwelling there, by letting sleeping dogs lie. Unfortunately, the sad reality is that most of us have simply blocked out the past and pressed forward, not realizing that the very thing, which you thought was out of sight and out of mind, is still there, paralyzing you, preventing you—even killing you, albeit slowly and silently. True, we can't live in our past, but we must deal with it before we can move on. Sadly, most of us don't. All of us have had occurrences in our past (hurt, loss and / or lack) that will prevent us from living a full present, and let's be completely frank, my friend, any time we're living on a level less than our best, when we are embittered by hurt or loss or lack, we are depressed.

The verse at the opening of this chapter states that *a sad face is good for the heart.* The wisdom to be gleaned is that sometimes before we can be truly happy, we must first be willing to become sad. Many of us have let our hearts remain unhealed, because, consciously or subconsciously, we know it's going to be painful to revisit the distressing past. The path to enduring joy winds through the valley of sorrows. We avoid the hard path, and our heart remains damaged—broken, bruised, crushed, maybe even shattered. We may not know it, but it hasn't functioned fully for years. The root of bitterness must be extracted. To do this, we must face the root cause.

Think about how life would change if you no longer had the use of an arm, an eye, a leg, or your liver. Your life would be altered. Yet the human heart, soul, and spirit are so much more important than any of these physical organs. Consequently, the effects are more lasting, affecting our ability to relate to our world, our God, others, even ourselves. Relationships are impaired, our potential is thwarted, our happiness hampered. We stop having intimate, close relationships with friends. Our anger is uncontrolled, our tongue becomes a weapon. We no longer trust others. Our fellowship with God is just a fraction of where it was, or could be. The list goes on.

To be sure, our past, if not properly dealt with, will also prevent our future from being filled with joy. Our present and future state of well-being, or lack of well-being, can be attributed to the extent to which we have successfully settled, or not settled, our early years. Living without a healed and whole heart also risks living outside of our true purpose (doing what we have been called to do by our Creator). It risks not being able to live life and experience life to the fullest. Here's what I mean.

Like It or Not, You'll Face it Again

At some point in time in our lives we've been hurt. To protect ourselves from the pain, to cope with the pain, we find ways to defend ourselves from any further possible harm. We are in "prevent" defense so we never have time for our offensive game. Some then decide never to take that course of action (the one that led to the pain) again, not realizing that in order to live a healthy life, we may have to visit that path again. We do a few mental gymnastics with our pain so that we can function, thinking we've straightened things out, not realizing we've become bent, living twisted lives thereafter.

Moses felt he was called to rescue his people. He tried it and failed— and the attempt nearly cost him his life. Ironically, he was called to do it again. To be able to respond to that purpose, Moses would have to face his earlier failure. — the same people, the same place, just a different time. Without being healed of the earlier incident he would not have been able to walk into his calling.

Our lives are no different. A little boy abandoned by his father makes a vow that he will never cry again. He doesn't realize that a man may need to cry at times. So the boy grows contorted—safe, but without emotion.

A young girl is teased and humiliated. She reacts by resolving to become the standard of external perfection. Her insides remain shards. She fails to see her natural beauty. She has lost the beauty of openness and transparency. She covers and hides, failing to see how these actions prevent her growth.

A child is emotionally beaten, day after day, never feeling the warmth of genuine, true love. He protects himself, growing colder and colder. To survive in society, he tones down the coldness. We call these people, "mellow." Married, and with children now, his pain resurfaces. He snaps, again and again. His family and friends wonder at the source of his "sudden" outbursts. As a father and husband, he's called to love. No one realizes that this little, four-letter, word had been put away a long, long time ago. Now he must choose whether or not to face it again.

Many trusting persons, when rejected, vow they will never take a risk again. Yet, they do not realize that to walk in greatness requires great risk. We must risk and forgive, continually. That individual does not recognize that the books to be written inside of him, the songs to be sung, the business ventures, and God's Kingdom — none will be unleashed unless he risks everything and decides to genuinely love and be loved again.

The Blame Game

Some of us have even forgotten what caused us to become twisted in the first place. Others remember. Either way, the result is the same: We're less than our best. We have yet to reckon with our past.

We blame our parents for poor parenting, and our spouses for poor "spouse-ing." By carrying the baggage of our past—and our past abuses—we become agents of blame, anger, guilt, and frustration. We're angry at ourselves for our failures. Incapable of loving our self, we become incapable of loving others. We become incessantly needy, so, instead of giving to others, we continually take. We've suffered rejection, hurt, humiliation, and abuse. Therefore, we do what we know: We reject, hurt, humiliate, and abuse others.

We feel un-accomplished and so become mired in guilt. We blame others for our failures. We blame ourselves. Our failures and unmet expectations lead to ill-will, discontentment, resentment, jealousy, and a critical spirit. We condemn others because we've been condemned.

Men who suffer from their unresolved past are unfulfilled, feeling powerless. These men know nothing of their purpose, and the ignorance is killing them. Loath to have this revealed, they overcompensate, becoming controllers. They constantly tell others—especially loved ones—how to live, what to do, and how to do it. They're unhappy individuals, yet try to appear as Cool-Hand Luke. Their frustrations cause them to attack, be it verbally, passively, or physically. They're ever critical, never satisfied. Afterwards they regret their behavior. They don't realize that what is in them must come out, and what is in them is rejection, resentment, bitterness, hurt, and anger.

Those who have been elevated, elevate. Those who have been pulled down, pull down.

Life Photos from a Friend

Let me give you another example. This is an excerpt from my friend Rachel's diary, beginning with childhood and spanning quite a few years. (She was born in an average, Caucasian, suburban city in Northern California.)

Saturday, September 29, 1984

Last Tuesday my mom, dad and brother got into a fight. Me and my mom moved to my Grandma's. Last night we came home. My mom wants my dad to move out.

Next Entry

We got kicked out of our house on Poplar Road. So we had to move into my Grandma's 1-bedroom house but then my mom and grandma got into a fight so we had to sleep in the car with our 3 dogs.
Our bird stayed at my grandma's.

Wednesday, August 6, 1986

We didn't have any money for dinner the other night--so my dad borrowed money. I overheard my mom talking on the phone and she said that my dad was smoking or doing some drugs at our dining room table yesterday while I was over at Amber's. We have no money and my dad is wasting good money just so he can get high!! I just feel like killing him!! Well, I better go--see you later!! Sincerely Me--

Wednesday, September 1986

[My Mom and brother] got into an argument and my mom took away his '66 Mustang car...called him a "bastard" and smacked him twice! My brother couldn't take it--so he moved to his friend's house.
I was so sad! I was crying that night and when he walked out of his room with his things, I couldn't even look at him.
I didn't want him to see me crying! I said, "You're moving out?" He hesitated and said, "Ya." I could have died. I just told him, "That's stupid," because his friend does a lot of drugs! And I was afraid Ricky wouldn't do his homework and get into drugs!!

June '88

I look at other people who have so much and don't even know it—I feel like crying. I don't know—I look forward to the day when I can truly

be happy. I think that will be when I'm moved out and on my own--in charge of my own life. Then after that being married with someone who loves me (preferably Danny Major). Well, maybe in my dreams! Everyone says your teenage years are supposed to be the best years of your life —maybe I'm just getting off to a slow start.
I've thought of suicide more than a few times. But I would never do that to my family, and I love God too much!! I don't know.
Maybe I'll feel better sometime. Bye!

Next Entry
Well, a lot of stuff happened since I last wrote. My dad got busted for selling and possession of drugs. We have to pay $2,000 as a first payment for his lawyer but there is gonna be a lot more. Also, if my dad gets found guilty, then it's mandatory he gets 2 years in the state penitentiary. Also, it was in the Daily Review paper. It's all—"San Mateo man accused of selling drugs. Pete Allen – who lives on Gaelic Street..."
So that's "cool," my dad is a drug dealer and user. But him and Ronnie (my brother) said they're going to a rehab. But saying and doing are two different things. I mean I love my dad so much. And I can't help but feel mad at him for getting himself into that mess—and Ronnie.
I hate drugs. I hate people who do drugs. I just remember how hard my childhood was. Every one was constantly fighting. Especially my mom and Ronnie–& dad & Sean. Well, I guess everyone. It was pretty stressful but still, there were times when we were a good family. Well, it's 8:58 p.m. Golden Girls is gonna come on. My mom's gonna come in and say, "Golden Girls is on." I'll write you again later.

Thursday, 7:00 p.m., March 9, 1989
Well, right now I'm sitting on the bed and re-reading what I have written in here. Pretty weird stuff! I'm listening to Billy Squier's tape. "Nobody Knows." That song is so sad. It makes me sad. It makes me realize how worthless my life is--at least, seems. I don't know what's wrong

with me. I always feel like this lately. A couple of weeks ago I had a nervous break-down. I came so close to killing myself. I have never been so scared in my entire life. Now I know what Jason meant when he said, "you'd really know if you had a nervous breakdown." He was right 'cause before I thought I had one. But that night I'd really known I had had one. It was 10:30 p.m. I got all shaky and couldn't stop crying.

I called Loretta – it helped.

But I don't think she really understood the shape I was in.

In fact, I'm starting to feel like that right now & it's scaring me. It all boils down to Donnie. If he would call me one time—or if he asks me out once I'd be <u>so</u> happy. There'd be something there for me to look forward to. But right now there's not. I should stop feeling this way. It's hard to.

Maybe I can forget about how I'm just used by people and how I'm finding myself more and more wanting to get drunk every weekend to deal with stuff. But I'm gonna try not to anymore! Wish me luck! I say that now, but what was the first thing I thought about when I thought about this weekend coming up? Yep! Alcohol. Pitiful.

I'll write you maybe in a couple days and say what I did over the weekend. I'm sure it was lots! Sike- Bye—Love, ME.

Monday, August 31, 1992.

I can't stand my dad living here most of the time. He can be cool—but then he'll just snap and say, "F- you! F- off, #%$" to me and my mom. He even slammed me up against the wall. About a month ago my mom snapped and threw my glass lamp at me and broke it on my back. Well, I realize more and more how important God is. I think that's the only thing that keeps me sane. I'm tired now, I'll write later.

Good night.

Rejection – Depression's Seedling

I want to highlight a couple points from Rachel's story. I know your story will be different. Maybe your story is much worse, much more violent, traumatic, and protracted. Maybe your story is not so dramatic. Regardless, please don't let that distract you from the principles you'll find relevant to your own story.

Rachel's experiences resulted in a damaged heart. For a child to have a healthy heart he or she must get the following from his or her parents: Unconditional love. Basic provisions. Discipline and forgiveness. Modeling of a pure and faithful fellowship with God. Modeling acceptance, honor, and value.

I've had the opportunities to take part in many inner-healing conferences and have learned from a great many professional counselors, teachers, and pastors. Here's what I have found: When we don't get these essentials from our parents or others, our hearts suffer damage. When a child experiences physical, sexual, or verbal abuse, a heart is damaged. A parent's departure (through separation or divorce) places undue responsibility and pain on a child, and a heart is wounded.

Those wounds are the seeds of rejection. As this root of rejection begins to grow, so too do its branches: insecurity, isolation, apathy, guilt, self-pity, false compassion, and conditional love. These branches begin to produce fruit of resentment, impatience, anger, strife, hate, cursing, retaliation, and vengeance. The results—and our sinful bodies' ultimate attempts to protect us from any further rejection—are rebellion, selfishness, deception, pride, faultfinding, suspicion, and control (via manipulation, possessiveness and, ultimately, witchcraft).

So let me ask you, when you walk into a room full of people, do you find yourself wondering if people are talking negatively about you? Do you often feel you're the only one in a group who is "different"? Do you often go to the movies alone, read books upon books, and avoid others? Do you get slightly upset or hurt at others for not greeting you when passing by? Do you feel hurt or angry when people don't call you right back or don't return your call at all? How would you respond if, just days before a party, you were invited by a "mere" phone call, when others had been formally invited months before by a mailed invitation?

When was the last time you initiated a genuine, verbal apology to someone? Was it last week, last month, last year? Has it been so long you can't remember? If you answered yes to either of the last two, you may need to consider getting out of denial about some past, unresolved issues in your life. I can tell you now that they're most likely pushing you down; keeping you from progressing higher.

Do you feel that people don't do nice things for you in the same way that you do nice things for them—that you've been short-changed? Is it common for you to simply adopt a "whatever" attitude toward life and others? If so, consider reading this chapter from the point of view that you are living life with a wounded heart—and that it's preventing you from leading a richer, fuller, happier life. The main symptoms of one suffering from the pain of rejection is a life lacking in rich relationships, in full and satisfying endeavors, in peace, contentment, and happiness.

May we dig a little deeper? (And for those who would like extra credit, also ask someone who knows you well to answer the following questions.) Remember, going through the pain is a necessary process to get to the gladness. So take the risk of being brutally honest with yourself, even if it hurts, even if it feels like it's too much—and begin the work of healing.

* Are there incidents that have happened to you that still cause you to feel anger and resentment toward another?
* Do you find yourself getting into arguments with others on a weekly, even daily basis?
* Do you feel like everyone else in the world misunderstands you?
* Do you have thoughts of wanting to get people back for the things they've done to you?
* Do you feel miserable when someone points out one of your faults?

✳ When someone corrects you, corrects something you said or did, do you get mad or quickly say something to defend yourself or show that they're wrong or, at least, that you weren't wrong?

✳ Can someone speak truth into your life (possibly revealing your faults) without your walls going up? How do you receive it? Do you wisely appreciate it and thank them or do you foolishly deny it, replacing it with blame and fault finding? How about asking family members how you respond in these situations?

✳ When was the last time you said *sorry* to someone?

✳ Do you find it difficult, nearly impossible, to apologize?

✳ Do you ask people to do things for you by first appealing to their emotions?

✳ Do you use guilt, anger, threats or manipulation to get what you want?

If so, please beware, because the seeds of your past wounds are beginning to grow roots.

Got Issues?

Is it any wonder, then, that the Bible states, *"Guard your heart, for out of it flow the issues of life"* (Proverbs 4:23). Funny, isn't it? Even back then they were telling people, "You have issues, man." Many of us still have issues. Don't inspect yourself. Better yet, ask the Holy Spirit to inspect and reveal what's inside. Ask Him about your attitudes, habits, emotions, and reactions. How sensitive are you when criticized? How often do you criticize? How's your temper? Your self-esteem? Your battles with guilt and self-pity? Can you pick up the phone and call someone, or is your excuse that since they have your number as well, "They can call me?"

Are there scenes from your past that torment you at night? Might there be images from your past that you've pushed down so far that you no longer remember them? Are you willing to ask the Holy Spirit to reveal to you any areas of your heart that remain unhealed by His Holy hands?

Are you always alone? Do you feel alone? Do you hate being alone in the silence? Must you constantly hear the TV, the radio, or a friend's voice? Do you need alcohol to make you feel better? Do you need to immerse yourself in work, church, or other projects to feel better? Are many of your conversations about other people's lives? Do you feel unaccepted? Do you need to shop and buy something to feel better? Do you worry about what others will think of your hair, your clothes, your car, your house?

Take the time and have the courage to examine yourself under the guidance and direction of the Holy Spirit. At the end of the examination, maybe you'll conclude it's possible that a root of rejection remains.

　❋　Were your parents there for you as a child?
　❋　Was there abuse of any kind in the home?
　❋　Were you rejected at school by peers and / or teachers?
　❋　Were you rejected because of your looks?
　❋　Were you rejected because of your economic status?
　❋　Were you rejected because of your background or your size?

Ask God, through the power of the Holy Spirit, to walk back through your past and deal with it once and for all.

Is it any wonder that Christ said one of His main purposes in coming to earth was to heal the brokenhearted? (See Luke 4:18.) If you dare to return to your past and let Christ heal your broken heart, your life will never be the same, and your potential will be restored. Depression can lift like the morning fog, relationships can be reconciled, and life's beauty can be discovered again. Let's look at how all this can happen by getting back to Rachel.

As seen above, Rachel grew up with a damaged heart. As a result of having a father who abandoned his responsibilities as a spiritual leader, provider, and protector, rejection possessed Rachel's soul. Couple that with a physically and verbally abusive mother, and it's easy to see that Rachel grew up with tremendous wounds and insecurities, battling thoughts of hatred for herself and her parents, and even questioning God's love.

I want you to notice what happened to Rachel. In her earlier years she hated drugs and observed the damage they did to those who used them. Yet in spite of the hell she experienced as a result of the drugs' aftermath, she too ventured along the same path into alcohol and, eventually, drug use. It's also interesting to note her thoughts on what she thought she needed. *It all boils down to Donnie. If he would call me one time—or if he asks me out once I'd be **so** happy.*

Isn't that what we do? We project into the future what we think we need in order to be happy. If I were in a relationship, then I'd be happy. If only I could get out of this relationship, then I'd be happy. If only I could get this job. If only I could get (that). If only…if only…if only….

We fail to realize that it's not a future event that we need to bring our spirits up, but past events that have cast us down. For example, in order to cope, Rachel had to block out the persistent pain of an addicted father, an abusive mother, and a household riddled with strife. Our bodies are smart: Just like we have defensive mechanisms to protect us from physical danger (the release of chemicals for fight or flight to boost our energy levels), we also have defense mechanisms to protect us from emotional danger.

However, just because our bodies blocked these memories long ago—even consciously forgotten them—doesn't mean the issues have been dealt with. No, forgetting was simply our mind and body's way of handling the crisis. For example, a child simply can't (nor should ever have to) handle the fact that the person whose job was to protect, love, and provide for him or her did just the opposite--abandoned, hit, cursed, or sexually abused. (I tend to think the human heart was not built to have to endure such early trauma.) Many children can't cope (again, and shouldn't have to), and so to protect themselves, their mental faculties block out the event — or shove it down to the recesses of their subconscious. If their subconscious can't fully block it, then they might deny the abuse in their conscious thought—anything to prevent having to square with the nightmarish reality of their own existence. As a result, walls and defenses develop. Those defense mechanisms will stay until we're strong enough to let them go. Unfortunately, however, many live their whole lives embracing those childhood defense (or coping) mechanisms.

The Great Connection

The problem is that those things that get locked inside of us, no matter how securely, eventually and inevitably will come out. Indeed, in some form or another, it will all come out. Be it anxiety, anger, or addictions; be it nightmares, passivity, dependency, or co-dependency; be it a critical spirit, a fearful spirit, or a wounded spirit—it will come out.

Often, however, because those things start seeping out after a lapse in time, it's easy to miss the connection between today's turmoil and yesterday's trauma. There is a connection.

As a result, we cannot adequately deal with the subject of depression without examining events in our life that may have wounded, damaged, or even broken our hearts and spirits. What's more, the soul is in many ways like an onion—it has many layers. Consequently, though we feel we've received healing in one area, there may be other areas that remain in disrepair.

"Indeed, in our hearts we felt the sentence of death. But this happened that we might not rely on ourselves but on God, who raises the dead. He has delivered us from such a deadly peril, and He will deliver us. On Him we have set our hope that He will continue to deliver us, as you help us by your prayers" (2 Corinthians 1:9-11).

Note the process: He has delivered, He will deliver, and He will continue to deliver.

How does our deliverance come? Here's a helpful list of ten steps to repair the broken heart.

I. Authorized to Mourn: Tell yourself that it's okay to grieve. Let the guards down. Give up the calm, cool, and collected facade. *"Blessed are those who mourn…."* Enough with the strong, independent act. Stop with the "always-in-control" routine. Don't be deceived. Better yet, stop deceiving yourself. It's okay to grieve. It's all right to mourn. It's good to cry. Force yourself to be aware of this. Begin to feel—and begin to heal.

II. Acknowledge the Loss: Be honest with yourself and recognize what you lost. Were you robbed of your childhood--your innocence? Did you lose someone whom you thought would always be your closest friend? Did you lose the love of your life? Did you lose the job you felt was your "calling." Put your finger on it. Were years of your life taken from you? Was trust taken? Was hope lost? Were dreams dashed? Take the time to acknowledge your particular loss.

III. Yell, Cry, Scream, and Kick: That's right, let it out. At night, in the morning, standing up, on your knees—whatever it takes and wherever it needs to happen, get it out. Cry your eyes out at night. Continue in the morning. Experience it fully. Refuse to let it stay stored up within you any longer. State what you're feeling, why you're feeling it, and whom you're feeling it towards. In order to forever remove the sting, you must first fully feel the sting. Pain is our body's way of telling us something is wrong and needs correcting. Feel it fully, and weep. If you suppress your pain, you'll also have to suppress other emotions—good ones, like joy and laughter. Don't sacrifice the beauty of possessing a full range of emotions for the sake of your reputation or ego. Let it go.

IV. Grow: Let the pain motivate you to grow. Recognize that this too will pass and the best thing to do in the present is to improve. Instead of dating the same person with a different name, determine to discover why you are drawn to people with these same issues. Resolve to work through the process in full confidence that when it's over you will be stronger and much better equipped to minister and help others who are in the place you once found yourself. Read books. Listen to sermons. Pray. Seek wise counsel. Rise to your next level.

V. Let Go: That's right—let it go. Let her go. Let him go. They're not coming back, and that may be a good thing. Stop deceiving yourself. Quit holding on. Let go of the pictures, of the memories, of the daydreams. She's gone. The season is over. Quit holding on. *"This one thing I do, forgetting those things which are behind, and reaching forth unto those things which are before, I press toward the mark for the prize of the high calling of God in Christ Jesus"* (Philippians 3:13b-14).

Forget those things that are behind you. Quit living in the fantasy. You are strong enough to live in the reality that they are gone, that life has changed, that what you once knew and clung to is no more. Things are going to be okay. Let it go. Give it to God and choose never to take it back—ever. You are growing up to a new you, and the old patterns of your life don't even fit you anymore. Free yourself from the bitterness of past hurts, as well, because now that you have grown, they will only hold you back from the destiny God has for your life. Now is the time.

VI. Forgive: In order to be free and whole, we must forgive. We must forgive others who have wronged us. We must forgive ourselves. When God said He'd remember our sin against us no more, it wasn't that He just ignored it, suppressed it or moved on, pretending it didn't happen. No, He dealt with it. He addressed it. He took action first. Ahhhh, but here is the key: He paid for it, sacrificing His Son. He forgave. Then, He removed them from you as far as the East is from the West.

We too must first forgive so that we may properly have mercy and receive the same mercy from God. We do not pin the sin on the person who has sinned against us, the same as the Father does not pin us with our sin once we have repented. This mercy and forgiveness on our part must come whether the person repents to us or not. Repentance is between that person and the Father. Forgiveness and mercy is between us and the Father. If we don't forgive, we cannot expect to be forgiven. Also, failing to forgive means not receiving healing from the bitterness that accompanies an unforgiving heart. This is imperative because, in order for us to be all that we're called to be, we must be healed from the inside out. That means that the inner man is whole. When we go into battle for the sake of God's kingdom, a facade of wholeness won't stand. The armor will be weak and the soldier will crumble. God's armor will only fit those who are prepared on the inside to wear it. God says, *"I desire truth in the inner parts."* For He knows that *"Out of the heart come the issues of life."*

It is time to forgive. It is also time to forgive ourselves of past mistakes and failures. Forgive yourself for wrong decisions and poor choices. Ask God to forgive you for going astray and wandering away from Him. Ask Him to forgive you and your family—even your predecessors (see Job 1:5). Forgive yourself. Ask God to show you through His Holy Spirit the hurts that need mending so that you can forgive and move on.

Then, as you begin to genuinely forgive others, going through the process that we just walked through, the failed expectations will no longer dismantle your joy. When we forgive others and ourselves, we grow another step closer to God. We have such a propensity to condemn ourselves when God has indeed forgiven us. Don't beat yourself up anymore. It is not about you, anyways. So quit making such a big deal about what you did – the mistake you made. You have repented, and it has been forgiven. The accuser of the brethren will bury you in self pity and false condemnation, rendering you powerless if you do not learn from your mistake and walk on. Remember to forgive others in the same way, and give up your right to be angry.

As we mentioned, God says He will not forgive us if we will not forgive others. Can you blame Him? Unforgiveness is the result of not understanding God's forgiveness of us. Who are we to judge, condemn, and criticize even those we do have very real and valid claims against? Doesn't God have some claims against us? Yet, He forgives willingly, lovingly, and completely. The whole point of forgiveness is *releasing* those who have wronged us. Forgive, for they know not (truly) what they do (or did).

When we judge others, harshly and continually, we forget our purpose and role. God sits on the judgment throne. He tells us that our position is to have mercy. Let Him do the judging. If we understood our purpose in this, then we wouldn't feel the need to judge. When we know our purpose—and that it is God ordained —we also know that no one can touch it. There's no need for jealousy, no vying for power, no fear of another's talents, and no need to defend ourselves. Our promotion comes from God, not man. Therefore, we can walk humbly, mercifully, and with a clean heart, with no need to put others in their place to ensure that we get "ours." Such tasks are within the Father's domain and we have already found our place in God.

Granted, forgiveness is easier said than done. So let's take a quick peek at how to really do this thing called, "forgiveness." First of all, remember that forgiveness is not saying that sins and misdeeds are acceptable. Second, take the time to specifically identify the person or persons with whom you are angry. Write down every wrong and/or perceived wrong they did to you. Go over this list of "wrongs" and state: "I forgive (name) for (event)." For example, "I forgive my father for leaving me when I was five and never returning to see me." List them all, every person, every event. Put them in God's hands, remembering that vengeance is the Lord's job, not ours. Put them in God's hands and forgive them by faith. Ask for God's help. Give it to God and let it go. Take the paper and get rid of it: throw it away, tear it up, burn it, whatever. Let it go, and never take it back again.

VII. Reconcile Truth and Reality: As Christians, this is one of the toughest areas I think many of us deal with. We need to reconcile the bad situation and, at the same time, the existence of a loving God. We must reconcile the apparent contradiction between the horrid situation and our loving God. "Where was God in all of this?" "I was the victim of these terrible things, yet you are supposed to be a loving God?" Our analytical minds just cannot comprehend God's reasoning.

Here, we'll have to recognize the place of sin and Satan—and of God lovingly giving mankind free will. We'll have to recognize that in God's original creation, everything was, in fact, GOOD. Sin, the fall, the flesh, and the enemy of our souls, not God, are responsible for bad things. The Bible says that all good things come from God. God allows things to happen, but He still causes all things to come together for good. Nonetheless, we first have to wrestle with these issues for ourselves. If we do not, deep down, unresolved anger and bitterness may mount up against our one Holy and Loving Father.

VIII. Let Patience Reign: The healing of our heart, like any wound, takes time. So give yourself time to heal. Don't jump back into a relationship. If you're not mended, don't put yourself in the company of those who have cut you—especially if they're still carrying the daggers! Don't put undue expectations on yourself for when you should be emotionally healed. Healing takes time. Give yourself time. However, if the process is taking years and years, seek a professional who may be able to point to specific areas you need to examine to promote a more speedy recovery.

IX. Embrace your present: Sometimes our wounds can make us feel totally helpless, hopeless, and incapable of living. This is a lie. Recognize it as such, and begin believing the truth: You can overcome! As soon as you are convinced of that, you will start to live again.

X. Believe in your future: Be convinced that God has planned something better.

"He regarded disgrace for the sake of Christ as of greater value than the treasures of Egypt, because He was looking ahead to his reward.... These were all commended for their faith.... God had planned something better..." (Hebrews 11:26, 39, 40).

That's right. God has something better, something good for your future. Stick with Him, and He will bring it to pass. It doesn't matter how old you are or what you've been through, your life is not over. God always brings us higher and higher, freer and freer, from glory to glory, greater to greater. All great men and women of faith learned this lesson. As you are already in Hebrews 11, take a look at the people listed here and read about them. Learn about them, and follow in their footsteps of greatness. A good future is yours. Believe it in your heart because that trust in God -- that hope -- is a healing balm for your wounds!

XI. Take a step: Refuse to remain in the ruts of your past. Take a step. Take a risk. Get out of bed. Do something new. Trust God: Do something fun. Break out of your isolation. Do what you feel God is asking you to do—no matter how small or grand. Just do it. Take the step, and begin living again. Soon, you'll be taking another step, and that, my friend, is learning a new walk into a new way of living.

"What saves a man is to take a step."
—Antoine De Saint-Exupery

XII. Lean Hard: When faced with "the process"—when faced with our own weaknesses, frailties, habits, and vices—it's easy to feel overwhelmed and inadequate. Our greatest strength is to acknowledge this inadequacy. Our greatest help comes when we admit to God our weaknesses and call on Him for strength. It is then that we obtain His Power. For God says that in our weakness, He is made strong. God gives His favor, power, and help to those who have this humble attitude. He opposes those who fail to recognize it. I've found that it's best to wholly acknowledge my holes, then He fills the holes and makes me complete. Imagine being filled with God Almighty. Yet those who refuse to acknowledge their holes remain filled with only their own strength and their own abilities. Don't you want more? Obtain more, by leaning hard on Him. He promises that He is not far. Call to Him; He will be there for you.

"Even in laughter the heart may ache,
and joy may end in grief" (Proverbs 14:13).
"Those who sow in tears will reap with songs of joy.
He who goes out weeping, carrying seed to sow,
will return with songs of joy, carrying sheaves with him"
(Psalm 126:5-6).

This is a prayer for you to say: *"Father, I come to You in the Name of Your Son, Jesus. I thank You that Jesus has come to heal the broken hearted. Lord, I come to You with much brokenness and pain. I ask Holy Spirit that You would search me and examine my heart—search out every place of wounds in my heart—and heal me. Lord, in those moments where I have been hurt and wounded; in times where words have been spoken to me that have penetrated and crushed me; where others have abused and robbed me of my dignity and respect; where I have been falsely accused; where I have been afflicted physically and sexually and emotionally; where I have been abandoned by those I loved; where I have been called names; Lord, in every place that has been hurt and pierced by sorrow and rejection, I ask that You would now heal. Lord, for every hole and empty place that has been filled with anger, isolation, self-pity, alcohol and drugs, apathy, cruelty, bitterness, callus attitudes, rebellion and ungodliness—I ask that You would heal. Fill me now with Your Presence and Your anointing that binds up the broken heart. With Your tender hands of compassion, create in me a clean heart and renew a right spirit within me. I choose today, with Your help, to forgive those that have wronged me, robbed me, hurt me and rejected me in any way. As You have forgiven me, I forgive them from my heart—they know not (truly) what they do. I ask that You would have mercy on them and even bless them. I thank You for turning what was intended to be evil for me into something that is good. I trust that my future and destiny and joy have not been stolen by any one; but that I shall obtain it in You. I thank You for the continued healing that You will do in my heart and mind in Christ Jesus. By faith, I take up the*

Christ Jesus. By faith, I take up the mind of Christ. I thank You for my complete healing and restoration in Jesus. I praise You because I am fearfully and wonderfully made in Your image! I thank You for making me as I am. I love You Lord. I love the way You made me. I fully accept myself, and fully love myself for who You made me to be. I choose to walk in love for You, for others and for myself. I let go of all anger and bitterness. I will walk in self-control. I will bridle my tongue. I will walk in forgiveness and love. In Jesus' name. Amen."

The Candy Kid

I'd like to tell you a story of the kid who grew up next door to me. He was raised in a typical looking house with a regular yard and a very friendly dog. Inside his house, however, was a different story altogether. His father, you see, was a hitter. It began as *just* a slap in the face--and it was always on the face-- slamming across his mouth.

At night, after work and a stop at the pub, his father would rant and rave and holler and scream about this and that and nothing at all. The poor kid, being forced to state a reason or plead his case or say something at all, would always, eventually, inevitably, get the same response—that's right, you guessed it…a swift slap in the face. Over and over, day after day, the blows would come across his cheek: a slap from the left, from the right, in the hall, in the kitchen.

His mother, however, was a giver. She gave out excuses and justifications, apologies and defenses, day after day, week after week, month after month, year after year. One day in those early years she gave her son something that would change his life forever: a candy. After one particularly jarring blow across his mouth, his mother, crying, came to his aid with a sweet little something in her hand to make her child's spirits rise, and with one taste in his mouth, his spirits did rise. In fact, they soared, causing his countenance to change from fear, fright and anger, to sheer happiness.

So became the pattern over the next several years. Though the slaps became harder and harder, eventually turning to outright, heavy-weight punches to the jaw, the candies kept coming as well. Eventually, to continually sweeten his mately, there was never a moment the boy did not have a candy in his mouth. While playing or daydreaming, reading or even eating, there was always, always a candy in his mouth. Only at night, after having gone to sleep, after his last one had dissolved, was there not a candy to be found in his mouth. It was also the night which plagued him with nightmares and restlessness...until the morning came, until the candy came.

Late in August, just before school started, I remember my friend being taken to the hospital. His father had punched him so hard in the mouth that the doctors had to re-set his jaw. Though the boy was amazed at the wonderful assortment of candies his mother had brought him this time, he was even more amazed at the wonder of the doctors who worked at healing his hurting mouth. It was then that he decided to become a doctor.

Become a doctor, he did — a renowned surgeon, in fact — a master at the use of his hands. More so, my friend had an additional gift, an amazing ability to diagnosis the wounds and infections of others. Yet, through all the years of college, of medical school, of residency, he constantly ate his candies. It turns out, the young doctor found that the abrasive motion of brushing his teeth, flossing and gargling actually irritated his mouth and really didn't seem to help the pain—at least not like the candies. Consequently, he stopped brushing and flossing and gargling, opting instead for stronger and sweeter candies.

Sure enough, his teeth began to yellow, brown, and actually rot. His breath, well, I'll let you imagine. His candies covered up most of the smell, and the colored ones masked the discoloration quite well. As a surgeon who was required to cover his nose and mouth with the little blue thingy, no one at his job was ever the wiser.

His friends, on the other hand, were. In fact, he chose not to associate with those who didn't eat candy—they weren't fun enough for him. Actually, he didn't associate with many people at all because he often thought they were staring or making fun of his rotting teeth. Sometimes they were, sometimes they weren't.

Most of his friends he had met on his days off, while visiting candy stores and various confectionaries. Often on these visits, on the streets of the city, his former patients would recognize him and thank him for saving their lives. Still, most of the time, he still felt alone.

Sure, he had friends come over the house to watch movies, shoot pool, and do the regular things people do. Sooner or later, someone would get close enough to actually see *into* his mouth and, naturally, feel inclined to say something. Of course, the doctor just knew that this "friend" was going to make fun of him and tease him, so he quickly counter-acted, and would swiftly kick them out. As it would happen, sometimes, a close friend would notice his dying and decaying mouth and reflexively reach over to point it out.

Unfortunately, the doctor thought this was an attempt similar to the ones years before by his father to hit him. To protect himself, he quickly counter-acted to this as well, and swiftly kicked them out in like fashion. As time wore on, as the candy continued, his mouth and teeth grew worse and worse, to the point of decay, to the point of severe infection, and eventually, if left unchanged, to the point of the doctor's death.

Over time, this pattern continued. Friends came into his world. Friends were kicked out of his world. Sure, some friends would stick around---they had simply learned the rule: Don't say a word. In any case, despite any ones' presence, he was truly, truly all alone. The only thing that remained, the only thing that never changed, was the candy.

--

So now, the reason for telling you my story: Can you help me? Tell me, please, how can I help my friend? Can I? Should I... and if so, what should I say? Please tell me. I would really appreciate it if you would. I think he needs me.

CRID

Chapter Ten

Making Sense of the Lows

"May God Himself, the God of peace, sanctify you through and through.
May your whole spirit, soul and body be kept blameless at
the coming of our Lord Jesus Christ. The one who calls you
is faithful and He will do it" (1 Thessalonians 5:23-24).

Arguably, one of the most frustrating consequences of depression, besides its debilitating effect upon the one experiencing it, is the fact that most of the non-depressed in the world haven't a clue as to what we are really going through. Sure, we try to explain it. With a dire need for even feigned empathy, we carefully, methodically, articulate what we're going through, our feelings, our experiences. Meanwhile, they continue staring blankly—waiting for the punch line. We throw our hands up in despair. "Don't they get it?"

Is It Really That Bad?

Well, I have some difficult news for you. Most people don't "get it," and they're right. Our situation isn't usually *that* bad. Now before you write me off as a turncoat, first hear me out.

Typically, most of us equate our circumstances with our emotional state. When things are going poorly, people feel sad, and vice versa. This is to be expected, and it is totally normal.

However, with depression, your situation may not be that bad, yet, you couldn't feel worse. This is the reason why it often seems impossible to describe to others the level of our torment. There are plaguing sorrows and currents of darkness that seem well beyond anything we can put into words. In the end, we feel like a wimp because in light of our actual circumstance (objectively viewed), we really don't have any concrete reason to feel this low.

Something doesn't add up and you know it. They know it too. You know what they're thinking. "Snap out of it buddy, it's can't be all that bad." From our vantage point, it *is* that bad! We just cannot explain why.

Because of that mystery, I vowed to never again explain to my close friend the extent of my depression. Attempts to do so only resulted in more grief and misery.

When I'd tell him how I was *feeling,* he'd ask me what I'd been *doing.* He saw the problem only with respect to the activities and events around me—my circumstances—and would therefore prescribe a logical remedy: "Dude," he'd tell me, "just stop doing (this)…and start doing (that)…." The solution seemed so simple for him.

I felt like drinking hemlock and he'd simply suggest switching from Coke to Pepsi. Didn't he see it? My inability to express my feelings, coupled with his inability to understand it, built a monument of helplessness in front of me. Nothing anyone said helped. Nothing I had to say, helped. Consequently, I spiraled downward.

The Park View

"For we are not ignorant of his devices" (2 Corinthians 2:11). For many of you, this chapter will be a shocker. It will offer a perspective on combating depression that you probably never considered. Since my aim is not shock value but, rather, spiritual edification, a brief foundation may be necessary to ease the way. My morning will serve as a good springboard.

Early today I drove a few miles from my house in Oakland to the nearby city of Alameda. Alameda's fame is primarily due to its naval base, though it remains a wonderfully quaint, often overlooked island just within the San Francisco Bay. Lately, I've been having my devotional times at one of its local parks.

Over the months I spent there, the park had become familiar. It contained all the accoutrements of a community park: baseball field, tennis and basketball courts, even an enclosed dog playground. I had also concluded from past visits that I was appreciably close to the waters of the Bay. At times, I could smell the ocean air or feel the gusty, ocean breeze. I just didn't know exactly where the shore was. Today's visit would change that.

This first day of spring had brought not only the warmth of the sun but also the enforcement of the parking meters. Being the cheapskate that I was, I opted to park a few blocks away, in a residential area, and trek to my destination. Although the new route led me a bit off the beaten path, I was no more than a block away from my usual parking spot.

However, before I even rounded the bend, something struck me as strange. The houses here were more reminiscent of the beach houses I'd been accustomed to seeing in Santa Cruz. The traffic flow had picked up; so too had the wind. Then, as I turned the corner, it hit me. At that moment, for the very first time, I realized I was no longer at my local city park, but rather in a massive, publicly accessible, coastal state park, with a majestic view.

Imagine that. All of my visits to the community park next door and I had never realized that just around the corner was a gorgeous public park with sandy beaches, free parking, a full view of the Bay and, to top it off, clean bathrooms. In one sweeping, panoramic motion, I could take in the Bay Bridge, downtown San Francisco and follow the bay all the way down to the San Mateo Bridge.

***You will never understand life in the Seen
without an understanding into the Unseen***

Matthew 24:35 says, *"Heaven and earth shall pass away but my words shall not pass away."* My discovery this morning led me to realize how critical it is to zoom back every now and then a bit farther from our perceived reality. My understanding of my immediate environment, however familiar, was limited because I had not panned back far enough. I had not explored and seen the full picture.

Life is like that. *By faith we understand that the universe was formed at God's command, so that what is seen was not made out of what was visible"* (Hebrews 11:3).

Strange as it may seem, what we cannot see is actually more real and more significant than what we can see. From Genesis to Revelation the Scriptures make clear that there is an unseen reality, an unseen struggle taking place in which mankind is a principal player. We are in a virtual reality game of the grandest kind.

We know that the world was formed from that which is not seen. Not only that, but the unseen will last forever, the seen only for a moment. Yet the world still tries to explain reality by what it sees.

"One day the angels came to present themselves before the LORD, and Satan also came with them. The LORD said to Satan, 'Where have you come from?' Satan answered the LORD, 'From roaming through the earth and going back and forth in it.' Then the LORD said to Satan, 'Have you considered my servant Job?'" (Job 1:6-8a).

The book of Job opens by explaining to the reader the background of what is about to take place in Job's life. The opening chapter gives a sequence of events taking place in the stars that put the rest of Job's sufferings on earth into proper context. Without this sneak preview, our understanding of the question of "why" would be lost.

For many of us, to gain a clearer picture of the predicament in which we may find ourselves, we'll have to peek into the unseen. We all know of God (Father, Son, and Holy Spirit), as well as Michael, the archangel and his buddy, Gabriel. We also know God has an enemy. So do you.

There is an unseen enemy, and this truth gives perspective to all truth, including God's mercy—and His ways. If we are to fully understand life, we must be willing to fully acknowledge the entire spiritual dimension and not simply ignore what we do not fully understand.

Inevitably, speaking about Satan and demons makes some people squeamish. Why do we have no problem with the idea of being "Touched by an Angel," but we deny the reality of the *rest* of the angels – the fallen ones? Many believe the Bible with respect to the existence of unseen forces of good, but often disregard the unseen forces of evil. We believe that God can "touch" our lives, but, because we are born-again, we think Satan cannot touch us.

Sadly, many *Harry Potter* readers understand more than most Christians about the dark forces of the spirit world. No, I don't subscribe to the "demon under every rock" theory, but I do believe that believers should walk in understanding. Any wise warrior knows that to know your enemy is a significant and necessary tactic in warfare, and we need to know that we are at war. Your enemy, Satan, seeks to devour and destroy you. This is written in God's Word.

Imagine being suddenly dropped onto another inhabited planet with the goal of understanding their way of life, culture, traditions, societal structure, government, etc. So you stand by the city streets, inside homes, along the country side and you watched how they live, how they talk, how they travel, what events transpire, their state of health, their emotions, etc. Suppose, however, that these inhabitants are undergoing a bloody, ongoing, and intensive *war* with another planet. (For a moment, try to think like a Star Treky, okay?) Well, if you knew that all-important fact, then you would automatically understand that their way of life has been significantly altered. You'd know that some events, in fact many events, are the result of the war.

Yet, many try to explain away school shootings, homicidal maniacs, international developments, tragedies, etc., without taking into account that there is an unseen enemy of the human race that is prowling about, bent on mankind's death, deceit, and destruction.

More Than Meets the Eye

"He sitteth in the lurking places of the villages: in the secret places doth he murder the innocent: his eyes are privily set against the poor. He lieth in wait secretly as a lion in his den: he lieth in wait to catch the poor: he doth catch the poor, when he draweth him into his net. He croucheth, and humbleth himself, that the poor may fall by his strong ones" (Psalm 10:8-10).

The above passage was a tremendous eye-opener for me in trying to understand why we, the depressed, often feel lower than our circumstances would ordinarily dictate. I'd encourage you to read the entire chapter in Psalms when time allows. Here are a few ideas to keep in mind as we examine the above passage in the Word.

The use of the word "poor" in Psalm 10 does not refer to economic standing or material status. The Hebrew word for poor used here is 1) "chelkah," which literally means "dark," "unhappy," "wretched," or "unfortunate," and 2) "aniy," which means "depressed," in mind or circumstances. It is the same word for "afflicted" mentioned earlier in the book. It is used to describe a depressed man or woman, the poor in spirit.

In addition, the psalmist is speaking of the deceitful, violent tendencies of his enemy, "the wicked." He likens his foe to a lion who looks for "poor," weak souls. As I understand it from watching "Predator Week" on *Animal Planet*, that's exactly how lions, wolves, hyenas, and even piranhas find their next prey. It is the way of the predator. They look to attack the weakest, the most isolated, the most vulnerable.

The implications are striking. The enemy of our souls—Lucifer, Satan—*"...prowls about like a roaring lion, seeking whom he may devour"* (see 1 Peter 5:8).

Now, do you see why you may be left feeling far lower than your circumstance? There is more at work to bring you down than meets the eye. The enemy sees—even looks for—those who are down. When he sees you down he simply grins, and starts kicking, harder and harder, and he works on keeping you from seeing the truth.

Our depression is a glaring beacon to the enemy, alerting him of our increased vulnerability. We now have an extra bull's-eye on our back. Once we've fallen emotionally and begin to limp and hang our heads, the enemy comes in and unleashes hell's battalion to keep us down for the count. He preys on the wounded. To those negative thoughts already plaguing us, the enemy adds more. To the lies we believe, they whisper an additional condemning word. Therefore, we fall deeper and deeper into a downward spiral of depression. We pick ourselves up for the moment only to later find ourselves crashing again, sinking lower and lower.

The reality is that those who are depressed are more vulnerable than others—and more subject to attack because of the enemy. Consequently, if we fail to properly respond in kind, we will continue to suffer emotional casualties well beyond what seems to be normal, and well beyond what is proper.

"For our struggle is not against flesh and blood, but against the rulers, against the authorities, against the powers of this dark world and against the spiritual forces of evil in the heavenly realm" (Ephesians 6:12).

The Truth is Out There

V.L. Parrington wrote the following about Herman Melville (author of *Moby Dick*): *"All the powers of darkness fought over him, all the devils plagued him. They drove him down into the gloom of his tormented soul, and if they did not conquer, they left him maimed and stricken...an arch romantic, he vainly sought to erect his romantic dreams as a defense against reality, and suffered disaster."*

Ghosts, goblins, witches, and warlocks aren't just parts of Hollywood story plots. As Christians we do have an enemy; one not given to idleness (see Ephesians 6 and 1 Peter 5:8). So why do we remain ignorant? We pretend these verses are somehow less real than John 3:16. Though he keeps throwing sand in our eyes, we prefer the ostrich approach and bury our heads in that very same sand.

Yes, our spirit is sealed (we are new creatures), but our soul is in process (therefore we must renew it). Consequently, the enemy of our souls attacks our minds. He magnifies (our problems). He distorts (our realities). He attempts to manipulate our thoughts with doubt, fear, deception, anger, and hate. Pairing with our flesh, he double-teams us. He sees those who are already down and discouraged and not only kicks us, but releases his attack dogs to finish the job. Yet, we remain perplexed as to why we could feel so low, why we have such morbid, defeating thoughts.

Fight Back!

"These are the nations the Lord left to test all those Israelites who had not experienced any of the wars in Canaan (He did this only to teach warfare to the descendants of the Israelites who had not had previous battle experience)..." (Judges 3:1-2).

When the Israelites entered the Promised Land, their enemies remained there. God left them there to test Israel and to teach them warfare. The younger generation needed to learn to fight.

God is a warrior, and we are made in His image. Therefore, He teaches us to war as well.

Paul reminds us of our continuous war as saints of the Most High. We fight and wrestle, though not against flesh and blood as did the children of the Old Testament. We wrestle (or, are *supposed* to wrestle) against principalities, powers, rulers of darkness of this world, and against spiritual wickedness in high places (see Ephesians 6:12).

God has given us the power to *heal sicknesses and cast out devils* so that we would in fact heal sicknesses and cast out devils (see Mark 3:15). We're seated with Christ. We're in Christ. Christ prophesied that we would do greater things than He did. Do we? Christ rebuked devils. Shouldn't we? It's written that those who believe will pick up snakes, drive out demons, lay hands on the sick and they will be well (see Mark 16:17). Do you?

If you haven't entered this fight, then perhaps you are suffering emotionally, physically, spiritually, and even financially well beyond what you ought.

Rise Above It

"Get thee behind me, Satan! You are a stumbling block to me..." (Matthew 16:23). By His own admission, Christ, God incarnate, declared that the enemy's words could have made Him fall. Likewise, the enemy will speak to us words that would make us fall. He will suggest to us that our future is hopeless: Our relationship failures are endless, our situation is impossible, and our God has forsaken us.

That's why what we listen to is vital. It can make us or break us. We can live in victory or remain defeated, based entirely on the thoughts we listen to. If Jesus rebuked the enemy, why are we still wondering WWJD?

The choice is up to us. Sure, we can hide from this truth, deny this truth, or simply pretend it's not worth the fight. Or, we can fight. We can entertain thoughts contrary to God's Word and let them torment and defeat us daily, or we can literally cast down every thought that sets itself up against the knowledge of God (see 2 Corinthians 10:3-7). We can either indulge in our lusts, fears, and anger, or we can demolish strongholds. We can despair because the battle against our mind rages, or we can proclaim victory over our mind and thoughts. I have chosen to fight. So can you.

Fight like Christ: Rebuke. Fight like the Apostles: Drive out. Be imitators of God and fight. Fight with God. Win. (See 2 Corinthians 10:4-6.)

I cannot tell you how many victories I've had over bouts of depression by rebuking the enemy. It's amazing the change that has resulted time and time again—from sadness to gladness—the moment I began to fight back.

What do I do, exactly? I command every foul spirit of depression, lies, condemnation, fear, doubt, anger, loneliness, lust (whatever the Lord leads or whatever I am afflicted with) to *go* in the name of Jesus Christ of Nazareth. I command these spirits, in the name of Jesus, never to return or retaliate. I command them to go to the footstool of Jesus. I renounce them. I rebuke them with a loud voice in the authority of Christ Jesus. I cast down every imagination and thought that sets itself up against the knowledge of God. Basically, I wield the Sword against my enemy.

Then I take back every gift stolen from me and my family (see Ephesians 4:8). I wrestle. I resist. Then, I take back peace. I take back joy. I take back my position and prosperity in Christ. I command the unclean spirits to give back what they've stolen. As led, I speak healing and the light of Jesus Christ into my life, my body, and my family.

Some of you must recognize that the ungodly thoughts you wrestle with—thoughts that criticize yourself and others, thoughts that say you won't have a successful career, marriage or future, that say you won't make it, you're going to die, your loved ones will die—are not your thoughts. They are contrary to the Word of God concerning you. You must command them to go. Christ anointed you with power over the enemy. You have a Sword, so use it. Don't ask Christ to do it—Christ commissioned *you* to do it. That is why it is a powerful thing to know the Word of God, it is the Sword of the Spirit that we use against the enemy.

Remember, our enemy is called the Accuser and the Deceiver. That's what he is really good at doing, accusing and deceiving. So he accuses you of your wrongdoing, deceiving you into thinking that that is who you are, a wrongdoer instead of the righteousness of God. He condemns you, plagues your thoughts that you have failed and all will fail, and that you are disqualified from the favor and blessings of God. Now remember this: our enemy has been disarmed!

So then, just as you received Christ Jesus as Lord, continue to live in him, rooted and built up in him, strengthened in the faith as you were taught, and overflowing with thankfulness.

See to it that no one takes you captive through hollow and deceptive philosophy, which depends on human tradition and the basic principles of this world rather than on Christ. For in Christ all the fullness of the Deity lives in bodily form, and you have been given fullness in Christ, who is the head over every power and authority. In him you were also circumcised, in the putting off of the sinful nature, not with a circumcision done by the hands of men but with the circumcision done by Christ, having been buried with him in baptism and raised with him through your faith in the power of God, who raised him from the dead.

When you were dead in your sins and in the uncircumcision of your sinful nature, God made you alive with Christ. **He forgave us all our sins, having canceled the written code, with its regulations, that was against us and that stood opposed to us; he took it away, nailing it to the cross. And having disarmed the powers and authorities, he made a public spectacle of them, triumphing over them by the cross** (Colossians 2:6-15, Amplified) (emphasis added).

Man, I love those verses! Can you visualize the scene? Christ took all the accusations against us—all the pronouncements in the law, the code of rules, the regulations that condemned us, Christ took it away and nailed it to the cross! This gave the enemy no more weapons. The enemy of our souls can no longer bring an accusation against us because Christ fulfilled them all! We are in Christ! Hallelujah! The accuser of the brethren cannot hold the law of requirements against us any longer as a means to disqualify us from the blessing of the Lord. He can try to deceive us. He can try to make us not believe it. Yet he holds no power because the truth is that we are now no longer under the law – we are in Christ. God's grace covers us because of the blood! Therefore, Christ is our Advocate, our defender, not our own works or efforts. (Praise God for that!) That's why we remain in victory and power over the enemy. Don't allow his accusations to cling to your mind any longer. As we affirm the truth of our righteousness in Christ alone, the enemy's accusations must fall to the ground. Therefore, use your weapon of your righteousness in Christ. Speak it out. Declare it. Believe it.

Yes, you do need to be led by the Spirit of the Living God before entering this fight. You must be fully equipped. Our fight first begins in time alone with God (read Matthew 17:21). Make sure Christ is Lord of your life (1 Peter 3:15). Ask for understanding that you might recognize when you are being attacked. Then realize that greater is He that is in you than he that is in the world (1 John 4:4). We are sons and daughters of God. If said in faith, those spirits must heed our rebuke. They must flee (James 4:7). Get violent about it. Get mad and take back what is yours. Reclaim your life and see your joy restored. For many of you, to have peace and joy returned to your life, you must incorporate this fight into your everyday life. It is part of the calling. That's why you've been given the authorization and power over it. *"Behold, I give you the authority to trample on serpents and scorpions, and over **all** the power of the enemy, and nothing shall by any means hurt you"* (Luke 10:19 emphasis mine). We sit around waiting on God and wailing to Him when He is telling us that He's given us all the ammunition we need. This is why we get frustrated with God, and it seems that He is not answering our prayers. He has equipped us. Our prayers are already answered.

The joy that comes following these battles is amazing. Sure, the demons get in a few blows, and it hurts, but you will learn their tactics. You will soon learn that he knows the buttons to push and, not to let him on the elevator. I've learned to just start speaking the Word of God. Satan can't stand the Word of God. He can't stand to see us worshipping Jesus or calling on His Name. If we do it every time he pushes those buttons, he'll get off the elevator. The Bible tells us that if we resit him, he will flee.

Wile E. ("E" Is For Enemy)

For a season it will seem like a very close wrestling match. The tide of victory will seem to ebb and flow, back and forth, from the good guys (that's us) to the bad guys (the bad spirits). Yes, they will fight back. They have gained ground that they do not want to give up. Your job is to keep battling until the ground is swept clean and they are only but a temporary nuisance. Just keep fighting through it. Eventually, you'll break their hold. Eventually, they'll flee, and you'll come into your season of rest. As time goes on, they'll harass you less and less. Your reputation as a fighter will precede you. You'll feel a noticeable difference in your life. Soon, you'll be able to fight for others—and begin walking in the anointing of Christ, who came to set the captives free (see Luke 4:19).

Because God is undefeated, so are we. So fight. Break generational curses. Through the authority of Christ Jesus, break every hex, curse, and spell placed on you. Speak it forth into the atmosphere with your words. Anoint your own head with oil. Rise up early, and seek the face of your Commander-in-Chief. Listen to His orders. Do His will—and begin to walk the face of the earth victoriously.

Incidentally, let me remind you that, just like in all wars, you are under a chain of command. Therein lays your authority. Hide yourself in the grace of God in Christ. Remove the law from before you. Place no confidence in the flesh. Make sure and get plugged into a strong church, under strong leadership, and with a strong covering. Spiritual warfare is not for the Lone Ranger. You must be prayed up to fight this one. Christ is our power source. You must abide in Him. If you are not daily abiding, you will be vulnerable. So abide.

Second, remember that our strength is in the name of Jesus. The Apostles did not heal people in the Father's Name. They healed in Jesus' name. It is not because there is no power in God; He holds all power. Nevertheless, we are connected to God, only through His Son, Jesus Christ. To tap into God's power, we must go through the connection, which is Christ. Therefore, everything we are able to do, all the power we have—to heal and deliver—is through Christ, by faith.

Finally, I cannot underscore the value and gains you will make in your life by fighting this fight. What feels like dark waves of depression will flee; fears will be immediately put to flight—if only we will fight.

I am no expert on spiritual warfare, but I have waged war against the enemy, and I have gained joy and victory as a result. The thing about God's Word is that we don't have to be an expert in warfare, we only have to know His Word and apply it. It is an amazing thing to enter beyond the third dimension. It is a struggle, and the enemy does fight back. Our punches strike harder though and last longer. When these evil spirits go (and they must go), God's peace prevails. His peace can prevail for you too, if you fear not and have the faith to fight. All the faith you need is already in you. You just need to pick up the Word of God and start reading it and using it and stop listening to the lies of Satan. He is one sad individual and he knows his days are numbered. If he can't take you with him to hell, he is going to try to make your life on this earth miserable, and at the very least, unproductive for the Kingdom of God. He doesn't have your soul, don't give him your peace and joy.

This is how we must fight, daily. Remember, the battle belongs to the Lord. Speak to whatever afflicts you. Command the enemy to go. Use your Christ-given abilities to take authority over that which is trying to exert authority over you. Don't stay in your affliction a second longer. Take up the Word and start swinging back. Use *your* voice and let *your* words shape a new reality for your life. Submit to God. Resist the devil. He will flee from you.

Here is a prayer you may want to say: *"Father, I thank You that my name is written in the book of life through the blood of the Lamb of God who takes away the sins of the world, Your Son, my Savior Jesus Christ. I thank You for the power and authority You have given us in Christ. I thank You that You have given us authority to trample upon snakes and scorpions and over all the power of the enemy. LORD God, I submit myself to You and I resist the enemy. I thank You that according to Your Word, he must flee from me. According to Your Word I take up the full armor of God. I take up the helmet of salvation, the breastplate of righteousness, the belt of Truth, the shoes for the preparation of the gospel of peace; the sword of the Spirit, which is the Word of God, and the shield of faith to extinguish all the flaming arrows of the enemy. Father, lead me by the Holy Spirit to remove any object or possession in my house that is displeasing to You and that is an open door of the enemy. I renounce all promiscuous behavior and sexual immorality. I will no longer allow the enemy to magnify problems and concerns in my life. I will resist the enemy in my life, recognizing that I wrestle not against flesh and blood but against spiritual forces of darkness. I take my stand, therefore, in the Name of Jesus Christ. I command every foul spirit that has been assigned against me to leave me now in the Name of Jesus and to go now to the footstool of Jesus Christ. I command in the Name of Jesus, every spirit of fear, depression, deception, anger, lust, lies, false teaching and deafness and darkness to leave me now and never return in the Name of Jesus. I cover myself and my family with the blood of Jesus. Father, I ask that Your angels encamp about me and my household. Father, I ask that You would fill me with Your Holy Spirit as you have commanded in Your Word. I ask that You would fill me with Your peace and Your presence. Father, I rest in Your covering for my life. You are my refuge. You are my life. I renounce the love of this world, the lust of the flesh, the lust of the eyes and the boastful pride of life. I long to do Your will. I worship You this day. I praise Your Holy Name. You alone are worthy. I come boldly into Your presence through the blood of Christ, I bow before You and exalt You as Holy, as pure, as good and loving. Thank You for Your covering. I thank You that by Your stripes I am healed. I receive my healing by faith in Jesus' Name. Teach me how to pray Holy Spirit. May I be still and know that You are God. May I spend time each day to hear from You and hear what You would have me to do. Help me to be quick to hear Your voice and obey. For therein is Your blessing on my life. Thank You Father. You are my Source. I find my rest in You. I rest in You this day. In Jesus' Name. Amen."*

Chapter Eleven
Healthy, Wealthy and Wise

"Happy is the man that findeth wisdom,
and the man that getteth understanding"
(Proverbs 3:13).

Wisdom's Wake-up Call

I don't mean to invoke the paranormal unnecessarily, but I first heard the voice of Wisdom in a dream. Please hear me carefully. I did not say vision, trance, or revelation. I was not translated in the Spirit before an angel to the heavens. I did not see seven golden lamp stands before a throne room. I said "*a dream*," just like the kind you may have had last night. Only this was one of those dreams you remember for the rest of your life. It was one of those traumatic dreams that jolts you awake for a brief moment of disorientation.

In my dream, I was hanging on a rope in the middle of a great chasm. It was a vast divide, immensely deep, separating two cliffs, similar to the Grand Canyon. I was swinging back and forth, to and fro'. I was never able to come close enough to land on either side. Consequently, I remained swinging, back and forth, for what seemed like an eternity.

At the edge of one precipice, loved ones stood. Though desperately trying with all my might to make it there, I could never gain enough momentum. I continued swinging, back and forth, back and forth. In my dream, years had literally passed by in an instant. Aged and wrinkled, I was still dangling, swinging back and forth, back and forth, never able to reach the sides. When I did finally make it to the other side, I had aged considerably.

I was profoundly shaken, and I knew this dream was different than other dreams I had had. (Most of my dreams involved me flying around L.A., like Superman—but in baggy blue jeans, not tights—or playing in the Super Bowl, heroic crime fighting, you know, the normal guy stuff.) I knew that this "Grand Canyon" dream represented real life—my life. I knew that if I continued my life without making some changes, I would spend the rest of my years hanging stagnantly, and, though swinging, never able to attain real progress. I would wear myself out to old age never amounting to anything. I would make it eventually, but I would have wasted my whole life in the process.

Without question, I knew that Wisdom had given me its warning. Before this night, depression itself had been trying to give me clues. I just wasn't listening. It was clear now: If I didn't start doing things differently, I would continue withering and squander all. Yes, Wisdom had awakened me. Its message was clear: Change or Die.

"Happy is the man that findeth wisdom, and the man that getteth understanding" (Proverbs 3:13).

"Wisdom brightens a man's face and changes its hard appearance" (Ecclesiastes 7:15).

The Bible states that happiness and wisdom are intimately interrelated, so we, especially those suffering from depression's sorrow, would be wise to possess them. However, as the Scripture above alludes, neither comes naturally. As with most precious commodities, one must procure them. Wisdom is "found"—suggesting that one must look for it. Understanding must be "gotten"—therefore, one must grab it.

In this chapter, we'll find wisdom and understanding. In doing so, we will, as the proverb suggests, become glad.

Pointing the Right Finger

"A man's own folly ruins his life, yet his heart rages against the Lord" (Proverbs 19:3).

For many of us, our depression stems from the fact that we're in a difficult situation. We find ourselves in hopeless situations, unsatisfying relationships, unfulfilling jobs, a miserable home, shameful finances, and the list goes on. We are dangling on the rope of life's circumstances. The Bible says that often, when in these straits, a person will start pointing the finger at God. Yet, the harsh reality is that our problems are often due to our own past and present foolish behavior. Therefore, to get out of our dangling despair and reach out for happiness, we need to change the way we live and land on the path of wisdom. This is the walk of wisdom, and here's how it works:

Wisdom: A Matter of the Heart

"Wherefore is there a price in the hand of a fool to get wisdom, seeing he hath no heart to it?" (Proverbs 17:16).

"So teach us to number our days, that we may apply our hearts unto wisdom" (Psalm 90:12).

Knowledge, apart from the knowledge of God, is a matter of the mind. It's the ability to recollect and resuscitate facts and figures, dates and data. The apostle Paul declares that the world's knowledge puffs up (1 Corinthians 8:1).

Wisdom, on the other hand, is a matter of the heart. Whereas knowledge wearies the soul, wisdom makes it glad (see Ecclesiastes 12:12 and Proverbs 3:13).

"The fear of the Lord is the beginning of wisdom; all who follow his precepts have good understanding" (Psalms 111:10).

A wise person is a happy person. A wise person has the right heart. A fool would like to be wise, but cannot be. He (or she) lacks the right heart. Here's how it works: God declares that the fear (awesome reverence) of the Lord is the beginning of wisdom. As a starting point, then, the heart that fears and reveres the Lord is on the right path to discovering the riches of wisdom. God also pronounces that the fear of the Lord is the hatred of evil as we see Proverbs 8:13. Accordingly, the hatred of evil is also the beginning of wisdom.

To put it together then, one who fears the Lord is one who hates evil, who will grow wise, and who finds happiness.

"The fool hath said in his heart, There is no God. They are corrupt, they have done abominable works, there is none that doeth good" (Psalms 14:1).

"In the mouth of the foolish is a rod of pride" (Proverbs 14:3).

A fool is wholly bereft of wisdom. A fool says no to God, or declares that there is no God. A fool maintains pride in his heart. A fool proudly resists God.

The wise, on the other hand, humbly revere Him. The one who lays hold of wisdom maintains awesome reverence for God. That reverence manifests itself, daily in our actions.

"He that walketh in his uprightness feareth the Lord; but he that is perverse in his ways despiseth Him" (Proverbs 14:2).

Let me make this a little more plain.

The fear of the Lord looks like this: The one who fears the Lord will keep His commandments, regardless of whether anyone is looking or not. You see, there are many who live as if they hate evil but do not. They live prudently for fear of earthly reprisal only. They do not steal for they fear jail. They do not murder for they fear the death penalty. They do not lie lest they be caught in the lie.

Yet, those who fear the Lord heed His commands simply because he or she reveres God. This obedience has nothing to do with prisons, jails, or pride—it also has nothing to do with the works of the flesh, or righteousness under the law (as discussed in previous chapters). It has nothing to do with local, state, or federal regulations. It has everything to do with God and our devotion to Him because He has saved us, set us free, and adopted us as sons and daughters. It is obedience based not on the mind's rationale, but due to the attitude of the heart through the power of God's Spirit operating in our lives.

"The fear of the Lord is to hate evil: pride, and arrogancy, and the evil way, and the froward mouth, do I hate" (Proverbs 8:13).

When the fear of God is in you, you're not only reluctant to lie, cheat, and steal, but you also seek to shun every proud and selfish thought. You don't want to lust, judge, criticize, or even litter—regardless of whether anyone will ever find out. With the fear of God comes an awareness that God knows your every action. That alone is all important to you. That is the beginning of living wisely. To live a life apart from the fear of the Lord is the way of the fool, however intelligent he (or she) may be.

"Folly is joy to him that is destitute of wisdom: but a man of understanding walketh uprightly" (Proverbs 15:21).

The Merits of Magnanimity

"The heathen are sunk down in the pit that they made: in the net which they hid is their own foot taken. The LORD is known by the judgment which He executeh: the wicked is snared in the work of his own hands" (Psalm 9:15).

What does our living circumspectly in the fear of God have to do with the acquisition of wisdom and happiness? Everything. Already, just because you've begun to live in line with His admonitions, you've begun to walk wisely. God honors that in a very real way.

"Like a father pitieth his children, so the Lord pitieth them that fear Him" (Psalms 103:13).

In addition, the Bible makes clear, again and again, the cause-and-effect, reap-what-you-sow, life principle. If we sow discord, evil, and violence, we'll reap the same. If we sow compassion, goodness, and peace, we'll reap compassion, goodness, and peace. Such "if, then" scenarios comprise the bulk of Proverbs, the book of wisdom. Let me remind you, however, that we're not speaking of the operation of works as bearing on salvation, but rather on the operation of works coming to bear on our lives.

Hence, it is written, *"Whoever would love life and see good days must keep his tongue from evil and his lips from deceitful speech. He must turn from evil and do good; he must seek peace and pursue it"* (Psalm 34:12-16).

"For the eyes of the Lord are on the righteous and His ears are attentive to their prayer, but the face of the Lord is against those who do evil" (1 Peter 3:10-12).

Similarly, Proverbs 17:20 declares, *"He that hath a froward heart findeth no good: and he that hath a perverse tongue falleth into mischief."*

Often, then, our heart determines our circumstances in life. For example, we may have few, if any, real friends because we have yet to learn the art of being a friend (see Proverbs 18:24). We wonder why so many of our relationships have turned sour, yet we lie, criticize, backbite, judge, talk too much, listen too little, deceive in our hearts, are quick to anger, gossip and don't forgive from our heart when offended.

We're constantly strapped for money. Yet we are spendthrifts and impulse buyers who love toys, love keeping up with the Joneses, hate hard work and have zero faith that God is our Provider. We never feel that close to God, yet we rarely spend substantial periods of time alone with Him.

This reality of reaping and sowing, replete throughout the Proverbs, can be a harsh reality, especially on our pride. It is too much for some of us to admit the fact that our present crisis is due to our past and present bad practices. So instead of blaming ourselves, we blame everyone else: We blame The Man. Men. The Media. The Market. The Liberals. Conservatives. The IRS. Minorities. God. We especially like to blame God. The Bible even tells us that we do. (see Proverbs 18:24; Proverbs 10:4; Proverbs 10:18-21).

"A man's own folly ruins his life, yet his heart rages against the Lord" (Proverbs 19:3).

I know what you're thinking. *This is way too difficult. I can't keep track of all of this! I've already got more issues than the New York Times. My father wasn't around to show me how to invest. My parents were never around for me. I was never told.... I never knew.... It's not my fault. I don't deserve this.*

That may be true. Many of us have had childhood traumas that are not our fault. Please realize that I'm not trying to browbeat anyone. It may just be true, however, that the tight spot we find ourselves in may be due to our own folly. Furthermore, we may have had ample, advanced warning. "By whom," you ask?

"By Wisdom herself," I would say to you.

Has Wisdom Called Your Name?

Listen to the voice of Wisdom: *How long will you simple ones love your simple ways? How long will mockers delight in mockery and fools hate knowledge? If you had responded to my **rebuke**, I would have poured out my heart to you and made my thoughts known to you.*

*But since you rejected me when I called and no one gave heed when I stretched out my hand, since you ignored all my **advice** and would not accept my **rebuke**, I in turn will laugh at your disaster; I will mock when calamity overtakes you - when calamity overtakes you like a storm, when disaster sweeps over you like a whirlwind, when distress and trouble overwhelm you.*

*Then they will call to me but I will not answer; they will look for me but will not find me. Since they hated knowledge and did not choose to fear the Lord, since they would not accept my **advice** and spurned my **rebuke**, they will eat the fruit of their ways and be filled with the fruit of their schemes.*

For the waywardness of the simple will kill them, and the complacency of fools will destroy them; but whoever listens to me will live in safety and be at ease, without fear of harm (Proverbs 1:22-33, emphasis added).

"Wisdom calls aloud in the street, she raises her voice in the public squares; at the head of the noisy streets she cries out, in the gateways of the city she makes her speech..." (Proverbs 1:20-21).

Here, the personification of wisdom makes it resoundingly clear that since she speaks in such a conspicuous manner, no one is without notice. She cries aloud, raising her voice, in the most public places. Everyone is within earshot of her voice. Even today, you and I can hear her call.

Do you say you are looking for wisdom but cannot hear her call? I'd bet you have, but wisdom's voice comes from an unsuspected source.

Have you ever felt that life was hitting you over the head with a two-by-four? Have you ever felt that life was getting the best of you, rather than the other way around? Have you ever felt that circumstances were beating you down, whipping you, and slapping you across the face?

Have you ever opted for a course of action that was in complete contradiction to the advice of those older and wiser? Have you heard, "I told you so," time and again? Are you living your life with secrets?

If so, you have probably heard the voice of wisdom. You see, her voice is often that of rebuke. When life seems to be chastening and spanking you—when others, those older and wiser than you, seem to be challenging you; when your pastor speaks against your lifestyle; when your parents have counseled you otherwise; when life keeps turning you flip side—wisdom is calling.

You see, wisdom's voice is not some mysterious, ghostly voice we hear while crossing the street. It is the voice of rebuke. It's the advice of wise counsel. It's heard when life buffets us, and the world about us seems to scold us. So wake up. You may have just heard the voice of wisdom.

"The wise in heart will receive commandments: but a prating fool shall fall" (Proverbs 10:8).

"Reprove not a scorner, lest he hate thee: rebuke a wise man, and he will love thee.

Give instruction to a wise man and he will be yet wiser: teach a just man, and he will increase in learning" (Proverbs 9:8-9).

"He is in the way of life that keepeth instruction: but he that refuseth reproof erreth" (Proverbs 10:17).

Imagine how many bad marriages could have been avoided if young daughters had listened to the instruction of caring fathers. Consider the many bad investments averted if husbands listened to the cautions of their discerning wives. Ponder the state of our prisons if young boys heeded the instructions of parents and guidance counselors. Contemplate the condition of our schools if children hearkened to the voice of a teacher. Imagine the state of man if we would give ear to the voice of the Lord and forgive liberally, exude kindness continually, work diligently, love abundantly, pray incessantly, speak truthfully, live humbly, walk holy, and worship adoringly.

Instead, though we hear instruction, we simply choose to ignore it. We're given advice but opt to do otherwise. We've been taught to do *this* but continue to do *that*. We've been told to forgive. We've been told to submit to those in authority. We've been told to be on time. We've been told to do our homework. We've been instructed to treat our sisters with all purity. We know we are to treat our elders with respect. We know we are to honor our parents.

Yet now, we're failing school, fired from our jobs, imprisoned, impregnated and hated, yet we still ponder why.

Look, folks, I'm not trying to be a major downer here. This is just another key piece to the puzzle of life and happiness. This is just a necessary dose of reality. Though not easy, following good advice is crucial to our success, spiritually and naturally. So please know that I'm not trying to beat you up, but, rather, build you up.

Many of us have heard the voice of wisdom; we've simply chosen not to abide by it. We say, "My way or the highway," and now we're living the consequences. Life has turned sour and we continue wondering what went wrong.

Turning to Live

"He, that being often reproved hardeneth his neck, shall suddenly be destroyed, and that without remedy" (Proverbs 29:1).

In my "younger" days, I used to go skiing quite often. My friends and I lived for jumps. Forget moguls, forget powder, forget ski bunnies, we wanted air. (This was before the onslaught of Age and his ruthless associates, Aching Back, Sore Knees and Stiff Neck.)

Finally, the day came when it was time to learn the much-hyped 360 (that's what we called it in the "olden days"). The secret to the 360, I was told by a friend more capable than I, was all in the head.

He wasn't talking psychologically—the need to psyche oneself up for an act of sheer stupidity (that had been achieved long before)—but, rather, physically: "If you turn your head, the body will follow," he told me.

As it turned out, he was right. When in the air I turned my head, my body followed. Mission accomplished. With my newly discovered intelligence, the trick seemed all too easy.

Brothers and sisters in the Lord, that's what the wise writer in Psalm 29 meant. When you are being reproved (chastised, refuted, chastened, rebuked) by life, don't harden your neck. Turn it. The rest will follow.

"He is in the way of life that keepeth instruction: but he that refuseth reproof erreth" (Proverbs 10:17).

"A reproof entereth more into a wise man than a hundred stripes into a fool" (Proverbs 17:10).

It is said that insanity is doing the same thing over and over again yet expecting a different result. Truth be told, many of us are toeing lunacy's line and don't even realize it. We face misfortune after misfortune yet resign ourselves to think that we're simply given to bad luck. We feel disaster is our lot. We think our fate is not ours to shape, but it is.

So we continue to do the same things day after day. We think the same thoughts night after night. We live our lives unchanged, yet all the while we wait for change to come. My friend, that is insanity! We are creating the very rut we are so miserably existing within!

Let me repeat this passage: *"He, that being often reproved hardeneth his neck, shall suddenly be destroyed, and that without remedy"* (Proverbs 29:1).

When you're being reproved (chastised, refuted, chastened, rebuked) by life, don't harden your neck.

When life keeps giving you headaches, sorrow, and unrest, maybe you're being reproved? Maybe wisdom is calling? Wake up! Turn your head so that your body will follow. Take steps to live life differently. Change — that you might live.

Often, unfortunately, instead of turning our head — we stiffen it. We brace for more future shocks, thinking we'll tough it out. Instead of turning away from sin, we take on others, and we take it out on others. Instead of changing, we start hating. We get hurt and grow bitter. Still, we do not turn. We do not change.

The Cool Breeze of Change

"The ear that heareth the reproof of life abideth among the wise" (Proverbs 15:31).

A profound and powerful reality is found in our capacity to change. It is that which makes us human (and accountable)—it is that which makes life beautiful.

A husband can become a new husband. A musician can become a better musician. A "C" student can become a "B" student. A tyrant can become an altruist. A wallflower can become a Travolta. The weak can be made strong. The boastful can bow.

We can achieve dreams that seemed impossible before. Add discipline, drive, determination, discretion, and a hardy dose of tenacity, and success awaits. Because of the life we live today, the life we live tomorrow can be different from the life we lived yesterday.

Still, we want our lives to change, but we don't want to do the changing. We want more money, but we don't want more responsibility. We want the rewards, but we refuse to take on the risks. We want those elements of life that have a higher price tag, but we don't want to pay the price. We want more, but want to stay the same. We pray, "Bless me, Lord." We sing, "Bless me, Lord." We cry, "Bless me, Lord." Yet, we don't change.

"Your heart shall live that seek God" (Psalm 69:32). Never forget, your ability to change is found first in the finished work of Christ – the work He has already done for you, by grace. Receive it today and receive His life and power in you, and your ability to reign! (Romans 5:17).

The Price is Life

"The blessing of the Lord, it maketh rich, and he addeth no sorrow with it" (Proverbs 10:22).

We've just examined how God blesses with wisdom those who fear (reverence) Him. We've seen that those who fear Him are those who keep His commands and hate evil. We've seen that the one who finds wisdom is happy. (In case you forgot, happiness is what we're looking for.) However, "the fear of the Lord" is also to be had elsewhere. I'd like to show you a sure fast way to obtain this fear of the Lord—a way that bears the promise of joy.

Throughout the books of the Law, God required that His people read His Word so that they'd learn to fear Him, and in doing so enjoy a long-lasting life (see Deuteronomy 4:10; 6:2; 24). He also told them to do something else to learn the fear of the Lord: tithing. That's right, tithing (giving the first 10% of your gross earnings to the LORD). It is the one thing that God even told us to test Him regarding, that if we would do this, our storehouses would be full to overflowing.

"Thou shalt truly tithe all the increase of thy seed, that the field bringeth forth year by year.

*And thou shalt eat before the Lord thy God, in the place which he shall choose to place his name there, the tithe of thy corn, of thy wine, and of thine oil, and the firstlings of thy herds and of thy flocks; **that thou mayest learn to fear the LORD thy God always"*** (Deuteronomy 14: 22-23, emphasis added).

Yes, when God implemented the tithe, it served to teach His people the fear of the Lord. Those who tithe to the Lord demonstrate a fear of God in their heart. Why? Because where your treasure is, there is your heart also. There's no government mandate to tithe. There is no earthly punishment for not tithing. It's only a reflection of reverence to God. Those who fail to tithe do so because they lack holy fear. They fear poverty more than God. Indeed, we are no longer under the law. However, in the New Testament, the standard of giving is actually higher. The early Church didn't just give 10%, they actually sold their possessions to meet the needs of the people. Christ commended the poor woman who gave all. We, ourselves, are not the Lord's 10%, but totally. We are to totally consecrate our lives to Him, daily, all day, not just on Sunday mornings or for a little prayer before we begin our day.

The beauty of tithing—and of all giving to God, the poor, the alien (sorry Trekkies, the other aliens) and the widow—is that a blessing is always attached (see Deuteronomy 15: 7-11; 14:29; 26:15). It's no less than reaping and sowing. God always blesses the giver. (The exception is the one who gives to the rich, i.e., bribery. See Proverbs 22:16.)

In looking over my life, it's undeniable that my breakthroughs, though, came as I began to tithe. Indeed, I'd always given a tenth since my parents taught me from the days I was a boy, receiving allowances for house chores. My real breakthroughs—in my walk with God, in understanding my purpose in life, etc.—came as I began to tithe from my payroll checks—the gross, not the net and sowed my seed in faith, believing for specific promises of God in my life each time I gave.

I know many of you are thinking I'm being legalistic, too hung up on the details; after all, God looks at the heart, and He knows that I'd *like* to give more, but I simply *can't*. Sorry, I don't buy it.

Yes, He does understand what you think is lack, but if you want the blessing, you'd understand that and more. More to the point, I'd venture to say that, in all due respect, you don't fear God enough, my friend, nor have a correct understanding of God as your Provider.

As a friend explained to me, tithing from the net is giving to God *after* Uncle Sam has dipped in, the state has dipped in and your 401(k) and anything and everything else has dipped in. God wants first fruits. He always has. Give it to Him. Learn to fear Him. He will bless you. He promises. You'll grow in the wisdom of God, for it comes by the fear of God. My friend, do not let this be a burden of the law, but an encouragement. This is one of God's ways toward financial freedom for your life. It is found in giving. Does not Proverbs 11:25 state: *"The liberal person shall be enriched, and he who waters shall himself be watered?"*

Please remember that throughout the Word of God we are told that *the earth is the Lord's* (I Chronicles 29:11; Psalm 24:1; I Corinthians 10:26). We must understand that all that we have belongs to the Lord. We are mere stewards. We are called to be faithful to all that He has entrusted to us. That means that the 10% is His as well as the other 90%! Just because we have given our first fruits to the Lord doesn't mean that we can be spendthrifts with the rest. It is all His. We should be continuously listening to Him regarding our giving as well as our spending. To God be the glory.

Finally, keep in mind that when I originally wrote this chapter I was not a Pastor, and regardless, it's of no fiscal consequence to me if you give or not, but I implore you still. Blessings await you. *"He that hath a bountiful eye shall be blessed; for he giveth of his bread to the poor"* (Proverbs 22:9).

If you don't believe me, I recommend you study giving. Look at what happened to those in the past who did it. Examine the promises God gives to those who do it. Look at the prosperous lives of our Godly patriarchs. Read the blessings dictated in Deuteronomy by God for those who give. We reap what we sow. God is not mocked. God is a good God. Those who kindly give will be given in kind.

"Blessed (happy) is every one that feareth the LORD; that walketh in his ways.   For thou shalt eat the labour of thine hands: happy shalt thou be, and it shall be well with thee.   Thy wife shall be as a fruitful vine by the sides of thine house: thy children like olive plants round about thy table.

Behold, that thus shall the man be blessed that feareth the Lord" Psalm 128:1-4. *"Praise the LORD. Blessed (happy) is the man that feareth the LORD, that delighteth greatly in his commandments. His seed shall be mighty upon earth: the generation of the upright shall be blessed. Wealth and riches shall be in his house: and his righteousness endureth for ever"* (Psalm 112:1-3).

Dreaming Reality

Going back to the dream I had — you remember me swinging from a rope for what seemed a whole lifetime. Its meaning became shockingly apparent as I read James 1. James speaks of enduring trials with patience. He adds that if we lack wisdom we ought to ask God for it. *"But,"* he adds, *"let him ask in faith, nothing wavering: for he that wavereth is like a wave of the sea driven with the wind and tossed. For let not that man think that he shall receive any thing of the Lord. A double-minded man is unstable in all his ways"* (James 1:6b-8).

As I looked up the word, *waver* in my Greek/Hebrew dictionary I was amazed to find it meant *to doubt, to hesitate*, and, you guessed it, *to swing back and forth*. Sadly enough, that was me. What I was doing in the dream, I was doing in my life as well. Though I loved God, loved His Word, and loved His people, I wavered, doubted, and hesitated over many significant details in my life, including career choices.

Over the years, I had put my hands to a great many exploits. My intellect and talents told me I could do anything. When I did, eventually doubt and hesitation caused me to give up. I'd never fixed my mind on a goal, or turned my head to one direction, determining to pursue relentlessly any real success in life. As a result, I never stuck to anything long enough for it to bear fruit. Instead of maintaining dogged persistence, I let real and perceived obstacles create doubt and fear. Upon reading that first chapter in James, I realized that God uses time to produce victories in our lives. I just had never waited long enough. I simply changed my course and pursued something else altogether. Never constant, I was the essence of a double-minded man.

Consequently, I had very few victories. Though greatly talented, I was utterly failing —and, as a result, greatly tormented as well – because I had concocted visions of failure in my mind instead of believing for success.

Today, I praise God for revealing to me these errors. I thank Him for His rebuke. I am so thankful for His discipline. I asked for Wisdom. In giving me insight into my jeopardy, He answered, with correction. He loved me too much not to warn me. To this day, I thank Him for allowing me the chance to change.

Today, I have a fixed purpose and have resolved that I will not relent until I have finished the course. I am committed to one purpose. Come what may, I will not waver. Since the time I utterly rejected doubt, hesitation, and the constant questioning of self, I have finally found uncompromising peace and joy.

I have found the beauty and calm that commitment and diligence bring to a confused and divided mind.

Is Wisdom calling you? If it is, heed her voice. I implore you. God's Word says riches untold—including happiness—await those who heed her call.

"Blessed (happy) is every one that feareth the Lord;
that walketh in His ways. For thou shalt eat the labour of thine hands:
happy shalt thou be,and it shall be well with thee.
Thy wife shall be as a fruitful vine by the sides of thine
house: thy children like olive plants round about thy table.
Behold, that thus shall the man be blessed that feareth the Lord"
(Psalm 128:1-4).
"Now therefore hearken unto me, O ye children:
for blessed are they that keep my ways.
Hear instruction, and be wise, and refuse it not.

...For whoso findeth me findeth life, and shall
obtain favour of the Lord.
But he that sinneth against me wrongeth his own soul:
all they that hate me love death" (Proverbs 8:33, 35, 36).
"The ear that heareth the reproof of life abideth among the wise"
(Proverbs 15:31).

I leave you with this prayer to keep from dangling: *"Father God in heaven, Holy is Your Name. Thank You for giving us all that we need to live this life in peace and prosperity in Christ. Lord, I receive Your Spirit of Wisdom and Revelation. Holy Spirit, I thank You for revealing to me the will of the Father concerning my life, my career, my finances, my relationships—all that I need. Father, forgive me and my forefathers for trespassing Your command to give. Forgive me for walking in fear and lack and thereby withholding from those in need. Forgive me for withholding my first-fruits, the tithe, from Your house. From this day I will give to Your ministry a tenth of all my increase. I will trust in You to be my Source, not riches. I hear Your voice of correction and will turn. Thank You for Your loving discipline. I put my foolish ways behind me and choose Your Ways and Your Word to direct my footsteps. Lord Jesus, You be the Ruler and Owner of my life. Take over the command of my life. I choose You. Thank You for Your Wisdom with which You have and will continue to give me. It is more precious than gold. Thank You for Your blessing. Thank You for creative ideas and the strength to implement them in Your time, Your way. You are my strength. I rest in You. I love You Lord. I thank You. I bless You. In Jesus name. Amen."*

ᏟᎡᎬᎾ

Chapter Twelve
The Four P's of Hap "pp" piness

"That ye be not slothful, but followers of them who through
faith and patience inherit the promise"
(Hebrews 6:12).

Mongrels, Inc.

My mother is of Italian/Sicilian descent, my father African-American, and for many years of my life I felt haunted by my identity. Left somewhere in the middle of two distinct races, I felt I was indeed of the "mongrel" generation loathed by the likes of former Alabama Governor, George C. Wallace. I always felt as if I was something of a hybrid: to blacks, I was too white, and to whites, I was too black.

My life was becoming a clutter of painful incidents of rejection by both camps—sometimes intentional and sometimes unintentional. After all, how close could I really be to my "white" friends once I overheard them utter the "N-" word? Then again, how close were my "black" friends who spoke ill of whites? In trying to find my place in this world, I nearly concluded there wasn't one.

That I didn't really "fit" became sorely obvious to me as I grew older. It seemed to crush me at every turn. It was killing me. Well beyond depression, I was slowly dying, and I knew it.

Finding Our Place in the World

"Jesus saith unto her, Woman, what have I to do with thee? Mine hour is not yet come" (John 2:4).

As I (slowly) began to mature, I realized that the class of persons who didn't "fit" was larger than I thought. I came across the indigent boy feeling at odds with his affluent classmates; the Hispanic reared in a town of "others"; the Asian living in Kansas; the Black boy in Beverly Hills.

As I grew, so too did my list: the orphan reared in a dozen foster families, the little boy teased for want of dexterity on the playing field, the young girl abused, the odd-looking, the odd-shaped, and the outcast.

Then I stumbled on an article concerning the ever-revered rapper Tupac Shakur. He, too, was quoted as saying the same: "I never really fit in."

Can you believe that? The powerful, hip-hop, T.H.U.G. life-preachin', potty-mouthed, often-imitated rapper of angst with long eyelashes, tattoos, and an early demise—Tupac—never really "fit in." This issue bothered him tremendously.

In reality, we each have something that separates us from everyone else, besides our DNA. We all have that which would cause us to separate and withdraw from others. I realized then I was not alone, and neither was anyone else. I was the world, and the world, me. We are all crimsoned stained together by rejection, pain, isolation, hurt, insecurity, bondage, struggle, and strife. We all have had our crosses to bear. In that, we're all unique.

Because we are unique, we alone are singularly qualified to do that which we've been called to do. Often, our past struggles, obstacles, and malicious treatment equip us specifically for our divine purpose, more than any formal education or training could ever give. God can put all of our "junk" to good use.

This is the peculiar thing about life. That which makes us not "fit in" is often that which makes us uniquely qualified. What has the potential for a negative outcome can be turned for great good.

Unfortunately, to get from "improper fit" to "unique" takes time, patience and understanding. If handled improperly or impatiently instead of our allowing God to work it out for our good, the "delay" can lead to a path of hate, anger, rebellion, destruction, and isolation.

"P" Number 1: People Make the Difference

"A man who isolates himself seeks his own desire; He rages against all wise judgment" (Proverbs 18:1).

"And let us consider one another in order to stir up love and good works, not forsaking the assembling of ourselves together, as is the manner of some..." (Hebrews 10:24-25).

No matter who you are, no matter where you're from, there are things about you that can make you feel alone and different. To be sure, we're all different. However, the Bible makes evident that we're bettered, we're healed, we're developed, and we're made glad in direct proportion to our ability to have intimate relationships.

That's the quandary: Life's forces of pain cause us to want to close up, clam up, and retreat within. We suppress our true feelings and thoughts. Inevitably, we become fools. Our thoughts won't match reality because they're never checked by others. Therefore, parts of our lives begin to rot, decay, and die.

Consequently, it's imperative to resist the urge to retreat. It's urgent to fight the tendency to *"...forsake the assembling of the believers"* (see Hebrews 10:25). Yes, people will hurt and offend you. You will see hypocrisy. People, yes, even Christian people, will do wrong. Yet, you make mistakes too. Maybe these people have been put in your life to teach you grace, compassion, and patience.

Iron sharpens iron. We can remain dull, tucked safely away in our isolation. If we never open up to others, we forfeit that process of sharpening.

In order that we may become more valuable to Him, He causes us to undergo more refining—and the refining process often hurts.

In order to refine us, God uses people—if we dare to draw near enough to God, and to people. The problem, however, is that instead of being shaped into something of value as a result of our intimate relationships and friendships, we become isolated, abandoning friends, communities and churches and remain unshaped—unperfected, and immature. Failing to see the log in our own eye, our pride causes us to continue placing the fault on others.

Yes, God uses His word to teach us. God uses His pastors and teachers. There may even be times where God is calling us to a temporary season of solitude, but God uses relationships. We're all parts of a body. Some of us are lacking emotionally, spiritually, and financially because God has put people around us to fill those needs, but our withdrawal and retreat prevents them from being able to pour their healing balm into our life. We miss out on friendships and much joy in life because we choose to be an island. God designed our bodies with the need to get rid of waste. If we don't do so, we die. It's the same with our emotional well-being. Regarding the bad stuff, you gotta get it out!

We need bonds of friendship to vent, to bounce our nutty ideas around with, get a different viewpoint, receive correction, etc. We should have at least one person in our life with whom we can share our deepest fears, frustrations, and vices. We should have someone to confess to, besides the Lord, and we should be a listening ear to another as well.

All of this is to say that we're all created to be connected—to God and others. Unfortunately, many of us are deceived into thinking that our connection to others is not that important. As a result, we're left lacking.

Beloved, learn the beauty of sharing. Stop stuffing and suppressing. It's killing you. Force yourself to be relational. Open up to a trustworthy soul. Therein you'll find relief, rest, and joy found nowhere else.

"P" Number 2: Patience is a Must

*"Consider it pure joy, my brothers, whenever you face trials of **many kinds**, because you know that the testing of your faith develops persever-*

ance (patience). Perseverance (patience) must finish its work so that you may be mature and complete, not lacking anything" (James 1:2-5, emphasis added).

In addition to connecting, if we're ever to become the men and women of God we desperately long to become, then we'll have to learn patience. It's not a glamorous concept, for we learn it best in periods of discomfort. We learn it best when God makes us wait. We learn it when thrust into loathed environments. We learn it in trials of "many kinds." There are no cheap substitutes. God wants quality. This does not come easy. If we want to be complete, this is our reality. In my struggle to find my place in life, the requirement of patience topped the list.

Making Cold Calls

Psalms 105 chronicles Joseph's life. While Joseph was still a teenager, God called him to be a great leader, and Joseph knew it. Deep down, quietly, like a gentle whisper inside of him, Joseph always knew it. However, for many years to follow, life held for him only the contrary. He was hated and despised by his brothers, who sold him into slavery. He was falsely accused as a rapist, thrown into prison, and the list goes on. *"He was sold for a servant, his feet hurt with fetters: he was laid in iron: until the time that his word came: the word of the Lord tried him"* (Psalm 105:18-19).

God had called Joseph to do great things. So he waited, and waited, only to receive greater and greater affliction. The Bible says that until the day Joseph came into his purpose, the word God spoke to him tried him. Do not be surprised if your life mirrors some of these people in the Word as you are being groomed by God to be one of His chosen.

Imagine how frustration could have plagued Jesus' soul and spirit if He didn't know the season of His call. He knew He had unmatched potential. Yet, He'd have to pass through thirty years before He'd enter His formal calling. Without an understanding of time, of patience, and of God's perfect calendar, His mind could have been racked with anxiety.

Are you growing frustrated? Are you feeling stuck, as if you aren't where you need to be? Do you feel that life holds for you something bigger than where you are? If so, don't assume you're necessarily missing God's involvement in your life; that you're out of His will, or in sin. Your time, perhaps, has simply not yet come. *"Mine hour is not yet come"* (John 2:4).

Don't Enter Without It

I know we hate to hear it, but patience is imperative for this Christian walk. What we often fail to realize is that patience can be a source of fresh air to our soul. On the other hand, lack of patience can be a source of tremendous defeat.

Frequently, many of us become tired of waiting out the hard times. If left unchecked, these feelings become fertile soil for the germination of sin and depression. We know that Psalm 23 says *"The Lord is my shepherd, I shall not want,"* but we feel we are in want. We feel we lack every good thing that everyone else has around us. All we lack is patience.

God is doing a work in us. He uses time to do it. When we lose patience with God, when we're unable to wait on God, we begin to feel we're lacking something. We begin to look away from God to find what we need. Once we do that, we're worshipping idols. We're coveting. We desire gain from something or someone other than God.

Be patient therefore, brethren, unto the coming of the Lord. See how the farmer waits for the land to yield its valuable crop and how patient he is for the autumn and spring rains. You too, be patient and stand firm, because the Lord's coming is near.

Take, my brethren, the prophets, who have spoken in the Name of the Lord, for an example of suffering, affliction, and of patience. Behold, we count them happy which endure. Ye have heard of the patience of Job, and have seen the end of the Lord; that the Lord is very pitiful, and of tender mercy (James 5:10-11).

Patience can be a refreshing aid to a weary soul. Breathe it in. Don't be in such a hurry. God is there. Look up and be patient. God often brings us much needed respite during these hours of waiting. If we use these times to draw closer to Him, He promises to draw closer to us. Without patience we're imperfect vessels, always wanting. Wanting brings grief. Patience yields contentment—and contentment brings joy.

I began this chapter by stating that I once resented my parents for inter-marrying. Today, I have thanked them. I would want it no other way. More and more, the benefits of living on both sides of the racial divide become apparent. I've found my calling. It took time. It required patience. Yes, eventually God came through for me. Finding my calling was a lesson hard won, but when learned well, it serves well. It brings a sweet calm to an anxious and weary spirit and peace to a tormented mind. I pray that you, in time, will find the same.

"That ye be not slothful, but followers of them who through faith and patience inherit the promises" (Hebrews 6:12).

"P" Number 3: The Pride of Perfectionism: Perilously and Perfectly Flawed*!*

*"As it is written: "There is no **one righteous**,*
*   **not** even **one"** (*Romans 3:10).

I remember not wanting to go to school one day because there was going to be a quiz. Can you believe I actually vomited because the anxiety was so great? A minor school quiz and I was in a panic. And did I mention that I was in the third grade?

Yes, I know, pathetic story, but through the years I have found that there are many more like me. OK, maybe not that bad, but not healthy either. I've also found that it seems to be those of us prone to the artsy-fartsy (as I affectionately call us) side of life. We are perfectionist, which means the bar set for ourselves is pretty darn high. I have heard that it is that same perfectionism that causes procrastination and eventually, paralysis. We put off projects and events and phone calls because we over analyze and over play its significance and the need for it to be done perfectly. Additionally, we are quite sensitive—as to our own feelings and towards the feelings of others. This also gives us an over active, "*What if-er?*" We go through the laundry list of, *What if he does this, What if she thinks that, What if, what if, what if...*

On the one hand, with respect to our giftings, be it writing, music, drawing, etc., that sensitivity is an amazing plus, allowing us to strike the chords of emotions in our work and empathize genuinely with those around us. However, the down side is that we can be extremely hard on ourselves because the expectations we place on ourselves is so rigorous. Consciously or not, we place that same bar on others—causing us to be hurt just as quickly as we find ourselves beating ourselves up. The need for us to receive and accept grace in our lives has been covered elsewhere in this book so we will not go into detail here as well. Suffice it to say, for us to function in the arena of happiness, we must ease up on ourselves.

Don't give up on yourself when you fail. Learn to get back up again. Like yourself, even while being imperfect. Yes, even love yourself with all of your flaws, weaknesses and frailties. God does, why shouldn't you? Let this be a constant air of comfort and ease as you navigate your day with people, commitments and responsibilities. Life is imperfect. So are you. That is the beauty of our ability to love—in spite of. Oh how the flesh longs to follow its former master. Oh how pride performs in many a matter. May it fall from heaven, the superstar, that the Bright and Morning star may arise.

"P" Number 4: Created for Purpose—Know it!

"Where there is no vision, the people perish" (Proverbs 29:18).

Can you think back to a time when you were driving along in your car only to realize that you were completely and undeniably lost? Maybe you forgot the directions, the Thomas Guide, Mapquest directions, GPS or the cellular phone. Maybe time was against you; and with no gas station in sight, the distinction between arriving fashionably late or shamefully tardy began to blur.

Remember how frustrating the experience? I do. It happens to me every time I drive into San Francisco. It also happened to me for nearly thirty years of my life.

That's right. For nearly thirty years of my life, I had no direction. I was lost. I didn't know my purpose in life. I cannot describe the unbearable frustration of that experience. I suffered greatly under its weight.

God created us on purpose, and for purpose. Consequently, where there's no purpose, there's no peace. You go to work everyday, but the daily dissatisfaction of life reminds you that you are a lost and aimless number in the crowd: Married with children, yet lost; fulfilling the American dream, yet lost; accolades to the brim, yet lost. We force ourselves to ignore the reality, lest we grow mad. Instead, we measure the success of our lives based on the level of cluttered activities we have for the day. All the while, we remain lost.

I'm convinced that many today linger in depression because they have no purpose – no destiny. Gifts and skills within lie dormant. Talents remain untapped. Inevitably, our failure to use those talents resonates deep within us—and frustration ensues. We feel empty and don't know why. Life seems meaningless, but the cause eludes us. We feel unfulfilled, yet puzzled.

For some of you, there is a writer inside, waiting to be discovered. For some, a fashion designer, for others an interior decorator, or a master craftsman, a teacher, a manager, a preacher, a Hollywood producer, a songwriter, a musician, an architect, a graphics designer, an owner of your own company doing what you love to do best—all of these and more lie within—literally, you are dying to be let out. God has called you to a specific assignment on the earth—if you are not about the Father's business for your own life, that end is the deepest depression known to mankind.

Inevitably, if we fail to tap into that which lies deep within us, the void will begin to torment us. Whether we realize the cause or not, that internal frustration will produce a constant murmur of depression that cannot be satisfied by anything else. You must seek God's will for your life in order to fill that void and fulfill our destiny.

Even more than depression, the proverb above makes clear that without a vision, death awaits. How do we go about getting out of our depressed meandering through life and discover our purpose?

People on Purpose

Christ, more than any other person, came with purpose. He knew His purpose. He knew not only what He was here for, but also what He was not here for. With focused intensity, Christ lived deliberately, intentionally, and effectively. Thus, throughout the gospels Christ declares, *"I am not come to... or, I am come to...."* We are created in Christ Jesus (see Ephesians 2:10). Therefore, we, too, are created for purpose. We are to live on purpose.

"...the way of man is not in himself: it is not in man that walketh to direct his steps" (Jeremiah 10:23).

In effect, the prophet Jeremiah writes that we can't walk the earth in sandals and travel to distant lands, crossing seas, valleys, and mountaintops and think we'll someday find ourselves. Our purpose is found with our Creator. He created us, so He knows what's inside of us. Therefore, if you're looking outward or inward or anywhere but upward to find yourself, you're looking in the wrong place.

*"Eye has not seen, nor ear heard, nor have entered into the heart of man the things which **God has prepared** for those who love Him. But God has revealed them to us through His Spirit"* (1 Corinthians 2:9-10 emphasis mine).

As the verse suggests, God desires to reveal to us our purpose. However, the Bible also suggests there are reasons why some will never tap into their potential or purpose.

The Talented Tenth

Again it will be like a man going on a journey, who called his servants and entrusted his property to them. To one he gave five talents of money, to another two talents and to another one talent, each according to his ability. Then he went on his journey. The man who had received the five talents went at once and put his money to work and gained five more. So also, the one with the two talents gained two more. But the man who had received the one talent went off, dug a hole in the ground and hid his master's money. After a long time the master of those servants returned and settled accounts with them. The man who had received the five talents brought the other five. "Master," he said, "you entrusted me with five talents. See, I have gained five more." His master replied, "Well done, good and faithful servant! You have been faithful with a few things; I will put you in charge of many things. Come and share your master's happiness!" The man with the two talents also came. "Master," he said, "you entrusted me with two talents; see, I have gained two more." His master replied, "Well done, good and faithful servant! You have been faithful with a few things; I will put you in charge of many things. Come and share your master's happiness!

Then the man who had received the one talent came. "Master," he said, "I knew that you are a hard man, harvesting where you have not sown and gathering where you have not scattered seed. So I was afraid and went out and hid your talent in the ground. See, here is what belongs to you." His master replied, "You wicked, lazy servant! So you knew that I harvest where I have not sown and gather where I have not scattered seed? Well then, you should have put my money on deposit with the bankers, so that when I returned I would have received it back with interest. Take the talent from him and give it to the one who has the ten talents. For everyone who has will be given more, and he will have an abundance. Whoever does not have,

188 | THE DEPRESSED CHRISTIAN

even what he has will be taken from him. And throw that worthless servant outside, into the darkness, where there will be weeping and gnashing of teeth" (Matthew 25:14-30).

Obstacle #1 to a Life on Purpose: Fear

In the parable of the talents cited above, note that the servant who buried his talents tells us exactly why he did so: *"So I was afraid..."* he tells his master. His fear caused him to put his talent in a hole in the ground, rather than out into the world. It's the same reason that I had buried mine. Likely, it is the same reason you've buried yours. Fear.

Fear causes us to doubt ourselves. We doubt whether we're smart enough, capable enough, or talented enough. We doubt we have all the requisite materials to get started. We doubt we have the time, or the energy. Fear causes us to question whether others will accept our talents, or whether they think our plan will work. Fear causes us to doubt whether friends and loved ones will still love us if we try this new thing, this small desire we have within us. That fear paralyzes us. That fear causes us to waver back and forth. That fear causes us to keep those talents and gifts buried deep within us; never offering our gift to the world—or to God.

We go on in our lives, skeptical as to whether these things will work out. We errantly regard the reactions of others to our gifts and this causes us to hesitate. We procrastinate, and soon, like the unfruitful servant, our gift is buried.

Perhaps you, too, have let fear rule your life. I know we covered faith earlier, but it's vital to keep in mind the following: Fear is more than a harmless human emotion—it's also the fodder for buried dreams. We have had faith in God for our salvation and believed that His Son died on a cross and rose again, why can't we believe God to care about our lives and bring our dreams to fruition? We can, we choose not to and that mindset must change.

As we've discussed before, the Bible says that anything not done in faith is sin (see Romans 14:23). We also know that fear is diametrically opposed to faith. Fear is not of God. We know Abraham's faith was counted unto him as righteousness. Our faith is counted unto us as righteousness. If we lack faith in God, we have no righteousness. For this reason the fearful servant was called, "wicked," and the Israelites, "rebellious."

Whereas fear is often masked and misperceived as humility, it's actually—and ultimately—an issue of pride. When we operate in fear we're by nature looking to self to see us through the situation. We look to our own understanding, our own strength (or lack thereof) or our own resources and talents, and when they don't seem to alleviate the situation in front of us, fear follows. Faith, on the other hand, does not look to self, but upward toward our Savior—and there peace, life, and joy ensue.

It's no surprise that in the parable of the talents, the fellow who operated in fear and buried his talents was called "wicked." He was called wicked not for sleeping around, not for cussing out the guy on the freeway, not for erupting in anger at the bank teller—but because he succumbed to his fear and buried his talents. It is time for us to lay aside every excuse and obstacle that hinders us from living life full of purpose and passion.

Have faith in God, and do it!

Obstacle #2 to a Life on Purpose: **Giants in the Sunshine State**

*"His master replied, You wicked, **lazy** servant!"*

Here's the second greatest obstacle to our hearing and answering the call of purpose in our life. You may not like it. You may not like me, but it's true nonetheless. This obstacle is a giant, and if you can slay it—and believe me, you can—walking in your true purpose will be close. This giant is laziness.

On the day that David killed Goliath, he killed his own giant. By doing so, David sparked his very purpose into existence. On that day, he shook hands with destiny—and entered into his chapter of dominion. David's actions turned the tide of the battle, and the rest of the Israelite army routed the Philistines (see 1 Samuel 17). The same is true for you. When you face and slay your giants, victories follow.

There was a time in my life where I thought an extra hour of sleep in the morning, every morning, was the one thing that kept me going. Man, I thought I needed sleep. Then, there were the afternoon naps. Yep, needed those too, or so I thought. I wasn't about to do anything beyond securing the bare necessities for sustaining life. I didn't have time, couldn't fit it into my schedule, wasn't feeling up to it…blah, blah, blah. I was lazy—and it was killing me.

It was one of the sins that so easily beset me (see Hebrews 12:1). It was a part of me that had to be cut off by any means necessary, however drastic, gruesome, or bloody (see Matthew 5:29-30).

I finally became convinced that if I was ever going to know and do God's will, I'd have to hit it hard; seek God earnestly. God had rebuked me—and it hurt.

Soon, I felt compelled to rise up very early in the morning and meet with God. So I did. Every morning I woke up at 4:30, brewed a cup of java, worshipped, read His Word, prayed, and listened. I was studying for the Bar at the time, by any certain time. Nevertheless, I had to get up. No, I didn't have to wake up that early for the sake of my salvation, or to be at a meeting or class. I had to get up that early because I was tired of despair. I wanted to have purpose. I had to for the sake of my soul's need for Him—for answers, direction, and leading. I had to for the sake of accomplishing my purpose.

I could have tried waking up just a few minutes earlier; maybe a half-hour or so. But it was time to get serious. David didn't have to cut off the Philistine's head—but he did!

Looking back, it's unmistakably clear that those early mornings were instrumental in God revealing His purposes for me, the tasks He would require, and the necessary healing and filling He would need to do in my life.

Just as there were collateral victories for Israel after the initial defeat of Goliath, so too were there collateral victories once I beheaded my own giant. My joy, peace, productivity—and my sense of God in my life—all increased. I now live in more happiness than I've ever known possible. Mornings are now my best time of the day. I have greater energy with fewer hours of sleep. God is my strength.

This is not a sermon on sleep, but a personal testimony of the power of beheading that which so easily besets us. Laziness—in our pursuit of God and in pursuit of our God-given dreams—will kill us. It has the power to eat us alive—yet quietly, often with no one else even realizing it. Therefore, it's time to wake up. It is time to ask God for His grace to empower us to slay this giant. Cut off its head. Get aggressive about it. Victory awaits those who are bold!

Make no mistake; there are giants in the land today. Your destiny awaits you on the other side. Your task? Kill your Goliath. Don't be surprised if God gives you a similar challenge. He has done it to countless others since the beginning of time. There are risks to be taken today. There are victories to be won today—to the end that the living God is glorified on the earth. The question is, "Will you partake?"

What other giant might be preventing your reaching your destiny? Is its name Anger? Pride? Lust? Theft? Lying? Bitterness? Self-Reliance? Rebellion? Self-Pity? Rejection? Alcohol? Fornication? What is its name?

If you don't know what it is, spend time with the Lord. Let Him reveal what He wills. Spend time in the Word, and in prayer, and listen to His leading. Obey immediately. Whatever you have to do, whatever God is leading you to do, do it.

Do not be lazy in obedience. Has God asked you to make amends and you haven't? Has He given you an idea and you're sitting on it? Does He want you to forgive? To re-pay? To re-start? To re-build? However small or grand, whatever the Lord has pressed upon you to do, do it.

Again, these decisions should not be borne out of our own thinking, meditations, or ruminations, but should be by the leading of the Holy Spirit. This is what propels us to accomplish God's work here and now. These decisions set us apart as His children. Loving obedience makes us men and women of God, abiding in His house as good and faithful servants. Failure to do so puts at risk our purposes for the Master. Compliance sets our destiny in motion.

Obstacle #3 to a Life on Purpose: Ouch! This may hurt!

I realize I might have been a little rough in the last few sections, so I'll keep this section light. Let's now turn to the third and final obstacle that prevents many from walking in true purpose. It is also found in the parable of the talents. It's what the master called the one who buried his talents: *a wicked, lazy servant*. We've covered lazy, so that only leaves one more adjective: *wicked*. This word describes a person who has not made the Master's business priority number one. The Bible says, *"Seek first the kingdom of God and His righteousness..."* (see Matthew 6:33). The man who buried his talents took the easy way out by hiding the talent and then simply carrying on with the rest of *his* business. The other good and faithful servants prioritized the master's business and, as a result, entered into the "joy of the master." Prioritizing in our life the business of the King (notice I did not say busyness in the Kingdom) is a sure and fast way to unlocking joy within.

Consider your life today: What are you pursuing and why? Who is your Lord (Owner, Ruler and Leader)? Who owns your dreams, desires, relationships, and finances? What is your life priority? Is it *your* life, or is your life submitted and surrendered to the Father? If the Lord is not your Lord in every area, stop now and consider your course and its consequences. Then consider that the best thing you can ever do—the strongest position you can ever attain—is to be submitted under the mighty hand of God, making your life a living sacrifice to the Father's will. Therein lies your true purpose in Christ.

Baby Steps

With that foundation, I'd like to set out some practical applications of finding our purpose. Understanding that the process is long, and at times difficult, I'd like to reduce the process to a few, short, easily stated steps.

A problem many of us have in discovering purpose is that we spend our time thinking about what we want to be at sixty-five. What we fail to realize is that what a person does when he or she is fifty years old is the culmination of forty-nine plus preceding years. To be sure, some people (my brother, for example) have always known how they wanted to spend their life. God bless them, but I'm sure not one of them. The rest of us must recognize that the answer to what exactly we'll be doing at age fifty may not come until our forty-ninth birthday. Yet here we are, trying to figure it out at seventeen.

The key I've discovered to knowing purpose is taking "baby steps." The question is not where do I want to be in fifty years, but five years. Life is a progression; a series of stepping stones. To get us going, the important thing is not to determine what's on the floor above, but to see the next step ahead of you. Plan for that next step and don't worry if you can't see the entire floor plan.

A friend summed up the above by pointing out the following verse: *"The steps of a good man are ordered by the Lord: and He delighteth in his way"* (Psalms 37:23).

He reminded me that God often only gives us the next step, not the whole map. Ask God for the next step, and give it some time before needing to know your life's calling. Ask God to expand your vision. Ask Him for a vision for your own life. Then ask God what He would have you accomplish in one year, not for your entire life. Set a six-month goal. Ask God for a one-year, three-year, or five-year plan. He may just give you one thing to do. Do it. It may just be for that day. Again, do it. After-ward, plan the next step with Him.

Then spend a good chunk of time with God, reading His Word and praying. Seek your direction passionately. Listen to His still, small voice. Now, unencumbered by fear and laziness, listen to what's inside of you. Uncover it.

Stop running, remove your fig leaf and return to God, daily. When you have a word from Him, you'll have life. You'll have something to wake up to each day. You'll love life because life holds your purpose. Even better, God's purpose is exactly what you're best suited for. His direction for you will match all of your interests, talents, wants, and needs. It will make life joyful. Because it's God's plan, it will bless others. Because it's God's plan, it will be a blessing to you.

Quick Plots to Purpose

I've found the following disciplines to be quite useful in finding our flow in life. I think you'll find them helpful too.

Pray hard: Spend time in the Word. Learn how to worship God. Humble yourself. Confess your sins. Fully expect that God will come through. (Fasting never hurts either.)

Inform yourself: Do your homework. Know your strengths and weaknesses. Familiarize yourself with your aptitudes and giftings. Do you thrive while interacting with others? Are you gifted with your hands? Are you an abstract thinker? (Philosophy, teaching.) Do you think three-dimensionally? (Architects, engineers.) Do you work well under a given set of instructions? Do you prefer generating ideas, or implementing them? What are your interests? What excites you? What makes you cry? What do you believe in? What are your passions? What have you enjoyed in the past? Are you drawn to the arts? Sciences? What gives you pleasure? What do you do well naturally? What do you enjoy so much that you'd do it for free? Consult wise counselors. Talk with those who know you best and are worthy of your trust.

Make Decisions: Make hard and fast rules to narrow your path and destiny. Life is not rigid, but you must sift through the chaff. Do you see paths that don't suit you? Cross them out. (Never let fear be a factor in your decision-making process.) Write down those paths that do suit you. Work on your list of likes and dislikes. The more time you spend on step two, the more you can do here. Make commitments to both sides of the ledger. Once you've decided to cross out a possible path, do not return to it. Once you've found areas of interest, investigate further.

Commit to it: Once you have a path, stick to it. Do not let doubt distract you; let nothing veer you from your path. Fear not.

Do it Tirelessly: Work hard at it. Study it. Be the best at what you do. Remember that God will supply the resources for the tasks He gives.

With Dogged Determination, Finish it: Stop at nothing short of completion. Don't give up. Don't give way to discouragement. Push away obstacles. Fight the good fight of faith. Finish the work.

Pray hard (some more): Entrust it to the Lord at all times. Seek Him as the source of your strength. Give Him all the glory. Be filled with the Holy Spirit.

Let us pray together regarding the obstacles of our lives: *"Father, I thank You for the plans that You have for me. I thank You for Your plans to prosper me, for good, and not for evil, for a desirous and excellent outcome. I will wait patiently for You and for Your plan and season. I thank You for the people that You have placed in my life. Help me to love others as myself. Help me learn my place within the body of Christ and to submit to the authority that You have place in my life. Father, I will not forsake the assembly of the believers in my community. I will learn to serve the body of Christ in love. Help me in this Lord, to have Your heart of love, the mind and attitude of Christ Jesus. Thank You for the Counselor. Thank You for your peace and patience. Lord, I will take no steps out of impatience or anxiety nor will I procrastinate due to fear or laziness. Father, I receive the strength of Christ each day and I thank You for giving me a diligent, industrious spirit. Lord, I will no longer allow the fear of man to ensnare my steps. I will not give undue thought, concern or attention to what others think, but will regard what You think more than the thoughts of man. I declare that this day I am free from the bonds of fear and doubt. By faith I receive the Spirit of Christ, of power, of love and a sound mind. I will not lose heart even though life may not have unfolded the way I would have wanted. I will wait upon You and continue to hope in You. I thank You for revealing to me day by day Your purpose for my life. Use me for Your kingdom. Father, make me a good and faithful servant who does a job well done. Father, make me Your humble servant who is faithful in all of your house. In Jesus name. Amen."*

Chapter Thirteen

The Balanced Body
Unlocking the Joy Within

"May God Himself, the God of peace, sanctify you through and through.
*May your whole spirit, soul and **body** be kept blameless*
at the coming of our Lord Jesus Christ.
The one who calls you is faithful and He will do it"
(I Thessalonians 5:23-24).

Lessons from Space

As many of you may know, the construction of the International Space Station is well under way. Did you know that the space station whirls around the earth at approximately 17,500 miles per hour?

At such speeds, the crew members experience "day" and "night" every forty-five minutes. Thus, during the forty-five minutes while on the sun side, the space jockeys experience temperatures well above 100° F and have to use gold visors to shield their eyes from the sun's intensity. Less than an hour later, as they rotate away from the sun, temperatures drop to well below 100°. During this time, the crew must turn on their heater-equipped gloves attached to their heavily insulated space suits to keep from freezing.

— interview with Jim Newman,
May 17, 2001, Fresh Air from WHYY
www.npr.org

What struck me the most about life on the space station was the unique properties of weightlessness. I know when most of us think of the effects of zero gravity we envision Neil Armstrong on that first historic walk on the moon, taking a small floating step which sends him soaring across the television screen. However, the absence of gravity actually plays out in much fuller detail. Example: If per chance one of the crew members had to tighten a bolt they could not simply take a wrench and turn. To do so would spend them spinning endlessly in circles in the opposite direction of the torque used on the bolt. Instead, he or she would need to be harnessed into place by anchoring his or her feet to something immobile, and then turning.

This is necessary because every action in space requires a reaction of equal, opposite force. Thus, even the downward force exerted by a finger typing on a computer would thrust the body flying upwards, unless the person is properly harnessed or, to use proper NASA lingo, they are "captive" to something. Again, without the distorting effects of gravity, elementary laws of physics exist: For every action, a reaction. In essence, it is the law of reaping and sowing.

For the most part, we understand this with respect to spirit and soul, but we are also a body. The early portions of this book have addressed the impact these two dimensions have upon our lives. In this chapter, we will turn to the body and how our treatment of it (action) affects our ability to function in a healthy, happy way (reaction).

Learn from a Lamborghini

I find it interesting the propensity of man to extremes. In the world, many are obsessed with the body (how we look, what we wear, our hair, nails, sun-tanning, laser-removals, lipo-suctions, tummy tucks, botox…). In the body of Christ, many neglect it. We must return to the right balance.

Earlier in Paul's letter to Timothy, we see another example of Paul's understanding of balance. In it, he explains to his young disciple that

"...physical training is of some value, but godliness has value for all things, holding promise for both the present life and the life to come" (1 Timothy 4:8).

Though conceding that godliness is the greater good, Paul nonetheless places some value on the merits of a conditioned body. Some people live as if Paul said that physical training was of absolutely no value. We do so by giving no thought to the foods we consume. We do so by shunning exercise.

Folks, we reap what we sow. If we continually put junk into our bodies, our bodies will respond accordingly. Our body is the most complex machine on the face of the earth. So why wouldn't we put in it optimum fuel for optimal performance?

As Christians we tend must resist the temptation to downsize the importance of a healthy body. Therefore, in light of all the mysteries of the spirit unfolded to Paul, he still concedes that *"physical training is of some value."* No, having "Abs of Steel," is not the all important thing in life, but it may help to prevent future backaches and a few other maladies, including depression!

Think of it this way: Liken the human body to a car. Now, think of a nice one. Consider the Italian thoroughbreds: the Lamborghini, the Ferrari, or the Maserati. Besides price, there is the matter of elegance, power, and craftsmanship. Ah, but there is also the subject of *handling*. The consequence of sound, skilled engineering is the ability to negotiate curves at breakneck speeds, climb hills and, over great spans of time, endure to be classics. Consider also that in the harshest conditions—hail, sleet, wind, snow—the better the condition of the car, the better its ability to handle them.

Did you know that our bodies are no different? The more we fine-tune ourselves—spirit, soul, *and body*—the better we can *handle* life's sure-to-come obstacles along the way. The less we take care of our physical temple, the less we're able to endure in life's harsher conditions.

When you are sleep-deprived and haven't eaten all day how well do you handle stress and stressful people? How prone are you to kindness and gentleness vs. irritation and strife?

For these reasons, while I was studying for the bar exam, my instructor encouraged us to not only spend time in Con Law, Property, Criminal Procedure and the like, but to also spend time in the gym, to eat right, and to rest. She knew that, come examination day, if we were operating on zero sleep, caffeine, and pure lethargy, our scores would plummet, regardless of how much information we had stored in our memory.

A flip through most any supermarket magazine will have an article or two on the merits of physical maintenance and exercise in relation to good ol' fashioned happiness. There are scores of studies that specify the ability of exercise to release endorphins—the feel good compound that gives us a natural "high" at the end of a period of physical exercise. Some of us haven't had a release of endorphins since being made to run around the track in our fifth-grade P.E. clothes—and you wonder why the sour face?

Personally, I started exercising twice a day. It's not because I need to lose weight either, I just love the enjoyment of the high! Our God made us this way. To many, this remains a river untapped towards finding joy in life. It's inside of you and it's time to get it out.

It never ceases to amaze me how much better I feel after a workout than before. No matter how tired I may feel before and how much I dread the thought of going to the gym, I've never once regretted going. It never ceases to lift my spirits. Therefore, no longer depreciate the value of a fine-tuned body and its effect upon your mood and daily outlook. Living a life with balance will aid our durability through the tough situations in life, both spiritual and natural.

OK, some of you are needing a little more scriptural backing for this. Well here you go: *Drink a little wine for thy stomach's sake and thine often infirmities"* (1 Timothy 5:23).

Drink a little wine!

Paul told Timothy to have a glass of wine now and again to ease his stomach sickness. True, Paul had healed the sick oftentimes before. Elsewhere in James we're told to have the elders lay on hands and anoint people. Here, however, Paul prescribes a physical remedy for a physical ailment. "Timothy, your stomach is hurting, so drink a little wine." (Incidentally, the medicinal value of wine has been noted throughout history.)

Funny thing is, Paul didn't lambaste Timothy for a lack of faith. Neither was Timothy suffering from sin. He simply had an upset stomach. Paul didn't tell Timothy to have more faith in God or to put his trust in God for his healing. Sure, those things are necessary; but this time, he says, drink some wine. Note that the great apostle did not give the same prescription for all of life's circumstances.

Our approach to understanding and conquering depression throughout this book has been no different. We feel sorrow for many reasons: Our own doing due to foolish living or sin, God's own doing in leading us through a wilderness season or testing, simply failing to place our wholehearted trust in God.

Simply put, it's the principle of balance as applied to our understanding of the variety and complexity of life. To me, that's the beauty of Paul's balance—neither too far to the left nor the right. That's the blessing of the gospel of Christ—purely balanced.

Accordingly, if you need to take medications, at this season in your life, don't condemn yourself or feel ashamed. Take them. See a Christian counselor. Yes, pray for healing; but if you need medication at this junction on your journey, then you may need medication. Don't let pride or religion keep you from living. Paul prescribed to Timothy a physical remedy, not a faith remedy, so why shouldn't you apply the same? You'd go to a doctor if you broke your leg, wouldn't you? In the same way, if you have a mental illness, it may be time to receive medical assistance. *Drink a little wine....* Just don't forsake the spiritual remedies first!

Regarding Balance-san

In my first year in law school everyone, I mean everyone, put in four to six or more hours of study, daily. It was a must. Stress was high and grades were low, even for the former collegiate all-stars. So one day when I asked my study partner why she wasn't in class, she simply told me that she was taking a "personal day." Well, immediately I asked for clarification, because I had never heard of such a day. Mother's Day, Labor Day, Secretary's Day yes, but "personal day?" No way Jose!

She simply replied that she needed to take a day off. No classes, no studying, no reading, nothing. Just plain old relaxation. "Are you mad?" I thought. She hadn't talked to her professors, the dean—no one for permission. It was just something she needed to take care of herself—to help her excel better in the long run, in the big picture.

At another time, in another year of law school, my wise study partner made a cool, powerful, and pointed observation of me. "Carmen," she said. "You take life too seriously."

"What do you mean I take life too seriously?" I mean, if there's a heaven and a hell, you gotta take life seriously, right?

Well, as I've come to realize, she was right. There is a danger in taking life too seriously. And if I were a betting man, I'd venture a bet that you're taking life too seriously as well. So this chapter is to help you not take yourself so seriously. Relax a bit. Take a breath. Feel God's breeze of *grace* upon you. Remember, it's grace, so you don't deserve it. So don't worry that you haven't earned it. And it's grace, so Gods favor is upon you. So learn how to bask in that each day, throughout the day. Then give it away. Yes, grace, give it away. Give it to others. Give it to yourself. Breathe it in, and breathe it out.

Okay, I know, I know, I'm getting too out there for some of you. Some of you want to see a Scripture—and quick. Well, here you go:

"Do not be overrighteous neither be overwise - why destroy yourself? Do not be overwicked, and do not be a fool—why die before your time?" (Matthew 25:30).

"It is good to grasp the one and not let go of the other. The man who fears God will avoid all extremes" (Ecclesiastes 7:15-18).

My friend, did you know that God created life so that we might enjoy it? Did you also know that Christ, during His stint on earth, also enjoyed it? Did you know that God—even in the midst of the craziness and mayhem going on around the world—is happy? God is waiting for many of you to start enjoying the life He has given you. Start by not taking yourself so seriously. Quit thinking that it's all about you. Not every one in the office is talking about you. Get over it. Even if they are talking about you, get over it. Take a deep breath and slowly let it out. Live life that way. Inhale the good. Exhale the bad. Enjoy the beauty of creation, of His creatures. Enjoy the uniqueness (and silliness) of the persons and personalities He's put on the earth.

Take time off. Take a Sabbath, once a week, and rest. Rest your body. Eat a nice meal. Swim in the ocean (yes, a recreational pool will do). Make a fool of yourself. Laugh. Discover the health and happiness of exercise. Start going to the gym. Stop putting garbage (foods with ingredients you can't pronounce) into your body. Eat the good of the land (stuff that's been around for a thousand or more years like fruits, vegetables, whole grains and fresh meats). Read the paper. Be informed. Laugh with a child. Visit the sick — and don't take yourself so seriously!

Abs of Steel

"Physical training is of some value..." (1 Timothy 4:8a).

The law of sowing and reaping really boils down to understanding that your life is no longer in the hands of destiny, but destiny is in your hands. What do you want to be known for years down the road? Whatever it is, start putting it into motion, today and every day after. Do you want a strong, in-shape body? Then sow for it. Cut back on processed foods. Eat healthy, daily. Drink water or 100% juices instead of sodas. Exercise. And when you don't feel like it, do it anyway.

In the same way that—throughout the earlier chapters of this book—we've been learning how to exercise our spirit and soul, add to it the exercise of your physical body. These things are the ingredients for a healthy body, mind and soul – a well rounded individual, with joy and purpose in life.

Do you want rippling muscles? Exert your muscles daily. Hit the bench press, the leg press, and the curl bar routinely, eat gobs of protein, and you will see results, no matter your current, scrawny size. Although anything impossible is possible with God, anything is possible with discipline plus time.

Do you want to lose weight? First examine your emotions—the health of your (unseen) heart. Get healing there. Then, eat less and exercise. There are no magic pills for this, just plain diligence and determination, faith that it will happen and discipline to do it. And, when you don't feel you have what it takes to accomplish your goal, what do you do? Yes, remember that in our weakness, He is made strong and ask God to fill every "hole" within and give you the strength to have the discipline to obtain the victory. The Holy Spirit will guide you. God promises to direct our path. He promises us the desires of our hearts to those who diligently seek Him.

"He that is slow to anger is better than the mighty; and he that ruleth his spirit than he that taketh a city" (Proverbs 16:32).

Mediocrity No More

"In all labour there is profit: but the talk of the lips tendeth only to penury" (Proverbs 14:23).

If you want to see positive gains in your life, you must be willing to do the work. The application of reaping and sowing, of hard work, applies to all areas of life. The word, "profit" (above) suggests superiority and preeminence. Labor suggests doing the work. The point? If you want to come out ahead, if you want to reap greatness in "all" things, you must be willing to work hard. We are to be diligent. We are to pursue. We are to put on. We are to cast off. We are to be doers and not hearers only. All of these things require action on our part. If you're willing to make difficult choices, to work at it even when you don't feel like it and it doesn't feel good, you'll be better for it.

Be it eating habits, exercise routines, academic study, or occupation, even in the working out of our salvation with fear and trembling, it is all labor. In *all labor, there is profit*. The proverbs tell us that talk is cheap and adds no return. That is why the ones who labor will advance in life and become future leaders, teachers, evangelists, business owners and the like — because labor requires difficult choices. When God knows we can be trusted to make the difficult choices to work out our salvation and make the sacrifices necessary to learn and grow, He can trust us with more. The commoner would rather sit on his butt, sleep, or watch television. Easy choices come easily. That is the state of many. Then, there are those who will labor, not just in body, but in matters of the spirit and soul. Will we answer the call?

"For bodily exercise profiteth little: but godliness is profitable unto all things, having promise of the life that now is, and of that which is to come" (1 Timothy 4:8).

Although Paul reminds us of the value of physical fitness, he, nevertheless, admonishes the recognition of proper priorities. Godliness is better. The benefits of a healthy spirit and soul far outweigh the benefits of a healthy body. So should be our understanding and our priority. It should be reflected in our daily routine. Further, because Paul knew that what one sows, one also reaps, he adds that a godly life is desired not just to ensure our future, but also to keep our present.

So the operative question here for you, as you read this book, is, what do you want? Do you want to be a person of prayer? Then spend time, lots of time, daily, in prayer. You won't become a prayer warrior by osmosis. It will take sacrifice. What do you have to lose? Sleep? (See Luke 9:32.)

Do you want to be a godly person, known for your faith in God. Do you want to be listed, in Heaven, among those in Hebrews 11? Then spend a quantity of quality time with God each day. This response to God's call on your life will require obedience and surrender. Consider the alternative: mediocrity.

> *"There are those who dream of worth accomplishments while others stay awake and accomplish them."*
> –from a billboard off the 710 freeway in Los Angeles

I've grown tired of living the mediocre life. I want joy and prosperity. I want to accomplish what my Creator created me to do. I want to profit. I'm tired of spiritual poverty. I'm sick of feeling poor and destitute in my soul (my heart and my mind). I'm tired of just talking about it. I want my spirit-man to thrive. I want my soul awake, in all of its fullness. I want to live on purpose.

To do that will require difficult choices. Easy choices make for a poor, mediocre, and boring life. It's a whole lot easier to watch movies than to read a book—or write a book! It's easier to listen to the radio than bow and worship in praise to God. It's easier to sleep than seek God. It's easier to feed our faces than fast. It's easier to watch the game than to work on making our dreams a reality. Let me tell you, an easy life never makes great gains.

You get what you invest. Remember, you reap what you sow. Living for God, over time, will produce a life that is beyond your present comprehension. By His Spirit, it is possible.

Good News for the Spirit of Heaviness!

That said, let me say this in conclusion, especially to those struggling with their weight. When Christ came onto the scene he quoted the first part of Isaiah 61, stating:

The Spirit of the Lord [is] upon Me, because He has anointed Me [the Anointed One, the Messiah] to preach the good news (the Gospel) to the poor; He has sent Me to announce release to the captives and recovery of sight to the blind, to send forth as delivered those who are oppressed [who are downtrodden, bruised, crushed, and broken down by calamity],

To proclaim the accepted and acceptable year of the Lord [the day when salvation and the free favors of God profusely abound.

Then He rolled up the book and gave it back to the attendant and sat down; and the eyes of all in the synagogue were gazing [attentively] at Him.

And He began to speak to them: Today this Scripture has been ful-filled while you are present and hearing (Luke 4:18-21, Amplified).

Isaiah 61 continues where Jesus left off, further delineating the benefits of the Anointing. In verse three, it states that the Anointed One also comes to *"appoint unto them...the garment of praise for the spirit of heaviness."* Would you take another look at those words, the spirit of heaviness. We know that the inner man is greater than the outward man, i.e., our soul is greater (wields more influence) than our body. Likewise, our spirit is greater than our soul. (We will discuss this in greater detail in the next chapter.) Accordingly, I believe that many of those who suffer from heaviness in their physical body are first and foremost suffering from a heaviness in their spirit. In essence, the spirit of heaviness upon that person has come to manifest in an actual physical heaviness. Here's one way I believe this occurs.

Remember in school, probably biology class, when you learned about our bodies fight or flight response system? If not, here's a brief recap. Let's say you were hiking and came across a bed of snakes. Sensing the danger, our body would release chemicals like adrenaline to give us an extra, quick surge of energy to be able to handle the imminent crisis – to be able to fight or flee. (I'm going to suggest the latter.) In this mode, our blood and heart rate changes as well as a number of other physiological adjustments. Our body has entered "attack" mode, so our senses are heightened, and we begin to see more and more through the lens of danger or possible threats. After the danger has subsided, the body returns to its normal state. In this mode our bodies would crave certain foods that would give them "quick energy" like simple carbohydrates.

However, today, most people's stress is not due to a bout with wild predators or physical dangers, but from stress related to jobs, finances, family and the like. It's not a one time crisis but a continuous, day in and day out running episode. Now do you see the problem? Our body never returns to its normal state. The fight or flight response switch remains perpetually on! Therefore, the release of these chemicals continue flooding in from this unending build up of stress. As a result, we remain extra-sensitive, in attack mode, and our bodies become over-loaded, taking its toll in the form of road rage, irritability, chronic fatigue, headaches, high blood pressure, digestive problems, immune system breakdowns and the list goes on. Furthermore, our bodies continue craving foods needed for fight or flight, i.e., junk food.

This is what happens when stress occurs. The spirit of heaviness operates in similar fashion, adding with it sorrow and condemnation. Many of you today are walking around feeling condemned and ashamed about your weight. Every time you eat, you feel condemned. With every look in the mirror, each and every time you shop for a new outfit, with every look at a slender waistline, condemnation meets you.

Dear sir or ma'am, today is the day that Christ wants you to end your condemnation forever. You are not under condemnation any longer. Christ has not only forgiven you, but He has freed you as well. Let God's grace freely given to you in Christ cause you to rejoice into thanksgiving. Let His grace elevate you to an attitude of trust. Let that trust rise to praise. Christ has given to you the garment of praise for you to clothe yourself so that you can take off the spirit of heaviness. So take it off. Throw it away. Give praise to Jesus for liberating you from ALL condemnation and shame, no matter what it is, for there is nothing too big that the blood of Jesus has not already washed! Receive it today and each day. There is *now no* condemnation in Christ Jesus. My friend, let that spirit of praise enter into every area in which you may feel condemned. Let that praise enter into every thought you have regarding your weight, your looks, even your finances and family—everything that may cause you worry, stress, anxiety or guilt. Let praise in Christ's work and death for you replace ALL heaviness. Let the praises of your righteousness in Christ lift every burden. Beloved, as you continue in this attitude, your atmosphere will change around you and inside of you. Your body will return to peace, for He is your Peace. By faith, enjoy now the riches of your inheritance in Christ. Enjoy Christ. Feed on Him and drink from the Eternal River of Life. Jesus is faithful!

Say this prayer with me: *"Father, I thank You so much for giving me this most precious gift of life. I thank You Lord for a mind and heart to know You, and for a body to serve You and my fellow man. Father, I admit I have been a pretty poor steward of the body You have given me. Father, I call upon Your Name and rely upon You and Your Spirit, by the grace in Christ Jesus, to give me self-discipline in the quantity and quality of all that I put into my body, Your temple. Father, I will treat my body with respect and not allow others to disrespect my body through impurity. I renounce the spirit of gluttony and lasciviousness. Father, I choose You, not food, to be my Comforter. Father, I call upon Your Name to help me eat all of my meals with Godly wisdom and discipline. Lord, help me live my life with Godly balance. I choose to guard what I allow to enter into my temple including the music that I listen to and the television, movies that I watch. Father, I thank You for self-discipline this day and Your Spirit of Wisdom in every choice I make. Thank you that I am not condemned, but rather righteous in Christ Jesus. May You be glorified in my life this day. Thank You for life today, Father. I bless Your Name. I ask all of this in the Name of Your Son Jesus Christ. Amen."*

Chapter Fourteen
Christianity 101:
It's Not What You Think

Personality Tests?

I used to love personality tests, and I've taken a lot. You know the ones I'm talking about, you answer a few painless questions and flip to the back of the book, usually it's Appendix B or C, and they tell you who you are, who you should marry and what you should do for the rest of your life. Admittedly, the initial fun isn't so much the joy of learning about yourself but the new-found pleasure of labeling everyone else. So now you introduce your boss as Mr. Type A, Anal Retentive Choleric (outside his presence of course), your sister as Susie "the self spotlight" Sanguine (most assuredly within her presence), your boyfriend for-the-last-six-years-and-counting is, unfortunately for you, the ever-slow-moving and ever-so-cautious-but-kind "Phlegmatic," and, last but not least, the Gloomy and Moody "Melancholy" remains you, at least for now.

The thin-skinned may want to stick to those other tests that make you feel slightly less odious. In those tests, you wind up either a lion, otter, golden retriever, or beaver—or any one of the possible combinations in between.

Upon taking one such test in a coffee shop in Westwood, California, I distinctly remember a spark of joy after simply discovering that there were other people out there who process life similar to the way I do, equally as crazy (and confused?). Better yet, I had an out, "It's not me, Mom, it's the golden retriever within." I was ecstatic. I was not alone. If not delivered I at least felt in good company.

Unfortunately, the joy dissipated as I sipped the last of my venti, non-fat, no-whip, extra-hot, triple-shot, soy-caramel macchiato. To my horror, of all the possible personality permutations, I possessed the worst possible combination of them all: the phlegmatic/melancholy.

For those who don't know what I'm talking about or care one bit for psychology, you must understand that all of those blessed tests contain the same boilerplate, feel-good language: "Every personality is unique, special and important, all possessing equivalent portions of both strengths and weaknesses...blah, blah, blah, blah." Well, Mama didn't raise no fool. I could tell by the writing. The very font belied the truth of stock assessments and generic words for the beguiled onlooker. Indeed, I alone, the phlegmatic/melancholy, had the lion's share of the weaknesses. No, this had nothing to do with my pessimistic tendencies. If you don't believe me? You do the math.

Not only was I despondent by my very nature (thanks to Mr. Melancholy), but if I ever did want to change, I'd instinctively go about it in the slowest possible manner—due to Sir Phlegmatic. Sure, they told me my strengths drew heavily in the creative fields, but who in their right mind *wants* to be a struggling, starving artist. That is not a strength, that is retribution. Give me a real personality, a real job, 9-5, a real life any day of the week. At least, that's what my dear ol' Grandmother's been waiting for.

Back to Basics

If anyone thirsts, let him come to Me and drink. He who believes in Me, as the Scripture has said, out of his heart (belly) will flow rivers of living water. But this He spoke of the concerning the Spirit, whom those believing in Him would receive; for the Holy Spirit was not yet given, because Jesus was not yet glorified (John 7:38).

Therefore do not let your good be spoken of as evil; for the kingdom of God is not eating and drinking, but righteousness and peace and joy in the Holy Spirit (Romans 14:17).

To walk in genuine, consistent joy and peace, there are certain "must haves"—and "must nots." To be sure, to avoid depression we mustn't care too much about what others think of us. Jesus certainly didn't (see Mark 12:14). We must trust steadfastly in our God, not in self or circumstance. We must not walk under the law; we must be healed from hurts; we must resist the enemy, and walk in purpose and balance, with patient hope.

However, there is one necessary ingredient—one glue, if you will—that makes all the above (and more) possible. I'm speaking of the Holy Spirit.

As I continued to search through Scriptures I realized that personality wasn't the issue. Yet, it bothered me to come across passages such as, *"Be led by the Spirit,* or *walk by the Spirit."* What was I to make of a passage like this: *"The Kingdom is not a matter of eating or drinking but of righteousness, peace and joy in the Holy Ghost"* (Romans 14:17).

These and similar passages bothered me because in the churches where I grew up the Holy Spirit was like the "untouchables" in a Christian caste system. We subscribed to a "Don't ask, don't tell" code of doctrine.

So growing up it always seemed odd that the Holy Spirit was a full *one-third of the whole Trinity, a full 33.3 percent of the whole God-thing—one out of three pieces of the entire enchilada*—yet I hadn't a clue as to who or what He was.

I figured that must not be a good thing—I mean, He's got to be at least kind of important, right? It's not like God Himself is going to have unnecessary parts like a tonsil or something. Yet, honestly speaking, even after being a Christian for years and years, I wouldn't have been able to recognize the Holy Spirit if He were to have slapped me in the face. With regard to His purpose, His presence, and His power, I did not have the faintest notion (which meant, incidentally, that I failed to experience His presence, His power, and *my* purpose).

I mean, Christ said we should be *glad* that He is leaving us so that we could have the Holy Spirit. It is odd that most of us act like Christ never left and that the Holy Spirit was never sent? Isn't this the One whom Christ said to stay and wait for, to not go anywhere, until you are empowered by Him? Christ said don't teach, don't preach, don't make disciples or converts—essentially, don't do a single thing — without the Holy Spirit's power emanating through you.

Later, in my pursuit of God, I came across Scriptures that said, *"Be led by the Spirit,"* or *"walk by the Spirit."* I read that the, *"The Kingdom is not a matter of eating or drinking but of righteousness, peace and joy in the Holy Ghost."*

Though it took a while, it became clear to me that the Holy Spirit (God Himself) was actually the "key" to living a successful Christian life. Because Christ is currently seated next to the Father, the Holy Spirit is actually the One who is here now to help us. He is our teacher who will lead us into all truth (see John 16:13). He is the One who gives us power to overcome, understanding into the hidden things, direction, knowledge, and comfort. How crafty the enemy is to bring the body's greatest division over the body's greatest force and source of strength and power.

I once heard a minister state that most Christians live out their Christianity (unfortunately, and in opposition to Scripture) from their souls and not from their spirit. Can you get a revelation of that for your own life and evaluate its truth? How much of your Christianity is lived out from your own thoughts and feelings and comprehension of God's Word, the world, and yourself? Yet, the Bible says to not lean on your own understanding. Am I living according to what I think or feel Jesus would do? If so, I am living from my soul. The soul is the limitations of our own mind.

Remember we spoke about how we are also spiritual beings. We have been created in the image of God, with a body, soul and spirit – a sort of trinity in ourselves.

As Christians, we should no longer be soul living, but, instead, we should be spirit living. Failure to do so eliminates our ability to walk in the fullness of the joy of the Lord, as well as it hinders our Lord's ability to rejoice in us.

I remember several years ago, when talking with a mentor regarding ministry, I was told that I needed get out of the way—to get my mind out of the way—and simply jump into the river.

Do you know that I hadn't the foggiest idea to what she was saying? I had been a Christian for more than twenty years and I didn't understand the basics of my own Christianity. Did not Christ say that, "*...out of His belly shall flow rivers...?*"

Funny how so many Christians ignore the plain writings and clear weight of the Word with respect to the Holy Spirit and gravitate instead toward their own thoughts, traditions, and fault-finding techniques. The flesh rages against the Spirit. Yet how long will God strive with man?

We are to be walking in another dimension—in the kingdom of God. Within this realm, there are provisions, guidance, and guarantees of right-eousness, peace, and joy. However, they are found as we walk in the Holy Spirit, as we, like Christ, die to self, bury the old man, and become resurrected with Christ by the same Spirit. That resurrected life is our new man, led by the Spirit, not our own self or our own thoughts.

An older, wiser, beloved brother in our congregation always asks me, "So what's the Lord speaking to you about?" He understands that the Lord is always speaking. That is not the problem. The issue is whether we continually put ourselves in a position of always listening—and obeying. The Lord is pouring out the River of Life, but if you are not a vessel set in position to receive that anointing – even by a few inches – you miss out on this power to transform and change the essence of your living. Compromise, lack of repentance and surrender and also lack of belief in the power of the Holy Spirit will keep you from this perfect posi-tion. We need not retreat to the mountains nor the oceans to hear from God, for He is always speaking.

> *"Why are so many Christians still thirsty? Why do they have to go back to get more water after drinking from the well? Because they are drinking from the wrong well. As long as our eyes are on the waters of this world, we will thirst again. The world could offer all that it had to Jesus, but He would neither enjoy it nor accept its offer. He refused to drink even a drop of the water of this world. Thus, He was fully satisfied."*
>
> --*Watchman Nee* "Secrets to Spirituality" (Whitaker House), *Pg 95*

The Holy Spirit is a person. Get to know Him. His greatest desire is to be with you (see James 4:5). Christ has given us life. By His Spirit we are enabled to live. Apart from Him we can do nothing.

> *"Every believer ought to know there are four things to be done attentively before God each morning: commun-ion, praise, Bible reading, and prayer. If one neglects any of these four, the day will declare it."*
>
> *A well-known pianist once remarked, 'If I do not prac-tice for one day, I notice something wrong. If I do not practice for two days, my wife notices something wrong. And if I do not practice for three days, the whole world notices something wrong.' How many Christians there are who wonder why the performance of their spiritual life is not worthy to be manifested before others, yet they are not willing to spend time with the Lord daily!*
>
> --*Watchman Nee*, "Secrets to Spirituality" (Whitaker House), *pg 102*

Learn to tap into the River. Let the Holy Spirit minister to you, comfort you, bring you peace, encouragement, direction, life, and power. That is His job and He does it well. If only we would let him. If only we would let go. From creation, when the Holy Spirit hovered over the face of the deep, waiting for the Word of God so that He could go to work, He waits for you to tap into the Word of God and speak the Word of God over your own life and trust that the Holy Spirit will bring it about.

Lean on the Holy Spirit. Rely on Him. Abandon self-sufficiency and with your spirit-man—not your mind—by faith—not by feelings—cleave to the Spirit of God within you. He is your source, your River of Life, your path alone to pure and lasting joy.

"Beloved, I pray that you may prosper in all things and be in health, just as your soul prospers" (3 John 2).

We're told that this Ghost Most Holy is the One who would Counsel us, lead us into all truth, Comfort us, quicken us, strengthen us, fill us, encourage us, give us joy, righteousness and peace—and yet He remains most wholly ignored!

How tragic.

How tragic our Christian lives are and will remain without Him.

The Bible states *"...the Spirit gives life"* (see 2 Corinthians 3:6). Yes, my friend, the essence of real living can be found nowhere else. It cannot be found in reliance on our own intellect (see Proverbs 3:5, 6), our emotions, or even our fleshly works, no matter how kind, noble, or moral. Imagine, in the face of Almighty God, considering ourselves to be wise. No wonder the Word says that if we think this way, we become utter and complete fools.

Our purpose, which gives life, is doing the work of the Father, who is Spirit. We will discover the work that the Father has for us to do on this earth by spirit-to-Spirit communion.

Sadly, many Christians are living as I did—not being able to locate my spirit, let alone understanding the leading of the Holy Spirit.

Did not Christ come to restore us to have continual communion with our Creator? Wasn't it Jesus' own prayer that we'd be One with the Father as He and God are One. That means that we have the Holy Spirit within us, just as Jesus did while He was here doing the work of the Father.

Sure, prayers are offered up to God, the Bible is read, hymns are sung, but communion and fellowship with the Father? Daily walking with the LORD in the garden in the cool of the day? These are the essentials of the Christian walk, and they are done through our spirit, with God's Spirit. If we do not acknowledge the Holy Spirit, He also cannot do the work of getting us out of depression because He is the One who reveals light to us, and reminds us of our righteousness in Christ.

The Holy Spirit is the One who brings ALL to repentance.

Yet, lest you feel we have strayed from our conversation of depression, consider still-

"Now may the God of peace Himself sanctify you completely; and may your whole spirit, soul, and body be preserved blameless at the coming of our Lord Jesus Christ" (1 Thessalonians 5:23).

First Things First

As the verse above alludes, man is spirit, soul, and body—in that order. Yet in dealing with depression, many, including those within Christian circles, would start by addressing either the body—proper firing of the neurotransmitters, trials of various SSRI's, examination of exercise, nutrition and the like, or the soul—negative emotions, unforgiveness, positive thinking, etc. However, actually we are first and foremost, spiritual beings. This is where we shall truly begin in our journey toward overcoming depression. Since our spirit is our predominant—and also most powerful and influential —essence, we would be wise to begin here and lay a proper foundation. To focus elsewhere, and lend too great attention to our secondary and tertiary elements would, even if temporal "happiness" is momentarily captured, result in a life incomplete, unfulfilled, and wholly bereft of true success—spiritual or otherwise.

Keys to Overcoming

"And they overcame him by the blood of the Lamb, and by the word of their testimony; and they loved not their lives unto the death. There-fore, rejoice..." (Revelation 12:11-12a).

I would like to continue to examine what I believe to be one of the greatest dangers affecting the world and the church today. It is the greatest hindrance of most Christians and, I believe, God's greatest obstacle toward implementing His Kingdom and His will. Incidentally, it also happens to be the greatest influencer of depression. In fact, it is depression's epicenter. It is a seldom-talked-about reality that you and I must be willing to face if we are to advance as Christians. It is one I pray you will not dismiss or gloss over until you have fully allowed the Lord to shed the truth of His light within you. Before we continue, we need a quick review and to explain some terminology.

We, the Temple

In the book of Beginning, we're told that in creating man, "...the LORD God formed man of the dust of the ground, and breathed into his nostrils the breath of life; and man became a living being [soul]" (Genesis 2:7). Three elements are revealed here – once again, in the image of God – our human trinity: the forming of the dust of the ground, the breath of life, and a living being. When the spirit (the breath of life) touched the body (formed from the dust of the ground) a living being or soul was created. Our life—who we are, our personality, likes, dislikes, that which makes us who we are—is our soul – this is our uniqueness, our "self." Yet, we also have a body and a spirit. That's why in 1 Thessalonians 5:23 Paul exhorts the brethren with the following statement: *"Now may the God of peace Himself sanctify you completely; and may your whole spirit, soul, and body be preserved blameless at the coming of our Lord Jesus Christ."* It is important to notice the order as well as the distinctions. Our spirit—which is first, and takes precedence over all other parts—is different from the soul, which is also different from the body.

Our body makes us conscious of the world through our senses: touch, feel, taste, sound, sight. Our soul makes us conscious of our self—our thoughts, will, and emotions. Our spirit makes us conscious of God. It is our spirit that has fellowship and communicates with Spirit (with God). Therefore, we know that man is made of three distinct parts, a tripartite being – our own trinity in the likeness of our Maker, as the Word says.

Another brilliant example given to us in the Old Testament is the intentional and God-planned, layout of the tabernacle of God—the residing place of the LORD God, Most High. In the temple, there was an outer court, which was open for all to see; next there was a Holy Place, which was where most of the priestly activity took place. Finally, there was the Holy of Holies. This was the true source of the direction of the entire temple, even though the majority of the activities took place elsewhere. This is where God resided, behind the curtain, in the depths of the temple, in the dark place, but this was the place of absolute power, decision making and direction for all of Israel – God's chosen people.

As believers, we become God's temple. We, by adoption, have become the seed of Abraham, the chosen people of God. We have a body that is available for all to see. We have a soul, which is the place of great activity—our thought life, our emotions, our will to do or not do, to choose, to accept or reject, etc. Yet in the deepest place of our being, in the place where there is no human light, the place where it takes the greatest of faith to locate within our own being, remains our spirit. All of which, God has created in us. As in the days of Israel's Tabernacle, this spiritual habitation is the place from where God directs. This is for us, as individuals, and for all of us as we become One in Him in the congregation. That is why it is so detrimental to the Body of Christ to disregard the power and facets of the Holy Spirit in our churches.

Our spirit is the mediator of the two worlds: that of the temporal and that of the eternal; that of the natural and that of the supernatural. Mediums, witches, warlocks, and the like exercise their spirits, but they do so to commune with fallen spirits of death and destruction. Be advised, there is truth to their dealings, but it is always for the darkness and toward fleshly and selfish ambition. The enemy always deals in partial truth. Do not forget the Garden of Eden and the simple eating of the "good" fruit. The enemy appeals to what looks good to the eye and what seems to be true. It is why there will be such a grand and complete deception in the end times. Be assured also that their end will be death and destruction unless they turn away from these practices and to Christ. As believers in Jesus Christ and the Holy Spirit, which He promised to send and did so at Pentecost, our spirit is to be properly set to commune with the Holy One. (That is why Paul explains the need for even our spirits to be preserved and blameless.)

The soul can influence and affect the lower order of the body. Our thoughts direct our bodily actions. Sadness (emotions, soul) can produce a teardrop (physical, body). In like manner, spirit can influence the lower orders, since it is at the top of the list. Therefore, the anointing of God (Spirit) can heal a broken heart (soul). The apostles laid hands (a spiritual exercise) and physical healings occurred in the body. Accordingly, this is life in the Spirit. That is why it is imperative to live in the Spirit to commune with God, spirit to Spirit. Yet, what overwhelming sorrow the Person of the Holy Spirit must feel as He is neglected day in and day out. How often do we ignore Him? How frequently do we instead seek help from the lower orders of our life – our soul and flesh? We seek to improve our bodies, comfort our hearts, bring calm to our minds—and yet our spirit-man, remains untouched! Beloved, this must not be. Therein lies the problem of our "spiritual" life. Therein lies the thirst that you cannot quench and the reason why. We must understand, before we became Christians, our primary existence was powered by our soul. We did what *we thought* was best, or whatsoever thing *we willed* to do. We *felt* a certain way, so *we acted* a certain way. We *liked* and *disliked, loved* and *hated,* all from our soul life, from our self. If we didn't act according to our soul, we followed our flesh and its carnal desires. Our spirit was dead before Christ, so our flesh—our body and soul—governed us.

Many Christians are deceived into thinking they are living a spiritual life, when in truth they have had little spirit-to–Spirit communion because their soul (the self) can "seem" to do a great many spiritual activities. With our mind, we study the Scriptures and tell others about God. With our emotions, we worship God in song and adoration. We can provide food and shelter to the hungry, bring comfort to the hurting, and other good works—even spiritual works—in the natural (our flesh). That is why even non-Christians, without a re-birth, can do many great works of love and those "random acts of kindness." What the Holy Spirit must bring to light for all of us is that we are not called to do the natural. We are called to that which is spiritual. Natural is temporal; spiritual is eternal. Holy Spirit-inspired works will bring eternal fruit. Natural works will have temporal results. That which is done in the natural exalts itself. Yet Scripture tells us that no flesh shall glory in His presence. All that is done in vain will be like chaff and will burn up in the time of judgment. Where our hearts are in surrender to the Holy Spirit, will be the true result of our works. This is our attitude and our true place of worship.

The problem with doing *anything* from the soul is that the soul has its root in independence. Self, not God, is at the center. Self, not the risen One, is the source of strength. A preacher might prepare a lesson for hours and days, studying, reading, and researching, yet never seeking desperately the wisdom and words from Father to see what He would have him say to the people. That is why a great many church activities are done, and many of them appearing quite successful, yet there has been no seeking the face of God. There has been no prayer in the matter—only good ideas and sincere, heartfelt compassion. Yes, even our righteousness is as filthy rags. Even the good we do, if its source is not from God, is no good at all. For no flesh shall glory in His presence.

Again, at the seat of living from one's soul, even in the greatest of "Christian activities," is self. Self-centeredness and independence are at the root. The foundation of utter and total dependence upon God is lacking.

Too many of us view being a soulish or carnal Christian as one who is still given over to the negative aspects of the flesh: fornication, lies, immorality, stealing, etc. Yet a carnal Christian is also one who is still working through the flesh (self), even in doing good works. Doing good, however good it is, if its source is self, is still not spiritual. That which is spiritual is that which has God as its source.

Why are we talking about such matters in a book on depression? The Bible states that life is in the Spirit. Therefore, we must know what is and what is not of the Spirit to have the real life that God offers us. The great deception and the greatest hindrance to true, and everlasting happiness, is to believe that happiness itself is the goal—the end all and be all. Our happiness is not the answer to life. The answer to life, the goal we should all be striving for, is accomplishing God's work—His will being done, for His kingdom to come upon this earth. His Kingdom is a spiritual kingdom. He reveals His will to us in the spirit realm. We must learn to go there, to be governed there—no longer believing *our own* thoughts concerning God and the works of God or *our own* emotions, or anything else that emanates from our self can please God, for flesh gives birth to flesh, and spirit gives birth to spirit.

Soul Check

Practically speaking, here is how living from our soul plays out. These are common aspects of believers who live soulishly:

- ✸ *Self-righteous:* Holding tenaciously to their own minute opinions.
- ✸ *Easily moved:* One moment extremely excited and happy, on another occasion despondent and sad.
- ✸ *Overly-sensitive:* Difficult to live with because they interpret every move around them as aimed at them.

✳ *Critical:* Condemn others but do not correct themselves. When learning new truths, such as those concerned here, they set about discerning and dissecting the soulish thoughts and acts not in their own lives but in those of others. The acquisition of knowledge has merely propelled them to judge someone else and not to help themselves.

✳ *Proud:* This is because they make self the center. These people feel greatly hurt if they are laid aside either in work or in the judgment of others. They cannot bear to be misunderstood or criticized because they—unlike their more spiritual brethren —still have not learned to accept gladly God's orderings.

✳ *First in works:* They are most active, zealous, and willing. But they do not labor because they have received God's order; they labor instead because they have zeal and capacity so to do. They believe doing God's work is good enough; they are unaware that only "righteous" work is that done in obedience to God's *appointment.* These individuals have neither the heart to trust nor the time to wait. They never sincerely seek God's will. On the contrary, they labor according to their ideas, as their mind teems with schemes and plans.

✳ *Dictated by feelings:* They take to work only when they feel up to it.

✳ *Unable to maintain calm in their spirits:* Outer confusion causes inner unrest.

✳ *Easily Discouraged:* They lack the quiet confidence that trusts God for His work.

✳ *Lacking in farsightedness:* They can see only what is immediately ahead. Momentary victory begets them joy, while temporary defeat renders them sad. They have not discovered how to see on to the end of a matter through the eyes of faith.

✳ *Experts at finding fault:* Quick to criticize and slow to forgive.

❋ *Hasty:* They cannot wait on God. They act from impulse rather than principle.

❋ *Wholly occupied by their own endeavors:* At times they presage a bright future (for their own endeavors), hence are beside themselves with joy; at other moments they see darkness and immediately become haunted by untold misery. Do they thereby think of their Lord? No, they think more of their labors.

❋ *Guided by sudden thoughts* that flash through the mind; lacking in spiritual insights, their words and works are therefore often inappropriate.

❋ *Delight in using high-sounding spectacular words and phrases.*

❋ *Vaunting Ambition:* The first place is often their desire. They are vainglorious in the Lord's work. They aspire to be powerful workers, greatly used by the Lord. Why? That they may gain a place, and obtain some glory.

❋ *Terribly self-satisfied:* Should the Lord use them to save one soul they will explode with joy and consider themselves spiritually successful. They take pride in themselves if they succeed but once—likened to a small vessel easily filled. They do not observe how vast and deep the ocean is. They have not been lost in God... If such boasting erupts upon winning only ten souls to the Lord, what will happen should a thousand souls be saved?

❋ *Uncommonly gifted, greatly talented, magnetic personalities:* It seems that God bestows abundant gifts upon the soulish in order that they may deliver their gifts to death voluntarily and then reclaim them renewed and glorified in resurrection. Yet such saints of God are loathe to consign these gifts to death and instead try to use them to the maximum. God-given abilities ought to be used by God for His glory, but carnal believers often regard these as theirs. So long as they serve God in this frame of mind they will continue to use them in accordance with their ideas without letting the Holy Spirit lead them. When successful, they render all glory to themselves. Naturally, such self-glorification and self-admiration are quite veiled. Nevertheless, however much they may try to humble themselves and to offer glory to God, they cannot avoid being self-centered. Glory to God, yes; but be it unto God—and to me!

* *Masters at self-pity!* Crushed, hurt, sad, and angry if not invited, if not commended or mentioned, if over-looked, if reprimanded or reproved.

* *They deplore feeling disrespected:* Similar to sensitivity, they feel hurt and angered if their ways are questioned, if their competency is scrutinized or their work suspected.

—*Watchman Nee*
"Secrets to Spirituality"
(Christian Fellowship Publishers), Pg 154-172

Let it Fall

When self is at the center, there is no real peace or joy; hurts, resentment, and frustrations follow. God uses these things—these people, which we think are against us, which we think are the problem—to expose the self in us. God exposes it so that we can confess it and get rid of it. God's refining fire will purge us of this if He sees in us a willingness to repent. What occurs is God's light exposing an area of darkness, not in them, but in us! The demonic have been relegated to dark places; places not just in the atmosphere, but in areas we've kept hidden; areas where the character of Christ does not reside within us. These are the areas where the Spirit has not been released because the outward sheath of our soul remains. The seed must fall to the ground and die. That death requires the outward shell of our soul to break, so that the inner man, the spirit, can come out. (I must give credit to great spiritual movers such as Myles Munroe, Smith Wigglesworth and Watchman Nee for introducing me to many of these concepts.)

The life of the Spirit flows when we put no confidence in our flesh, no matter how "good" that flesh may look. As we decrease, He is able to increase. Our dependence upon Him draws Him, our independence repels Him. Our tendency will always be to act independently—even in how we "serve" God. The tendency is for us to want to witness in our own strength, worship in our own strength, teach, serve, preach, and live the Christian life on our own! Though it may look like Christianity, it is far from it. That is what the church in Galatia fell into. They began in the spirit, and now were in the flesh—and didn't even know it. Obviously then, we are able, in the natural, to have a form of godliness in the natural (that is, it still looks good, like Christianity) yet still wholly miss the mark. That is why it is essential to have the Holy Spirit divide soul and the spirit so that He can separate that which derives from our self and that which is from the spirit. That is why we must deny ourselves, take up the cross and follow Christ daily!

Truly, the key to our life is not found in personality explorations (in fact, I feel a good argument can be made that they oppose Biblical truth) but in the Person of the Holy Spirit.

Our job is not to clean up our old man, but to learn to walk in our new man, created in Christ Jesus. We are to be powered daily, not by our personality, but by the Spirit of Christ, strengthened with might in our inner man, receiving grace to reign (see Ephesians 3:14-21 and Romans 5:17).

The Conclusion of the Matter

"Jesus said to him, "You shall love the LORD your God with all your heart, with all your soul, and with all your mind. This is the first and great commandment. And the second is like it: You shall love your neighbor as yourself. On these two commandments hang all the Law and the Prophets" (Matthew 22:39-41).

No discussion of foundational Christianity can be complete without discussion of the above verses (or their counterparts in the other gospels). In my experience, a great many Christians "say" they love God with all their heart, soul, mind, and strength, but there really is no evidence of it. My experience was no different. We desire God's promises of abundant life, His provision for our every needs, His peace, His power, His comfort, and His strength, but we forget, ignore, or put to the recesses of our mind the fact that Christ states that all of these—everything else—rests on these two commands, to love God with *all*, and love our neighbor as our self.

Here is how our reality plays out: We pray, we strive to please God, we tithe, we serve, we sing—we do all of these things, yet we fail in keeping the first command! If we were to honestly discern our innermost desires and wants, we'd find that what sits at the center is not to do all and be all for God but, rather, for self. In our fallen nature, we first seek to please ourselves and love ourselves, and then others. God sits at a distant third place. However, we were created to thrive when we do the opposite, by placing God at the forefront of our every thought, desire, action and will. After that, we are to love others and put their needs ahead of our own.

God reminds us, put first things first.

God asked Adam, "Where are you?" He was not asking for his location, whether Adam was by the mulberry bush, the apple orchard, or the east river, but rather, where was Adam in relation to the I AM. God asks us, "Where are you?" Where are our utmost desires and ambitions? Is our greatest desire to know Jesus and to see Him glorified on earth, or is it to simply live "my way." We all must answer this question—and we must not put it off.

Over the years, in my long-standing Christianity, I came to the point when I had to confess to God that I didn't *really* love Him. I knew I should have. I even apologized that I didn't, for I was sure that He was worthy of it, but deep down, if I were to be truly honest, I couldn't say that I did love the Lord with all my heart, soul, mind, and strength. Sure, if asked in Sunday school, I probably would have said I did. To really love God like the love one has for that special someone -- that simply was not the case. I confessed lukewarm love to God and asked for His help—to help me love Him as I ought.

I say all that to encourage you to return to your foundations. Our foundation begins with God, who is Spirit, and our fellowship with Him through Christ, in our spirit. At the center must be our Love for God and His will, His way, His kingdom. All else in our lives—including our lives—must subordinate to Him. Even if you find that your love for God falls short, begin even now to confess it aloud, and believe for it, even believing it for your life. Our love for God, for others and ourselves truly does fall short without the love that He lavishes on us. Only because He first loved us are we able to have this love. Understanding that it comes from Him first also helps us to understand that it is okay not to "feel" these things, but to have them in our spirit as God's truth. We walk in love and then soon, we will have the love.

Thank God now and each day for His glorious love. We have a God and Creator of all things who loves and cares about the tiniest of our detailed lives. This has been my prayer. I encourage you to make it yours. "LORD, I thank you that I shall love you with all my *heart, with all my soul, and with all of my mind, and that, by your power, I shall love my neighbor as myself.*"

Believer, on these two commands hang all…

"Let us hear the conclusion of the whole matter; Fear God nad keep His commandments, for this is man's all, including every secret think, whether good or evil" (Ecclesiastes 12:13-14).

Lastly, I want to thank you for accompanying me on this journey. You are mighty in God in Christ. I pray that you would daily receive God's favor and power for you, the riches of Christ's death and resurrection for you. God loves you. The Lord is with you.

As we conclude this journey, I would like to leave you with two of my favorite passages. The first we have discussed extensively in the early chapters of this book. These are powerful verses that can change your life. The first is this: *"Happy is the man (or woman) who puts his (or her) trust in the Lord."* My friend, you will be blessed in untold, countless ways as you learn to put your trust in the Lord in all areas of your life. As a Believer in Christ, may you be strengthened by the work of Christ to believe, and be blessed.

The second verse is found in Romans 5, verse 17: *For if because of one man's trespass (lapse, offense) death reigned through that one, much more surely will those who receive [God's] overflowing grace (unmerited favor) and the free gift of righteousness [putting them into right standing with Himself] reign as kings in life through the one Man Jesus Christ (the Messiah, the Anointed One).* Amplified.

Man, you have to love that one! Our means to reign as Kings in life through Christ: Receiving the abundance of grace and the gift of righteousness! I try to keep these two verses on the forefront of my conscious each day. My prayer for you is that you will put your trust in the Lord who loves you, believer in Christ, beyond comprehension; and may you receive God's abundant grace and gift of righteousness that you may not only banish depression from your life, but reign in life through the One, Jesus Christ!

Here is a prayer we can share as we remember who we are in Christ by the power of the Holy Spirit serving a living, loving and Holy Father:

"Father, thank You for Your provision. Thank You for providing for us a Helper, a Comforter, a Power, and that is the working of the Holy Spirit in our life. Father, forgive me for my self-sufficiency. LORD God, forgive me for ignoring You, Holy Spirit. Father, You told us in Your Word to, 'be filled with the Spirit,' and 'to be led by Your Spirit.' By faith today, then, I thank You for filling me with Your Spirit. By faith, I will be led by Your Spirit. I acknowledge that my life is found in doing Your will. I know that life is found in Your Spirit, and so I look to You, Holy Spirit, to guide me into all truth and life, and to be my strength to do the will of the Father, and keep His commands. I thank You that the fruit of Your Spirit is love and joy. I thank You that as I am filled up with You, I will be

filled with love, and joy. Father, I thank You for restoring to me joy in this life, in this day. I thank You for delivering me from death, darkness and depression and for bringing me into Your marvelous light. I thank You that I can rest and trust You in all things, and no matter what life may bring, I can rejoice in You, trust in You, smile, and give You praise. Because You are such an amazing, loving God, you have given to us a wonderful, rich, victorious and joyful life. Thank You for this life, Father. I bless Your Wonderful Name. In Jesus' Name, let it be so!"

Epilogue

(Yes, you should read this.)

The Bible forewarns us, predicting that in the last days, perilous or stressful times will come. Faulty economies, violence and terror, familial depravity, and the like will continue from bad to worse. Good will be spoken of as evil, and evil good. It is the inevitable progression when sin and lawlessness replace righteous and true living and lifestyles, be it in the home, the neighborhood or the nation.

The good news is that in heaven, there is peace, order, provision, stability and safety. We, as children of God, are to bring those things down here, on earth, as it is in heaven. That transformation first takes place within us. It is accomplished by faith. With the LORD God, we always have an answer, there is always a way out, we can always find a safe shelter, peace can always be found, there is enduring hope. Always. Certainly, we might as well partner up with the One whose finances and resources are not contingent upon the economies of the world. This is a real possibility, and the expected way for every believer—not trusting in religion and rules to guide, but learning His voice and guidance for our life, and following Him and Him alone. Money is nothing for God. Providing for us is not difficult for Him.

Ultimately, when all is said and done, when we pass from this life to the next, what will only matter is if we, during our brief stint here on earth, did what was requested of us by the eternal Creator God. The good news here is that this heavenly calling, the work He has given you to do, is also the very thing that will completely satisfy and fulfill and over joy you while on earth. It is that which banishes depression forever. It is that which brings the abundance of life. This life, my friend, is and has always been about our choices.

I implore you to answer the call that is upon your life. The successful navigation of the issues covered in this book should help you towards that end. Give yourself time and be patient. Renewing the mind is a process, a lifetime one at that. The Lord deals with us about different things at different times—this book is sort of all at once. Don't be overwhelmed—only prayerfully consider what is the Lord dealing with you about now. Then courageously obey in that area... You may need to go back over relevant sections in the book, asking the Holy Spirit's wisdom and guidance in each. Ask the Holy Spirit to show you the truth regarding the materials contained in this book. Yet, remember that knowing and doing are totally different matters. The demons know that Jesus is Lord, but He is not their Lord. Yes, know the truth, but do it also. Daily, surrender your will to the will of Father, and do the work. From your reliance upon Christ, and not of yourself, draw from the strength of Christ moment to moment throughout your day so that you may walk in His truth, character and calling for your life.

If you are having difficulty spending time in the Word of God, begin with the Psalms and Proverbs. Wake up each day and wash yourself with the Word of God. Spend time thanking and praising the Lord for every good thing in your life. Let His Word ignite faith in you. Let that faith build so that you are assured of His presence and help in your life for the day. Thank you for taking the time to read this book. My faith is there for you, that God's anointing is available for you to break the bondage of depression, fear, suicide, anger, gluttony, lust...whatever it is that has it's hold on you. God's power is available for you... Let your faith arise to believe it for yourself... Then begin to thank Him for it! It's yours.

Now, in that same faith in Him, in His strength, walk in it, and live it. And when you fail, get right back up again. His love for you endures forever.

"God made Him who had no sin to be sin for us, so that in Him we might become the righteousness of God" 2 Corinthians 5:21. *"For you know the grace of our Lord Jesus Christ, that though He was rich, yet for your sakes He became poor, so that you through His poverty might become rich"* (2 Corinthians 8:9).

Today, I was reading the second book of Corinthians and again was reminded of The Great Exchange, as I believe it has been called. I now would like to remind you of the exchange, of what Christ endured and of what we secured. As the first verse above explicitly states, Christ took up sin (became unrighteous) for us so that we might become the righteousness of God. I encourage you to remind yourself of this daily, verbally declaring to yourself, "Through Christ, I have become the righteousness of God." Similarly, the second verse reveals to us that Jesus gave up His wealth and became poor in order that we might become rich. That's right, you have an inheritance now in Christ Jesus. You are successful now in Christ Jesus. As you continue to believe it, you will continue to walk in it, because it is already yours. I would encourage you to continue to read His Word to find out what else is yours!

Not only did He become poor that we might be rich, but remember, He was beaten so that you might be healed. Therefore, healing is yours, today, through Christ. He died that we might have life. That's why each new day brings hope for a good life, a good outcome, a great end for you and your family in Christ. He was cursed so that we might be blessed. That means that you are successful! Success is in your hands. Regardless of the failures of the past, you must know and believe and declare that in Christ, who paid the price, you are successful. Would you be willing go repeat that out loud right now? Say to yourself, "I am successful in all things in Christ." In your relationships, in your work, in your body, in your school work, in your strategy for finances and business opportunities, you are successful! In fact, according to the Word of God, all is yours in Christ. Fix your eyes on Him and what He has done and given to you. Receive the abundance of grace he has secured for you. Receive His righteousness He has captured for you. O what an amazing loving God we serve. Blessed is His Name. Above all names, He alone is worthy of praise! Give thanks to the Lord for He is good and His grace lives on forever!

Would you now prayerfully consider making this, or something like it, your prayer during this season of your life?

"Father, I thank You for allowing me to know You, through the finished work of Your only Son, Jesus Christ. You alone, Lord God, are worthy of praise. I thank You Father that You have given to me everything that I need for life and for Godly living. Lord, forgive me for living in doubt and fear. Thank You for forgiving me for my lack of faith and not trusting in You. Lord, I now put my trust in You for every detail of my life. I trust that You will take good care of me. I thank You that I am forgiven in Christ Jesus, by His blood, and that You have declared that I am blessed and that all of my needs are met. Father, I will no longer live under the law, but I will be led and walk by Your Spirit. The Word of God will be a lamp to guide my path and instruct me. Father, I forgive all of those who have offended or hurt me. I let go of every offence and bitterness and ill-will towards all, including friends and family that have wronged me. In the same way that You have forgiven me completely, I now forgive them. In the same way that You have blessed me with grace that I don't deserve, I now bless them in Jesus Name. In the Name of Jesus, I take up the full armor of God. I take up the helmet of salvation, that

ness, the belt of truth and shoes for the preparation of the gospel of peace. I take up the sword of the Spirit, which is the Word of God. Lord, give me a hunger for Your Word. I ask for the Holy Spirit's help every time I read the Word, even Your Spirit of Wisdom and Revelation. I take up the shield of faith to extinguish every flaming arrow the enemy would hurl against me. I take up the garment of praise for the spirit of heaviness. I clothe myself with the humility of Christ Jesus. I submit myself to You, God, I resist you devil, and according to the Word of God, you must flee from me. I break off of my life every spell, every hex, every curse in the Name of Jesus! I command every unclean spirit of depression, fear, anger, resentment and bitterness, pride and false teaching to leave me now in the Name of Jesus and to go to the footstool of Jesus and never return or retaliate against me in Jesus name! Lord, I thank You for giving me Your Wisdom. I thank You for self-discipline in my life today in all that I do, say, eat and drink. I will heed Your corrections and submit to the authority that You have placed over me. I will be a first-fruits tither. I receive Your love for You and for others, that I might love You with all my heart, soul, mind and strength, and love my neighbor as myself. I will heed Your voice today and obey. Thank You Lord for Your love and mercy. Thank You that You are a God who is slow to anger, full of compassion and abounding in Love. I worship You. I praise Your Name. You alone are God. You alone are worthy of praise!"

Finally, this is my prayer of blessing for all of you, beloved people of God.

"May God's power strengthen you to accomplish all that He has given you to do upon this earth. I declare this day that you are blessed in Jesus name. You will do it! Not by might, nor by power, but by the Spirit of the Living God inside of you!"

THE SHOE

There was a time not long ago,
a vast expanse of time although,
when man did not wear <u>shoes</u>.

No glass on the streets,
neither thorns nor thistles,
there was <u>never</u> a need.
The terrain everywhere soft and cool,
exuding passions, life, innocence and joy.
The dark, rich, fertile soil,
the color of coffee, of cacao, <u>soothed</u> the sole.

No one seems to remember those days.
The recollection of man begins
when it was crushed - <u>the</u> foot that is.
As Time wore, so too, the significance.
By what and for what remain questions of inconsequence.
Of import is that the foot had
been damaged badly - swollen,
bruised and bleeding.
Internally and ex-.
Most then in modernity
wear shoes.
Our <u>Soul</u>,
the cobbler,
makes them:

236

The Cross-Trainer

Overwhelmingly popular are the cross-trainers. Men wear them at the
gym, working inexhaustibly the biceps and triceps, pecs and traps, lats,
delts, glutes and abs. Women too, day after day, striving for less of this
and that, yearning for more of them and those.
And, for a moment, the pain waxes thin.

The Work Shoe

Some simply choose to lace the work shoes. Ignoring the pain
and the infection, they have moved on.
And though the wound remains,
they never mention it and rarely
ruminate on its presence.

Running Shoes

Others simply prefer running shoes. Once they are shod,
the pain races away -- Forever seeking
new faces, new events and new horizons.
Only in stillness does it haunt.

Dress Shoes

Inadequacy and imbalance must flee in the presence of silk, sheer,
Egyptian cotton, Italian, patent leather shoes. The night is theirs. She
will wake and mourn. He will wake and run.
But tonight, they have on dress shoes.

The Open-Toe Shoe
Her sore is open for all to see
It is severely crushed indeed.
Expressing her woes to all she can, she hopes for concern,
and maybe a comment. No one ever does.
She pretends not to notice - but can't.

The Casual Shoe
Dressed with a ready smile, "Nothing's the problem." Racked with frustration, pain and guilt, they are always the proper fit and perfectly styled. They are the cool.
They are the ones to watch.

The Penny Loafer
He drives the nicest car, wears the most glamorous watches, and says the most scintillating of words. Nails pressed, suited and booted, a flawless mirage, she's the consummate queen. Having everything, yet still their toes waft stench. Unaware that what they need is not a thing.

The Sunday Church Shoe
They press to be first though speak of being last. Diminished during the week, deacons and deaconesses today demand. They, the spotlight. This their show. They cascade down the aisle as if a platform fashion fair. But at the end of each Sabbath, like all the rest before,
nylons and socks descend to reveal
the foulest of lesions.

Wrestling Shoes
Compete.

Golf Spikes
Condemn.

Boots
Control.

House Shoes
Hate.

Then I remembered the foot,
used for locomotion, progress and balance.
Then I heard the voice of the Lord, softly and calmly,
say unto me,

"TAKE OFF YOUR SHOES, YOU ARE ON HOLY GROUND."

_____

_____

_____

About the Author

C. Christopher Lindsay is a pastor at
Jubilee South Valley Church located in Morgan Hill, California.
He can be reached at:
carmen@thedepressedchristian.com

or simply go to the website at:
www.thedepressedchristian.com

*May the Lord richly bless you and yours
with a new found joy as you realize who you are in Christ!*

C. Christopher Lindsay

∞